DIARY
of a
PREDATOR

DIARY of a PREDATOR

a memoir

AMY HERDY

VINCENT
Publishing
House

Boulder, Colorado

Copyright © 2012 by Amy Herdy

All rights reserved. No part of this book may be used or reproduced in any matter whatsoever without the written permission of the publisher, except for brief quotations included in critical articles and reviews.

Published by
Vincent Publishing House
PO Box 19632
Boulder, CO 80301

Cover and book design by Sandra Jonas

Publisher's Cataloguing-in-Publication Data

Herdy, Amy.
　Diary of a predator : a memoir / Amy Herdy.
　Boulder, CO : Vincent Publishing House, 2012.

　　p. cm.

　　ISBN: 978-0-9831802-2-7
　　ISBN: 978-0-9831802-1-0 (ebook)

　　1. Brents, Brent J. 2. Sex offenders - Colorado - Biography. 3. Adult child abuse victims - Colorado - Biography.

HV6565 .C6 H47 2012　　364.15320978883 —dc22

2011927840

For Matt
I could not have done this
without you

Contents

Prologue *1*

1. A Hunter at Work — *5*
2. Predator and Prey — *10*
3. A Premonition — *17*
4. Legacies — *35*
5. A Man in My Life — *51*
6. Manhunt — *60*
7. The Interview — *73*
8. Finding a Victim — *82*
9. A Phone Call — *98*
10. Fallout — *113*
11. Down the Rabbit Hole — *124*
12. A Question — *135*
13. Excavating — *144*
14. A Purple Hippo — *154*
15. The Childhood — *166*
16. A Journal — *184*
17. The Sentencing — *207*
18. Aurora — *224*
19. Aftermath — *238*
20. Letters — *252*
21. Changes — *281*

Epilogue *301*

Acknowledgments 311

About the Author 313

I can't remember much about when I was real young except fear and shame and lack of courage.

—Brent Brents

Prologue

This is the story of one of America's most notorious sexual criminals, Brent Brents, from his childhood of horrific abuse to his adulthood on the streets of Denver, where he stalked, raped, and tortured multiple victims before police captured him in February 2005.

Brent pleaded guilty to eighty criminal charges, including sexual assault, kidnapping, and attempted murder, and in July 2005 received the largest sentence in Colorado history: 1,509 years.

At the time I started working on Brent's case, I was a *Denver Post* criminal justice reporter, cynical and driven. I've often said this is the tale of two predators—one a criminal, the other a journalist—for don't we as journalists often prey upon people for their story? So this is also the account of my own awakening.

The year before his case erupted, I coauthored an all-consuming investigative series about sexual assault and domestic violence in the military called "Betrayal in the Ranks." Fellow *Post* staffer Miles Moffeit and I invested every fiber of our beings into those stories to honor the amazing women who counted on us to be their voice, leaving behind our families, our friends, and our health in the process. The series prompted investigations and spurred congressional reforms, but left me empty and exhausted. It took me months to truly care about journalism again, and then the Brents case caught my attention.

The prospect of writing about sexual crime from the perspective of the perpetrator, not the survivor, revived my interest.

He was the most predatory criminal I'd ever encountered, and I hoped that through him, I would perhaps understand all the faceless men who had assaulted the hundreds of survivors whose stories I've told and carried all these years, like a heavy bag of so many broken hearts.

I scrutinized him as I would a bug under a microscope—indeed, that's what I told him. Yet my curiosity was never tinged with hate, a reaction that I soon learned to my surprise would alienate me from just about everyone I knew, especially those in my own newsroom. There's no such thing as objectivity in journalism.

Still, I was pumped by the amazing opportunity: Criminals on the scale of Brents rarely cooperate with efforts to pick their brain. Coincidentally, it was my lack of contempt that prompted Brents to continue to call and write me. As one former FBI profiler told me, "You did one thing right from the very beginning, and that's why he talked to you: You never judged him."

Instead, I began to judge myself.

I did not expect what would happen—that by probing Brents for the story of how he was made, I would uncover parts of myself in the process. His case affected me in ways I could not have predicted, for it illuminated my growing disillusionment with the callous media of which I was a part. Those effects continue to this day, as does the correspondence between us that began shortly after his capture and included him sending me his journal, a meticulous record of his crimes and his history. I have been able to verify his accounts by corroborating the details through interviews with officials and witnesses, as well as court records and criminal and medical reports.

Because of the unprecedented access he allowed me, this book is more than simply the true story of the crimes Brents committed. It is also the rare story of the psyche of the sociopathic man revealed and the impact it had on the journalist covering the case. Through Brents, I realized truths about the human condition and our assumptions of evil—that it is not assigned, but constructed. I also discovered I could no longer continue to be the reporter I once had been, forsaking myself and my family to pursue a story.

Throughout the book, I make use of excerpts from his journal, our letters, and interviews, in addition to the extensive research I conducted as a reporter. Anything attributed to Brents journal is exactly as he wrote it, including punctuation and spelling.

With his history and "jacket"—the notoriety of his crimes that accompanies him to prison—Brents expects to eventually be killed by other inmates. "My biggest fear," he wrote me, "is that I will die without ever having done anything good."

His experience of the world is violent, calculating, pathetic, and wrenching—but it is still the same world in which we all live. It is Brents' hope, and mine, that by presenting his life in unflinching fashion, we will learn something from it.

November 2010
To the reader:

As you read this book, you may find yourself experiencing a wide range of emotions. But I ask of you only to keep an open mind.

You may very well find yourself full of opinion towards myself and the author. No matter how you feel about me or my actions—hate me, be wary of my sincerity if you choose—please, if you are a parent, planning on being a parent or are someone who is responsible for the wellbeing of children: Treat them with dignity, respect and love. Be good role models. Teach them empathy, compassion and integrity. Regardless of your financial, emotional and physical situations, show them how to overcome and achieve. Be loving and attentive. Listen to them, hear them, spend time with them and nurture them. Most of all, give them your heart forever so that they will become good people.

—B. Brents

I could easily be Bundy i think he had the same fucked up brain the release was never Achievable. What realy hurts me deep is that there are a few things and people I can sincerely care for and love and would never hurt but the rest of Gods Green earth is fair Game. I am truly a fucked up dangerous person and were the opportunities to present themselves I would act. It hurts me to admit this. I am sorry for hurting all those other people, Truly but how can i be any kind of Good or decent if i cant stop my mind from Working Like it does. I look back to when i was a kid and i realy think i went crazy. Death is the only solution to this.

—**From Brent's journal**

ONE

A Hunter at Work

AUGUST 2004

Going to the *Denver Post* again every day was still feeling awkward and oddly formal, as though the newspaper and I were weary exes now embarrassed by the intimate secrets we had once whispered to each other.

I'd worried that my editors would tiptoe around me by asking me to cover fluff pieces, hesitant to assign me any gritty crime stories for fear I wasn't ready. After all, I had been gone four months. Yet that wasn't the case—they actually gave me nothing to do. So during those first few weeks, I would go through the motions of putting on a suit, makeup, and some jewelry, show up, dial a few perfunctory phone calls at my desk, take a long walk around the dirty Gotham City that is downtown Denver, and leave early.

It was at the start of one of those uneventful days that I stepped into the crowded elevator on the ground floor of the twenty-two-story, mud-brown *Denver Post* building at 16th and Broadway in the heart of downtown. The newsroom for the *Post* was on the fourth floor, and as the elevator groaned to a stop at each level for people to trundle out and begin their day, I had the distinct feeling someone was watching me. Glancing over my left shoulder, I was taken aback by a man staring at me with the intensity of a cobra.

He was about my height but muscle-thick, with military-short hair, wire-rimmed glasses, and dark, penetrating eyes. He wore a cheap, rumpled gray suit that fit like it belonged to someone else.

And he wasn't just glancing at me curiously, as if he somehow knew I didn't quite belong there. Nor did he casually drop his eyes, as most people do when busted for ogling. Instead, he held my questioning look with a flinty stare both unabashed and unwavering, almost as if he were . . . calculatedly appraising me. Like a wolf assessing its next meal.

Human beings are flesh-and-blood Rorschach tests I read for a living. This one said, "Darkness! Danger!" Although I pride myself on never dropping my eyes first during a confrontation, I did so now, quickly turning to face front again as my gut alarm tripped and my heart started to pound.

Instinctively deciding I didn't want him to know which floor was mine, I tensed my muscles and tightened my grip on the heavy black bag at my shoulder. When the elevator thudded to a halt at the next level, one floor below mine, I waited as two men shouldered their way out. Then just as the doors began to whine close, I darted after them, feeling the stranger's disconcerting stare continue from inside the elevator after the doors slid shut behind me. I felt like a laser had burned holes in my back.

I ran around the corner and up the stairs, taking them two at a time, adrenaline-fueled fear making my feet fly.

For the rest of the day, I couldn't help but search the newsroom for the frightening, stocky man in the wire-rimmed glasses. As the hours passed and I didn't spot him, I began to relax. It was just a random encounter, I told myself. He was gone and I would never see him again.

I was so very wrong.

Wednesday, February 16, 2005

10 a.m.
After raping her, Brent Brents handed Aida Bergfeld his hunting knife, wrapped her thin fingers around the handle, and asked her to kill him.

That morning, he had picked up Aida off Colfax Avenue near Cheesman Park in Denver, where he knew the twenty-seven-year-old prostitute with the baby face worked the street for money to get high.

"I bullshitted her," he would later say. "I told her I'd give her fifty dollars for a fuck."

He had known Aida as a drug-and-sex buddy for most of the seven months he'd been out of prison, where he had spent sixteen years for raping a six-year-old boy and a nine-year-old girl. Behind bars, he had honed his five-foot-eight body into an intimidating 185 pounds of muscle and perfected a flat stare, shaving off his thick, brown hair to add to the disconcerting effect. Once released, he kept his hair military short and often wore wire-rimmed glasses.

This day he had been smoking Ice, a combination of methamphetamine, heroin, and PCP, and he literally itched as he drove near downtown and watched women walk by, thickly bundled against the February cold. They were sheep, and he was a wolf. In his thirty-five years, Brent had become a relentless predator. Over the past six days alone, he had raped six times, including a grandmother and her two young granddaughters, in their own home, in their own beds.

He was consumed by the burning need to strike again. Then he saw Aida, wearing bulky clothes over her slight build, her large dark eyes framed in her angular face by a cloud of dark hair, and smiled with almost giddy relief as she got into his car.

Once inside the vacant Denver apartment where he used to hole up, he moved quickly. "I snatched her up, told her I was going to kill her, put the knife to her throat. I then put the knife on a heater and fucked her."

Usually, he tormented them and raped them in ways that gave them the most anguish, taking his time doing the things they begged him not to do. But not today, not with Aida, perhaps because he knew her. He finished quickly, moving away. A short time later when he faced her again, he held the knife.

Brent knew that like him, Aida had her demons, only hers were heroin and the easy money she could make for it turning tricks on

Colfax, known around the country as the stretch in Denver offering any kind of sex for sale.

Yet Aida's demons apparently did not clamor for pain. She shook her head as Brent, seated before her in the chilly room, lifted his chin. "Do it," he urged. "Do it!"

Slowly, Aida shook her head. "I can't, Brent," she said thickly, the hit of heroin she shot into her veins an hour before still deadening her expression. "I love you." She opened her hand, letting go of the knife.

Brent squeezed shut his eyes. He had wanted it to be over, the pounding agony in his head, the well of rage that rose in his chest, the hunger for suffering and release that he could not satisfy, no matter how many victims he took, no matter their age, no matter what he did to them, how they fought or screamed.

He wanted to stop seeing his mother's face.

He opened his eyes and looked at the young woman before him who was now rocking slowly back and forth. Her own mother was a prostitute and heroin addict, and Brent felt sure she knew about craving peace. She then met his eyes and touched his arm.

"I want it to be over too," she told Brent.

Soon, they would both get their wish, only not like either of them had hoped.

I'm sure some of those I hurt would like to see me butchered, beaten and murdered and maybe that would satisfy them. But what they don't know is that vengeance is not as sweet as it sounds.

I know.

I was and I am solely responsible for the actions I took. However people need to see how I was made. Then realize there are thousands of me out there and more still being made and do something about it. Something besides the "systems" answer.

It's not just feeling the surface pain, It's feeling and sharing what comes after and how they deal with it. Its Like trying to plug a crumbling dam, you plug one hole and another appears leaking your sanity. Plug it and one appears Leaking your sense of safety. Plug that one and another appears Leaking self confidence or self love. To many holes and not enough hands.

—From Brent's journal

TWO

Predator and Prey

Wednesday, February 16, 2005

Noon

Across the city, Denver Chief of Police Gerry Whitman finally got his call. A tall, rangy man with a long face, earnest hazel eyes, and a deliberate manner, Whitman could have been a poster child for the hardy Midwestern stock from which he hailed. Born and raised in Burlington, Iowa, he started his career as a patrol officer in Ames before leaving the state for Colorado, where he joined the Denver Police Department in 1982. He had methodically worked his way up—always within the patrol division—before being named chief in 2000.

This month marked his five-year anniversary. The recent spate of crimes was among the worst he'd encountered, and these streets were his. Even harder, he would later recall, was the fact that he had a wife and two children, including an eleven-year-old daughter—the same age as the twin girls who were Brents' last victims.

So when the lab results from the recent string of rapes were done, the first call was made to Whitman.

A lab technician from the Colorado Bureau of Investigations had determined that semen taken from five recent rape victims was a DNA match to a man whose information was on file with the Colorado Department of Corrections. Finally, they had his name: Brent Brents. Quickly, detectives in Denver's Crimes Against Persons Bureau began compiling information.

A check of Brents' lengthy criminal history was chilling. At the age of twelve, he had been sent to a boys' home for attacking other children and spent most of his youth in various juvenile detention facilities, where he was accused of sexually assaulting others as well as having "inappropriate relationships" with other inmates and staff.

As a teenager, Brents moved with his family to Colorado and again spent several years in and out of juvenile facilities. Then in 1988 in Denver, an eighteen-year-old Brents used the pretense of a lost cat to lure a six-year-old boy into an alley, where he raped him and then stuffed him into a trash bin. A few days later he hid next to a neighbor's house and grabbed their nine-year-old daughter as she climbed the fence to return home after walking to a nearby Burger King. Brents dragged the girl to the family's garage and raped her at knifepoint, threatening to kill her if she screamed. After the children identified their attacker, police issued a warrant for his arrest. Brents left the state in the middle of the night and was later arrested as he headed toward his mother's home near Las Vegas.

The case was worked by a Denver police sex crimes detective named Carrolyn Priest. The mother of a teenage girl, Carrolyn was married both to her job and to another driven Denver detective, Jon Priest, who worked in homicide. During the course of the investigation, she turned to her husband for help, and the case chewed at them.

Sixteen years later, Jon Priest would doggedly pursue Brents on his own.

But in the 1980s not much was known about pedophilia. In an effort to keep the young victims from the 1988 case from having to testify, prosecutors offered Brents a plea agreement of being guilty but legally insane. He was sentenced to twenty years, with the beginning of his sentence to be served in a state mental hospital "until restored to sanity," according to court records.

Brents remained at the Colorado Mental Health Institute in Pueblo for two years and four months before doctors there requested he be thrown out.

"For more than two years, staff have attempted to help Mr. Brents with his very traumatic past," wrote Eric Whyte, the acting chief of psychiatry for the hospital, in a memo to a Denver district judge dated

April 29, 1991. "He has made very little progress while in the hospital and exhibits very little insight into his illness . . . He has continued to act out his feelings impulsively, and recently stated that one method he uses to cope with painful feelings within himself is to inflict pain on other people."

Brents had become "assaultive with staff," Whyte wrote, and had been transferred three times for "inappropriate sexual behavior."

After that, officials moved Brents to various prisons throughout the state. Seven times, he waived a parole hearing as well as refused sexual offender treatment, taking the additional six months of prison over the supervision tied to parole. In July 2004, four years short of his twenty-year sentence and despite a history of sexual violence toward children, Brents was released without parole.

In September and October, he molested an eight-year-old boy, the son of an Aurora woman he dated briefly. The woman lived across the street from Derrick West, a Denver bank loan officer who met Brents in a King Soopers' grocery parking lot the first day of Brents' release from prison. West had offered the new ex-con a room in his Aurora townhome in exchange for remodeling work.

West's neighbor across the street, a stay-at-home mother of two young boys, was pregnant and alone. Brents began visiting her frequently after he arrived in the neighborhood in July 2004, and soon he was staying overnight at her house. Within weeks, however, the woman's family became wary of her new man, and the relationship exploded once her sister entered his name into a criminal database for a background check.

After questioning her sons, the woman called Aurora police in October and tearfully told them Brents had molested her eight-year-old boy. Detectives there began investigating Brents on November 9, but in a tangle of miscommunication that would later fracture the department, an arrest warrant was not issued until January 26, 2005. Since then, Aurora police said, they had been unable to find him.

His latest spree appeared to have begun the week before on Friday, February 11, and even the cryptic police accounts were shocking. At

1:45 p.m., a man armed with a knife raped a woman in her home on Adams Street, near Congress Park. Three hours later, another woman was sexually assaulted by a man with a knife inside her pet supply business near East Sixth Avenue. On Monday, a man broke into a house on Vine Street and sexually assaulted twin eleven-year-old girls and their sixty-seven-year-old grandmother, who was babysitting them while their parents were en route to Switzerland for a ski vacation. The man had ejaculated into every victim, in some cases both vaginally and anally. That semen was matched to Brents.

As more than a hundred officers began to scour the city, Whitman, normally taciturn with the media, called Sonny Jackson, one of his public information officers, a broad-shouldered former television photojournalist. They needed to hold a news conference and flash Brents' face across the five and six o'clock news.

"He is a career criminal, he's a parolee, he's a registered sex offender, he's a pedophile," Whitman grimly told reporters. "He's about as evil as you can be." Within minutes, tips on Brents began to pour in, and agents from the FBI began tracking leads of his whereabouts across Denver. He was reported to be in Exempla St. Joseph Hospital, so dozens of officers carrying his prison-booking photo began to scour the grounds. Then he was seen walking down a street. He was spotted leaving a pharmacy, then sitting in the rear of a downtown bus. After customers called in tips to police saying they recognized Brents, officers went to the Satire Lounge on East Colfax Avenue three times Wednesday night. Throughout the city, police scrambled from location to location as their radios crackled with urgency. Nothing panned out.

Across Denver, residents armed themselves with whatever they could find, including hockey sticks, mace, and baseball bats.

At 5:20 p.m., police dispatchers sent out a bulletin to look for a green Pontiac Grand Prix, which they believed Brents may have been driving. Later that evening, it was discovered in a King Soopers parking lot in Aurora.

At 6:40 p.m., a SWAT team stormed a townhome in the 15000 block of East Louisiana Avenue. The residence was owned by the parents of Brents' former roommate, Derrick West, the man who took him in from a King Soopers parking lot the day he was released from prison.

The team searched every room before leaving through the front door, nodding good night to the elderly couple who lived there.

Just before 8 p.m., investigators brought West in for questioning. He told them he had kicked Brent out because Aurora police kept coming to his home regarding the case involving the young boy. He had driven Brent to East Colfax Avenue and Race Street, he said, dropped him off, and urged him to turn himself in to police.

"I'll never go back to jail," Brent told him before walking away.

1969–1975

These first five and a half years were to me very good. Full of the fun a child should have. I adored my mom and idolized my dad.

My earliest memories, well they were all good accept a few accidents of my own doing. Grubbing the tail pipe of a motorcycle and badly burning my hand. Stepping on a broken bottle cutting my foot badly.

The good was living with my parents who never stayed in the same place long enough to establish a life. For a child i got to see so many beautiful places in the western u.s. I got to see wildlife that most people only see on tv or in books. I played with snakes, worms, fish and bugs like any normal boy. I climbed pine trees and still remember the fragrant smell of tall pine forests and the rotting of the forest floor. I built forts out of cushions and under trees and even a front porch. I played hide and go seek. I was an active independent child i suppose even though I tried to follow my dad everywhere. My best memories of him were of me and him and an ugly old orange pickup and our adventures in it. My favorite was me barely three feet tall and trying to follow in his footsteps (something i now regret) in sixteen inches of snow. What was a child's dogged determination to be where his dad was and to impress, quickly turned to frustration and fear he would leave me behind. But that giant man came back and carried me. I idolized him. Six foot five—three hundred pounds plus of muscle. The giant who always smelled good, smiled a lot, and whos giant arms were always a safe haven for a *small little boy when he needed it. Cledith Ronnie Brents. That man was my hero but like many things in life change happens.*

My Dad and Mom both told me years ago that first of all my Dad's father beat him and molested him when he was a kid. My Mom said her father raped and so did her brothers.

So they did it to me. I wonder if it's genetic.

My mom was so very beautiful in those days. Long dark hair. Beautiful smile and happy.

I had no understanding of our first sexual encounter when i was just four. But i remember being impatient and wanting to run up the road to where my dad was and see him. Even that first encounter couldnt obscure that little boys zest for life. Besides if its mom its ok, right?

Well as I said he travelled a lot and it was fun. Then in 1975 we end up in Hauchuca City Arizona. And for me 1975 was the year the Gates of hell opened up and swallowed me whole.

I know we were poor, really poor. We were starving, my shoes had holes. But when I turned six one day it was like a light switch went on and i became a sex toy for the two of them. My brother (Brandy) was just an infant. But they found plenty of time for sex with me. The first time he raped me i passed out from the pain. The beatings soon followed. Along with the harsh words. Your worthless, your to small, your weak. Your dumb, you stink. Your draining us. I'll cut you. I'll shoot you, you'll die. Run you little piece of shit. Broken, bloodied and destroyed, each day i became these things and more. The next five years I became what i knew.

—From Brent's journal

———————

THREE

A Premonition

WEDNESDAY, FEBRUARY 16, 2005

Late afternoon
From Brent's journal:

> I told Aida to kill me and go. But she would not do it. So we fucked, I drank, smoked some weed, she did some heroin, we fucked some more. Wed night I took her to see Million Dollar Baby my second time. That night we went to the Marion apt. I stopped and got Arbys for us. Got her some crack and some more vodka. We fucked hard, cuddled, talked, slept, fucked some more slept until we heard the glass repair people come. We hid in the Little Area where the boiler and the water heater were. When they left I checked around then we both went to Cheeseman Park . . . cuddled in the park then she tells me baby I wanna go back and fix and have a girl. Will you get me a girl . . . I picked up Angel took her to Aida and let them do there thing . . . took Angel home. In the morning I went and got us breakfast at Mickey D's. We slept for a while.

THURSDAY, FEBRUARY 17, 2005

Brents, a man with a history of raping children, had admitted to an Aurora police detective in November that he had molested his girlfriend's eight-year-old son, yet the detective let him walk away. By the time the warrant was filed, Brents could not be found, and the Denver media latched onto the story like a dog with a bone. Besieged all day with calls and requests for interviews, officials from the police department and the Arapahoe County District Attorney's Office acknowledged that something had gone very wrong and vowed to investigate.

Meanwhile, more than two hundred tips poured into Crime Stoppers, most of them worthless. Chief Whitman told a national cable news station that an arrest warrant with a $25 million bond was issued for one of the attacks. "We don't know if he's still in state at all, but we're following up on multiple leads across the country," Whitman told Fox News.

Producers from *America's Most Wanted* called, and an anonymous donor offered $20,000 for information leading to Brents' arrest.

At a community meeting at Bromwell Elementary School on Thursday night, residents spoke of their fear to the chief. "This guy is hunkered down somewhere," Whitman told the anxious crowd. "If you think you see him, you want to call us." He then urged them to keep their doors locked and not walk alone.

Investigators dug for scraps of information on Brents, and so did we reporters. As a forty-one-year-old criminal justice reporter at the *Denver Post* for more than two years and in the news business for fifteen, I knew the drill, but my heart was not in the story. I was newly married and, for the first time in a good while, trying to enjoy a part of my life I had long neglected.

I grew up in Kentucky, six blocks from a horse park—a huge facility of barns, fields, and paddocks—and I spent every minute I could there. I fled a depressed mother and a raging, drug-addicted brother by pedaling my greenish-blue three-speed bike like mad to the barns and then horseback riding until it was nearly too dark to see my way home. Since my German-sensibilities father immersed himself in his job as a civil engineer and my older brothers and sister were at home as little as possible, it was often just me and my mom.

I could tell her mood from the moment I came into the house. If every light was off and her bedroom door shut, it was a Bad Day. If I ran the vacuum or had the TV too loud in the living room, a resounding "SSHHH!" would erupt from the direction of her room.

I've since compared notes with siblings and come to realize our mother took a variety of drugs that included uppers and downers that physicians apparently prescribed like candy back in the '60s and '70s rather than propose therapy, especially to a woman. It certainly formed in me an early and strong aversion to drugs and doctors, although by the age of six, I knew how to renew her prescriptions. I would call them into the pharmacy, wait for the delivery boy at the front door, and then bring her the pills with a glass of water.

I remember once my mother sitting up in bed, crying and uttering something unintelligible, and I began to panic. As she rocked back and forth, sobbing inconsolably, I patted her back, but her tear-filled eyes only stared straight ahead, unseeing, while she moaned like a wounded animal. Finally, even though I knew it was frowned upon to disturb my dad at work, I climbed onto our black-and-white kitchen stepstool to reach the phone on our wall and call him to come home. I then went back to her room, wrapped my arms around her, and rocked with her until he arrived.

And so the role of rescuer locked itself down in the neural pathways of my brain. I eventually embarked upon a career documenting the tragedies of the human condition and upon more than one floundering relationship enabling a codependent man.

This didn't mean my heart was wide open—oh no, far from it. Even those who love me will readily acknowledge that I can be sharper than a paper cut. My brusqueness began in childhood and became the armor my emotionally orphaned self needed to protect my heart—if you weren't so sensitive, I would tell myself, you'd be a lot better off.

I learned that early on. For example: One winter afternoon when I was about five or six, my sister and I pulled on our brother's hand-me-down white long underwear under our clothes, then added coats, hats, scarves, and heavy black galoshes before we tramped through the snow to the golf course two blocks away. Once there, I decided to see just how frozen the deep ditches underneath a crossing bridge had become. I made it only a few steps onto the ice before the surface collapsed, and I was jarringly submerged in freezing, brackish water. I managed to clamber out and, dripping and scared and numbingly cold, bawled hot tears all the way home and through the backdoor of our house.

Our mother was sitting on the kitchen stool, talking on the phone, and when she looked at me with irritation, I realized it was a Bad Day. On days like that, any demand could be too much, and I think that rather than feel the despair brought on by feeling overwhelmed, she would become angry.

"Hell's bells, Amy," she said to me sharply, invoking one of her favorite curse phrases, "what are you crying about now?"

So I learned to suck it up. Then, I cultivated those same qualities professionally. I spent twelve years living in Tampa, and for seven of those, I worked as a crime reporter for the *St. Petersburg Times,* matter-of-factly documenting a never-ending litany of death and destruction in the Tampa Bay area. It was there that I realized how growing up in a dysfunctional household with my depressed mother and my violent, unpredictable brother named Dreux had an unlikely perk: It honed my skills of observation and emotional intelligence. At the newspaper those skills delivered interviews, time and time again, because I was able to analyze situations and relate to my subjects swiftly and on any level—they could hear in my voice, or see in my eyes, that I innately understood who they were and what they were feeling. There was no judgment. I learned at a very young age that we human beings are deeply flawed.

After work, however, I did my best to take off my reporter hat. I was a mother to three sons, four if you counted my oldest son's best friend who lived with us and called me "Mom." I always knew I wanted children of my own—perhaps to nurture someone who was capable of loving me back? But most of all, I think, because I had seen both ends of the human spectrum—the awful things we are capable of doing, as well as the selflessly heroic.

Like the story of the twisted young man who sexually assaulted a nine-month-old baby, then left her for dead in the woods. The Hillsborough sheriff's deputy who found her was also a parent, and he was filled with a sickening certainty when he saw her tiny hand sticking up out of a pile of leaves that he would find a dead child. Yet when he uncovered the baby, her open eyes blinked and she fixed her gaze on his. Disregarding his EMT training and reacting as a father, he promptly picked up the girl and cradled her to his chest, telling me later, "I will be there, at a distance, while she grows up."

Or the angry young man from the projects who helped steal a car from a wealthy young girl before he shot her in the head and left her to die. Against all odds, she lived, agonizingly crawling her way across a field to get help. And when the young man's father realized what his son had done, he turned him over to police, breaking his own heart and shattering his dreams that his son would find a better life off the streets.

Covering crime can be scarring, yes, but it also gave me a deep appreciation for the power and the potential of life—even if, at the same time, the darkness of what I learned every day could be isolating. There were many times I felt I knew too much.

While I was at the *Times*, my two youngest boys were preschoolers—I lovingly called them the Little People—and this fact was the only glue between me and most of the stay-at-home mothers on my street. They baked their own bread, breastfed until their babies were well past the toddler stage, and painted teddy bear stencils on their nursery walls.

I, on the other hand, was a soon-to-be divorced single mother with a live-in nanny. I responded to 4 a.m. calls about bullet-ridden bodies next to the Hillsborough River and kept my freezer stocked with microwavable dinners. Instead of doing arts and crafts, I let the Little People paint the garage while clad only in their Spider Man underwear. I didn't date and declined lunch requests with coworkers so I could leave the newsroom in time to have dinner with my boys. My only meaningful social contacts were the women who lived in my neighborhood, although more than one had told me she blamed me for divorcing my children's father. Three straight years of counseling could not fix what was wrong with our marriage, and one day I was done making excuses.

Despite my reservations about those women (except for Patty, who valiantly trained for and ran a marathon with me), one muggy, bug-infested summer night we all met at my neighbor Terry's house for Girls Night Out, an evening whose only mission was to drink too much and swap stories while their husbands and my babysitter stayed at home with the kids.

As Terry's indulgent ex-husband ran out for more wine (I always wondered how she managed that), the tone of the conversation turned confessional. One of the other women, a plump, meticulously dressed mother of one meticulously dressed son, divulged that years before, she really, truly did have sex with the mythological figure Pan, the half-man, half-goat, who suddenly appeared in her bedroom one night when her husband was out of town. The rest of us shrieked with laughter—"Pan? Are you kidding?"

"No, I'm not kidding," the woman steadfastly maintained, calmly folding her neatly manicured hands. "It was the best sex I ever had."

I was still hooting with laughter when she suddenly turned the conversation to me.

"What about you, Amy?" She stared at me hard, her arms crossing over her ample breasts.

Still chuckling, I shrugged—there was nothing to offer. At least, nothing I was willing to give up. Besides, how could I top Pan?

The next moment, as though I were a zebra and they were a pack of lionesses, those domestic divas began to rip me apart.

"You don't let anybody in."

"You come across as a snob."

"You'll never really be close to anyone."

"You're too hard."

And finally, "You have an edge."

They looked at me accusingly, and a long, uncomfortable silence filled the once-jovial room. I tilted my head to one side and considered their assessments. Then I lifted my glass of merlot and smiled. I was too drunk to be offended—indeed, drunk enough to be honest.

"I do have an edge," I admitted with a shrug. "And what's more, I *like* my edge. I *embrace* my edge. It has served me well over the years and helps me survive a job that's all crime and slime, and," I added as I stood unsteadily to leave, "it helps me tolerate all of you."

Go figure that none of us stayed in touch.

Florida is a terrific playground for adults, but not for children. As a crime reporter, I knew all too well the dangers lurking on the streets, and I began doing research to find a better place to raise my boys. The final straw came when someone cut the ropes and stole the cheerful blue-and-red Little Tykes swing that hung from the oak tree in our front yard. So I took a job as the criminal justice reporter at the *Denver Post*, a lesser paper but one located in a part of the country where my kids could leave their Trek bicycles in the front yard and they'd still be there the next morning.

Everything seems to move slower in the West. I wanted to be able to exhale.

Of course I did just the opposite.

In November 2003, the *Post* published a three-part investigative series I coauthored with another reporter, Miles Moffeit, about how the U.S. military mishandles cases of sexual assault and domestic violence. Like a birth, the series took us nine months to research and write, during which I traveled the country to interview more than sixty women veterans. Every one of them was a traumatized survivor of sexual assault.

Before my first interview with a military rape survivor, a courageous former combat medic named Sharon Mixon who at the time shook with trauma as if palsied, I resolved to protect myself by remaining clinical and unmoved. I focused so much on distancing myself from Sharon's palpable pain that later when I reviewed my notes, I found them worthless—I hadn't even double-checked the spelling of her last name.

When I called her back to schedule another interview, Sharon was more than gracious. "That's all right," she said in her Louisiana drawl. "When it comes to puttin' up walls to protect yourself, believe me, I get it."

After that, I made the conscious decision that it would be all or nothing for the story. I didn't yet know how to establish good, healthy limits and boundaries. So, like a sponge, I absorbed the despair of every victim I encountered, leaning in close while I talked with them for hours, writing their stories from the depths of their own trauma. My workdays lasted fourteen, sixteen hours, sometimes even longer. I put the Little People to bed every night, opened my laptop on the kitchen table, unwrapped a Nestlé triple chocolate ice cream cone, and plunged into those veterans' pools of pain. When I dreamed, it was about their rapes.

The series caused a national outcry. We followed it up with hard-hitting reports about women soldiers being sexually assaulted in the combat zone. The stories sparked coverage of the issue of military sexual trauma from media around the country, and Congress launched an investigation, as did Secretary of Defense Donald Rumsfeld, who cited our reports in his memo requesting action. When Miles and I attended the Senate Armed Services hearing, we were treated like heroes by the other media. A producer for *60 Minutes* gave us a bow when we walked in the room.

Reforms were enacted, including changes to the Uniform Code of Military Justice. The stories were nominated for a Pulitzer Prize. But the best nod I got was an unexpected bouquet of red roses from a women's trauma therapy group at the Los Angeles VA Medical Center, sent with a now-treasured card that read simply, "Thank you for being our voice."

I was gratified but exhausted, suffering from secondary post-traumatic stress disorder brought on by absorbing too much of other people's pain. Immediately following the military stories, *Post* editors assigned me another set of investigative reports, this time about female students' allegations of rape by football players and recruits at the University of Colorado at Boulder. Under pressure by an editor for a scoop, I felt like a hamster on a wheel. I was worried about my kids, worried for myself, and for the first time in my career, I decided to say so in an email I sent the editor the first week of February.

> **From:** Herdy, Amy
> **Sent:** Wednesday, February 04, 2004, 1:28 p.m.
> **Subject:** concerns
>
> I need to be honest in telling you I have concerns about becoming embroiled in the CU story. And they are personal--I don't think I realized what a toll the military stories have taken on me until I thought about taking on another project. I haven't had much of a life for a year now and was really, really looking forward to reclaiming one.
>
> I know what covering the CU story means: breaking stories on a daily basis. And believe me, the competitive side of me says Yes, I would be good at this as well as just the mindset of being a hard-core journalist. I go full tilt after every story. I'm not built any other way.
>
> But here's an example: My nine-year-old was a finalist in a spelling bee yesterday. Because he was the shortest kid there, they had to lower the microphone every time it was his turn--he still couldn't reach it, had to tiptoe and people laughed. He was mortified, did terribly and cried afterward. He cried last nite telling me about it.
>
> And the worst part of it was that when it was over, and all the kids ran to their parents, I wasn't there. I was in the newsroom, pushing and pushing on this story, trying to get the attorneys to get the victims to talk, feeling like

I couldn't leave it because we didn't know til the last hour if we had a daily or not. So of course no one was there, as I am a single mom.

And believe me, that hit hard. I know that years from now, the CU story won't matter one damn bit, but he will always remember that awful day. All last year, during the series, I kept telling him and his brother, Just hang in there, after Halloween, it will be over. Then after Thanksgiving . . . and it did ease, briefly.

Anyway, as far as CU--I've already established a really good rapport with the attorneys, and I know we will get the victims before anyone else does, as well as other info. But please, when it comes to the nuts and bolts of this, can someone else be assigned the full brunt of it? I realize what it means to do it right and I honestly don't think I have it in me right now.

Let me know.

Thanks,
Amy

His response was predictable:

Sent: Wednesday, February 04, 2004, 2:21 p.m.
To: Herdy, Amy
Subject: RE: concerns

Yes, Miles raised some of these issues with me, and they concerned me. I do want you to have a life and not to be burdened with an endless series of traumatic stories. On the other hand, I want to be able to tap your first-rate reporting skills. Why don't we sit down and talk about this in the office tomorrow?

Miles, bless him, was adamant about not being immediately involved in another difficult investigation and was allowed to beg off the CU story. Yet when I met with the editor, he flattered, cajoled, and pressed me into trying harder, and as usual, I ignored the warnings of my inner voice and agreed to meet the challenge. I worked around the clock for the next two weeks and finished the story, which documented a written apology by one of CU's football players to the young woman who had accused him of rape.

It ran on the front page. I did not care.

Their appetites whetted by this victory, the editors asked me for more. In an email I sent at the beginning of March, I told them no.

```
No one needs to push me. I do plenty of that on
my own. Victims call me all hours of the morning
and night and weekends. If you want me to track
all my hours, I'd be glad to, and maybe I should.

There are few reporters more competitive than me.
I don't want us to get scooped, either. But I hate
this CU story. I hate the nasty politics of it. I
hate the ugly air of desperation it has generated
in the newsroom.

I have never, in my life or in my career, said
Enough, I can't do this.

Until now.

Enough.
```

But it was too late. Around me, the walls of my life had already begun to crumble.

I'd been maintaining a long-distance relationship with a man also scarred by his work. He had been coaxing me to move back to Florida, and the change—leaving a job that caused me so much misery—sounded like a good idea. Plus, I had never warmed to Colorado's unpredictable ice.

I found a home in Florida three blocks from the beach in a pink stucco of a town called Gulfport, put a deposit on it, and listed my house in Colorado with a realtor. It sold within days, and my boyfriend came to Colorado to help move the boys and me into a temporary rental duplex, a small, boxy concrete structure I dubbed "the bomb shelter."

The entire situation made me edgy and anxious. Security is a huge issue for me because I spent much of my early years feeling abandoned. So over time, I created an independent life for that very reason. Selling my house and uprooting my children—again—for someone else made my heart pound with fear.

And if we focus on what we fear, that's what we'll get.

So was it the stress? Trauma? Or intentional sabotage? Whatever the reason, I told my boyfriend a lie—that I had gone to the doctor—when in fact I had cancelled the appointment because the very thought of going overwhelmed me. I did this in spite—or because?—of him often saying, "Don't ever lie to me": *his* biggest fear.

He returned to Florida and promptly broke up with me by email.

If I could have reached through my computer and snapped off his head, I would have. And in that moment, I decided to remain on the other side of the country, as far from him as possible.

My two older sons, who would be leaving for college in the fall, accepted the news stoically. The hardest part was telling the younger boys, who were seven and nine, that there'd be no new life away from the *Denver Post*, no house near the beach, no man who might have become a new dad. The night I told them, they held each other as they cried. I don't know which loss they mourned the most.

As for me, I balled my hands into fists while vacillating between what felt like overwhelming grief and inconsolable rage; the boyfriend had been the first man I had allowed to be in our lives since the divorce years earlier, and I had been blunt from the beginning. "My heart is one thing," I had warned him in full mother-bear mode, "but you better not hurt my boys."

I blamed him. I blamed myself.

I attempted to sort things out in my journal:

> I feel awful and I feel weak that it's devastated me this much ... Is there a pattern from my father? Was I never good

enough for his approval, or did I subvert my needs in order to always keep him happy? With a father, you keep on trying for connection. With a lover, you can do the same, especially if you're trying to fix that early paternal relationship. Why would I continue to move forward with someone who carries so much anger and has such rigid thinking?

His anger, in the end, reminded me of Dreux. Was I trying to rework that relationship? Or was it a sign of how unhealthy we'd become, and that I was clinging to it despite how awful it made me feel?

Everything stopped.

By now it was late March and the boys' spring break from school. I took a week off to spend long promised time with them. Once I settled, however, I couldn't fathom going back to the newsroom, and my body joined in the revolt. The very idea of driving toward Denver would give me an unrelenting headache. I began to have crying jags—as if finally releasing the anguish of every victim I had ever talked to—as well as my own.

I cried everywhere. I sobbed in the car, I dissolved into tears during dinner or while perusing the aisles at Blockbuster. I fell asleep clutching handfuls of tissues and awoke in the morning with white fuzz stuck to my face. I went to a therapist and wordlessly pointed to the tears as they streamed down my cheeks, as if they were a mystery. "*This*," I finally choked out as I looked into the kind eyes of a woman who would later become my anchor, "I can't seem to be able to stop doing *this*."

Yet when friends gently hinted that perhaps I should take something for depression, I resisted—no pills. I was already filled with a deep fear that I was becoming my mother. "I want to feel this pain," I told them. Instead, I got up every morning and forced myself to go through the familiar motions: Fix the boys breakfast and get them to school. Go for a run. Take a shower. Eat. Brush my teeth. Walk the dog. Feed the dog. Clean house. Drive to the grocery. Fix dinner for the boys. Put them to bed. Wash my face and brush my teeth. Try to sleep. Repeat.

I had no appetite, and when my clothes began to hang, I called friends and asked them to nag me to eat.

My sister, Sally, who lives in Missouri, became so alarmed at my persistent weepiness that she flew out to be with me, an act of love that proved to be the defibrillator my numbed heart needed. I have vivid memories of her cooking on the small, 1970s gold-colored electric stove in the bomb shelter and attacking its dusty windows with vinegar and water on every side. "You need to be able to see out," she said.

Time crawled on. Finally I sent an email to an editor, telling him, "I'm not coming in, and I'm not coming in to fill out paperwork to say I'm not coming in. Leave me alone."

And they did.

From Brent's journal:

> *16 years in prison. Drugs, Lovers, violence and Lies.*
>
> *I'll start with drugs. I went into prison a heroin junky clean for a couple of years. It didn't take Long though to seek it out. The stuff was readily available. I was lucky my source was a Guard so I seldom had to go to the cons for it. There was a time when most Guards knew who the junkies were and were content to leave them be. Hell Junkies are easy to manage when theres a steady flow of dope. I kept a heroin habit until 2000 then began a steady meth habit. Traded Tit for tat with a corrections officer to make sure my urines show clean. Sometimes I muled pot for people either by swallowing balloons in a visit or sticking an ounce or two wrapped in cellophane and a few balloons up my ass while on outside work detail. I got my cut either way.*
>
> *There were serious Incedents of violence over drugs.*

Mostly fights over my getting paid or not being able to pay. I won some Lost some.

Lovers. I had men and women. My first male Lover we will Just call him#1 was Just as fucked up in the head as I was so it was basicaly a perpetual cycle of Fighting and fucking. But for someone who was raised on a steady diet of perversion I couldn't seem to get away from it.

My first Female Lover in prison was a counselor, widowed and lonely.

Only once in my Adult time did someone try to Force me into being a bitch. It was a bloody Long fight and in the end my Attacker realized even If he won the fight I would have killed him. Sooner or later. This probably should have deterred me from doing the same shit but it didn't. I conned, manipulated and forced many weaker guys into Letting me fuck them. There were plenty of willing ones too. It's no badge of honor, I realy don't give a shit what anyone thinks.

How did I survive sixteen years in prison—easy. I created a new me, a solid believable story. Punk a chomo child molester, check a rat in the yard, Act Respectable. Take care of the bros when you can, get in good with the cops without being a snitch. Get the Guard you're fucking to hook your bro up with some head or a shot of pussy. Hell it was all easy but it only helped to further my mental destruction. After a while I believed my own Lies. I couldn't remember what I'd told whom and when. If I hadn't gotten out when I did I was bound to be found out and I probably would have been killed for it.

I played jacks with rattlesnakes every day for sixteen years. My sixteen years in prison was a continuous game for me. Bad relationships, drug use, contraband smuggling, sex, rape, violence, manipulation.

And i knew it would be only a matter of time before i raped when i got out.

April 2004

I took four months off from the *Post* to heal. I had just gotten a German Shepherd puppy my boys and I named Pike, and while they were in school, Pike and I explored trails in the mountains near our home outside of Boulder and began to train in search and rescue.

I traded my signature black suits—an editor once called me the Johnny Cash of reporters—for shorts and tank tops, and quickly grew tan, keeping my long, dark hair in a ponytail. It was a welcome relief to go without makeup and not wear dress clothes.

And while I had periodically gone to a therapist in the past—usually in response to a broken relationship with a man—I now threw myself into it. Twice a week, I saw Michelle Frieswyk-Johnson, the wise and compassionate woman who became my regular therapist, and once a week, I began doing an alternative form of therapy called "energy work." This practice is based on the idea that the energy fields inside us and around us can be manipulated, like a chiropractor can adjust a spine.

Whenever I tell someone this and they roll their eyes, I recite them a line from one of my favorite movies, *Phenomenon*, a film about an everyman played by John Travolta who suddenly becomes a genius and develops telekinetic abilities, which he demonstrates while being tested by the military. When asked how he can perform such feats, Travolta's character says to the doctor, "We're all made of energy, Bob. You know, the little pieces . . ."

Our energy can become blocked or disturbed, according to energy practitioners, who try to "feel" these areas and address them. They can also help release old trauma that has settled into the tissues of your body, and this is what the amazing energy therapist Doug Jones did for me. The first time I met Doug, I hid behind a curtain of my hair while I cried. Within a few weeks, I learned how to feel and control my own energy waves—and how to deflect negative ones from someone else. The ex-boyfriend had started calling my cell and home phone repeatedly, trying to reengage in our angry dance, so I used my new skills to energetically push him away.

Enlightened by this realization, I also began researching the use of crystals. Since my early childhood, I have collected different crystals, and now I learned that they have a vibrational energy of their own, which can be used for healing. Soon everywhere I went, I carried a deep purple chunk of amethyst for an overall healing stone, and for my heart, I fell asleep each night holding a piece of rose quartz in my hand.

Whatever it took, I was willing to do. I was as fervent in my quest to uncover the cause of my undoing as any story I ever pursued and to use the lessons wisely. It had taken me forty years and nearly being swallowed by the whale of depression to do it, and I wasn't gonna waste the life lesson: *There*, take *that*, the universe had said, knocking me on my ass. You're not superhuman after all.

I discovered that I was prone to repeating the dysfunctional roles from my childhood: perpetrator, victim, rescuer. My brother, my mother, me. If I wasn't replaying those roles, I was watching them endlessly unfold through my work as a crime reporter. To stop repeating them and live in a healthy way, I needed to be more conscious of every emotion, every reaction, every choice, every decision.

I learned that I had given myself away, both in my relationship and in my work, and that the breakup was only the symptom of a larger abandonment. For me, the seductive lure of journalism—of the dangling hope that this story, this time would make a difference, however small—carried with it a voraciousness that I sacrificed myself for all too often.

This was further compounded by the grind and competitive demands of daily deadline journalism—what reporters call "the Beast."

When the Beast growled, I fed it, even though it left me empty.

His social history from CSH indicates Mr. Brents grew up in an extremely chaotic and abusive home environment . . . Brent's father continued to be very abusive toward him, and indeed, fractured the orbit in his eye. He was hospitalized and Dependence and Neglect charges were filed; however, they were later dropped for some reason.

—Colorado State Hospital Social Summary report
on Brents, January 4, 1989

FOUR

Legacies

From Brent's journal:

4 July 1976, my head is spinning I'm sweating, sick to my stomach and drunk for the first time in my life. Hell everyone's drunk. We live in a little town just off base of Ft. Huachuca. I'm laying on my back in the weeds there's really not a lot of grass around. Teresa is holding my hand. The fireworks are not really memorable. Hell Teresa is with me. This was our first childhood feeling of love. This was probably the most honest innocent and happiest time of my life. We stole a bottle of Wild Turkey and got drunk and sick. My Dad got even drunker. But for once he did not try anything hurtful he just passed out in another field. Teresa's mom came and got us pretty late. Ok lovebirds she said time for bed. I remember thinking on the walk back to the trailer how my dad was going to kick my ass. I was scared. The next morning I only remember Dad saying bye and going to work.

I know shortly after the 4th Teresa moved to Tucson. It would be 2 years before I would see her again. I never stopped thinking about her.

Then my mom told me Teresa's mom died and we went to Tucson. It hurt when she died. Teresa's grandparents took her in and I know she was happy for a while. She was older than me. I remember one day she said Hey I'm getting boobs. Like I hadn't already known this. But she was right they seemed to have grown overnight. We moved to a little area and bought a store in the country. I missed her terribly but I found another girlfriend. Then her grandparents moved to the same little river valley just up the hill from us. First thing Teresa did was beat up my girlfriend and reclaim her man. Ah Life was grand. For some reason my dad was on a beat and rape break during this time. When they owned the store we actually got along and life was pretty happy.

Then the world caved in. My mom came out while I was feeding our goats and chickens. She told me Teresa died. I know now it was a lie. But I can tell you no physical pain ever hurt as bad as being told my girlfriend died. I've never known anything like what Teresa and I had. And Mom was jealous.

I know I wasn't a good kid after that either. I didn't get outright bitter but I lost something inside. Between Teresa and my Dad's wrath I changed mentally and it went downhill. The worse my Dad got the worse I got. I always felt ashamed at not having been stronger and demanded someone make him stop hurting me and my brother and sister and Mom. I've always felt I had some of the blame.

I had the chance to shoot him one night. I had the gun to his head. She begged and pleaded with me. Please baby don't kill him he's all me and your sister have. Over and over she kept saying that. I thought what about me you bitch. Don't I count for shit. What will happen to your sister she says. Looking back hell maybe it couldn't have been any worse.

Anyway my Dad began raping me in this trailer park in this tiny little trailer (in Ft. Huachuca) and not long after the beatings began in earnest. I did not wet the bed until this time either. After he began raping me I started to wet the bed and have a hard time controlling my bladder *and bowel movements. Which led to problems in school. I started having problems sleeping because I was scared to wet the bed for fear of getting hurt. I was afraid to go to the bathroom for fear of being screwed or forced to perform orally on him. So I would lye awake until I could not keep my eyes open and then it would happen. Either I would wake up or he would wake me up and sure as shit I would have wet the bed. He would drag me to the bathroom by my hair my throat an arm or leg he did not care. He would slap me, hit me, push my head in the toilet. Call me a pussy, a baby, lots of shit.*

Of course in the beginning in school I did not do well. Some behavioral problems but mostly being too tired to consentrate or in pain or fearing rape or beating when I got home. I did not realize it until years later that I never told for the same reasons no one ever confronted him. He was huge, scary as hell and he was a smooth talkin manipulator. He was intimidating to everyone he met and involved in everything. He was screwing men out of money and there wives sexually. He owned a chuck wagon and did that job in the mornings and his security job at night. He drank to excess did uppers and downers. Beat my Mom ruthlessly and I tried to help her and got my head beat on for interfearing. Sometimes I got beat for no reason at all and then sometimes for realy stoopid reasons. Once I cut my foot in a mint patch I accidentally stepped in. He took me to the doctor got my foot sewed up. Then beat the piss out of me for being clumsy. My Mom started molesting me (again) in Ft. Huachuca too. It felt ok so I didn't complain. That's how it began and went for 7 years.

Mom and I became realy realy entence, sexually and emotionally. It was weird. Like she and I were the husband and wife, Dad was furniture. Dad worked and stayed out and she would let me skip school to be with her. We'd hold hands talk, play. I would go to leave and she'd say don't not a command but like begging.

You know I always was selfish, thinking no one would understand what I went through as a child, or how I felt . . . feeling like people could look at me and see the ugliness and fear. Know I was screwing my mom or that i was a rapist or that i found love in cheap meaningless ways. Waking up in the night. Living 24 hours a day wondering why i have to be who i am. The reality that i am a sociopath and only truly care for a few people really sucks.

Ok the house North of Ft. Huachuca '79 Brandy and I started to play together a lot. For awhile it was ok there. Then with a vengeance he started back in on us. It was also about this time I started becoming aware of my body in a sexual way. I started doing sexual things with the younger girls and even the girls my age. Plus things with my mom started getting weird. I think I screwed up in school pretty bad to. I could not concentrate and I was out of school to often to real do good. Then came the night he raped Brandy for the first time him and my mom. And From There it got worse, raping him, locking him in the room, not feeding him.

To this day it haunts me, The memory of sitting there in the closet in the corner where I broke a small hole through the wall so i could sneak him food. How time after time he would beg me to stay at that hole and talk to him and play with him. He called me bubby, Bubby please stay and play with me. At night after my dad would fuck me or beat me i would Lay there on that closet floor and we would hold hands through that Little hole. Brandy was in that room for about two months Give or take. I don't know all that my dad did to him but i know he hurt him far worse than me. I remember in the day time when dad was gone I would beg my mom to open the door. Only once she did. Brandy wanted to go outside and play. But he had to bath first. I remember how i used to love his hair he had bright shiny blonde hair, I think maybe one reason for my dad's hatred of him. That day I was going to hide him somewhere but we were so terrified of my dad we went home and my mom locked him back in his room before dad came home.

I told a teacher about Brandy. Then they came and took him. I felt guilty, sad and truly Lost but at least he would not get hurt any more. They didn't know I told. I know Lots of people started coming around after that and Dad figured it was time to split. So we went to Wyoming. We lived in a small trailer in Casper.

I was changing mentaly and physicaly. I was going thru puberty and becoming self aware. I had this paper route me and my mom we delivered the local paper on one whole side of town. It was here I started Learning how to stalk and Remember the whos-whats-whens and wheres. I would take so many papers on my bike and deliver them and double back to Look in windows of women or girls. I Learned where there were abandoned houses and buildings, which alleys were safe to take young girls from school thru. I found trails down to the river and hid supplies anchored and waterproofed them in case of flood I started carrying a knife. I Learned I could now ejaculate and made the girls I was being sexual with or molesting Let me do it on Them Like I had seen in mom and dads porn. It seemed my mom and dad always had realy perverted friends to. My mom and dads Lover, she also became my molester-Lover. She was a junky and a prostitute. She didn't even blink when my dad told her to fuck me.

In Wyoming dad did not hurt me sexually to often but when he did it was fierce and Painful and usualy physicaly brutal as well. He'd get this crazy Look in his eye We need a hunting Trip Boy. My heart would sink, I'd scream inside. I loved to hunt and fish and camp but I never realy had fun *because I anticipated hurt from him. I sorta became two people. The abused Abuser and the free kid. I got molested and molested others.*

It took the courts a long time to catch up. But after my dad shattered my face I Lost it.

I was forty years old before I figured out just how angry I was over the loss of much of my childhood. And in that regard, just as I have her long French nose and love of words, I inherited my mother's rage as well.

The third oldest of nine in a Catholic family, my mom often told me the story of how her mother would hand her the latest baby before she, my grandmother, would slowly climb the winding oak staircase to the second floor of their enormous Southern house and go to bed.

After marrying and starting a family of her own, my mother vowed to be different. Fueled by an angry determination, she would leave for her job teaching school just as we woke up. She would teach all day, come home and cook dinner, and jump back in her car and commute an hour away to the university as she worked toward her master's degree in education. She was a whirlwind of tight-lipped efficiency, and we all knew not to cross her. Once, while she was teaching English at a rural high school, one of the farmer's sons nonchalantly sprawled out his long legs while he lit up a cigarette. My mother took it away from him, and when he defiantly reached for another, her temper flared.

"You light up that cigarette," she snapped, "and I'll do my damnedest to ram it down your throat." Without a word, the farmer's son put the cigarette away.

I was never sure if my mother mercilessly pushed herself only to create her own identity, or if part of it was to work toward the financial comfort she knew as a child from a wealthy family in a small Southern town. Money was often tight in my parents' household; my father's engineer salary and my mother's meager teaching pay were always stretched thin as they put their children—there were four of us—through private Catholic school. And not having money bothered our mother a great deal.

She often told me she married our father for his intelligence and his strong bone structure: "I wanted to have beautiful children," she said. She also wanted a beautiful house like the grand home she grew up in, and when my father bought some rocky acreage in the Shawnee National Forest in southern Illinois instead so he could camp and hike in the woods as he'd done in his childhood, I don't think she ever forgave him. Then my mother's health collapsed, the medical bills began to mount, and that was all she wrote.

When I was very young, a housekeeper came three times a week. Soon that became once a week, and then my parents let her go altogether. My father's idea of maintaining a house was only pragmatic; he would—and could—fix anything with duct tape. As her health declined and so did our house, my mother despised what was becoming her prison for its shabbiness and disrepair.

"I *hate* this house," she would say, eyeing the worn carpets and peeling paint with a mixture of contempt and hysteria, and every time she did, I would be flooded with sorrow and shame, as if it were also my fault she was so miserable. Then I'd tidy the house to try to cheer her up.

One day when I was about six, I looked at the worn brick wall framing the fireplace in our living room and realized the bricks were once the color of the red shoe polish I put on my sensible school shoes. So I opened the polish and, using the brush applicator, painted the worn part of the bricks so they would once again be a bright, happy red. The problem was, once the polish dried, it was no longer a shiny, red-delicious-apple color but an ugly, dull rust. And it wouldn't wipe off. I slunk guiltily out of the room and put the shoe polish away. No one ever said anything.

It felt like I had two mothers. On a Good Day, I remember her briskly typing up her latest school paper on her heavy black Smith Corona typewriter or pumping out leg lifts on the living room floor or carefully touching up her makeup in the bathroom mirror. At not quite five foot two, she was petite and quick and hummed with energy, and around the house, she'd often burst loudly into snippets of raucous songs, such as "Take it off, take it off, shouted the boys from the rear. Take it off, take it off, soon was all you could hear. And the band played a polka while she stripped!"

On a Good Day, she could be vivacious, funny, and loving, and throw a fabulous dinner party, served on the finely detailed German china, engraved silver, and delicate crystal that had been handed down through both sides of the family.

On a Bad Day, she alternated between harsh resentment of my father and a palpable despair that life had not turned out as she planned. On a Bad Day, she crawled under the covers and set her electric blanket on high, while time—and the rest of us—marched on without her.

Then when I was twelve, things took a turn for the worse. My mother was diagnosed with Ménière's disease, an inner ear disorder whose main symptom of vertigo can be so severe as to become crippling. She literally began to lean on my father just to walk across the floor, and this triggered something protective in him. Her once-absent husband started to dote on my mother as they visited doctor after doctor, none of whom could offer much relief. For the twelve years I lived in Tampa, the only time they came to visit me—and their grandchildren—was on their way to Sarasota to see yet another specialist.

After the official diagnosis, my mother pretty much stayed in bed. If she did manage to be up for a while, she would often regale me with stories of her childhood, and a common theme was her resentment about taking care of her own mother when my grandmother was hit with bouts of depression.

The pattern wasn't lost on me, but I vowed it would end with me. Once I had children of my own, I made it a point to try to *engage* with them, whether by reading them books or teaching them baseball or simply cuddling on the couch. It's a daily challenge to juggle all the demands of raising children *and* keeping a house *and* working a full-time job, and I had followed my mother's footsteps and married (and later divorced) a man whose absences were so pronounced that I nicknamed him "the Ghost." I wouldn't even think of giving up journalism, so I learned to live my life around it. So did my family.

I remember once while interviewing someone for a story, I glanced at the time and fretted about the baby, my youngest, waiting for me at home. Since I was still nursing, the thought alone was enough to make my milk come down, which is to say, my breasts filled up and started to leak. I carefully and firmly folded both arms across my chest in an attempt to staunch the flow while I abruptly finished up the interview. Nursing my children was a sweet part of their babyhood, and probably one of the few times in my life I didn't feel the need to justify my existence any other way. Although once I did try to nurse the baby *and* vacuum. It didn't work.

At any rate, I tried to put my children first and ended up going too far in the other direction. I always put my needs last. It's hard to give when you're empty or, in my case, exhausted. And it was years before I became comfortable with self-care as simple as taking a nap, because it always reminded me of my childhood and the lonely yet familiar sight of my mother's shadowy form curled in her bed, the thick beige curtains in her room drawn to keep out the light.

And I've never liked heavyset men, because they remind me of Dreux, my second-oldest brother, who was named for our French ancestors but resembled more of the stocky German side of the family. Our childhood affected all four of us. My oldest brother, Roger, and I immersed ourselves in work for recognition, and my sister, Sally, turned to God—but Dreux fueled his rage over abandonment with drugs or alcohol. He started by smoking and then dealing marijuana, and to this day I can't stand the smell of pot. I associate the musky, oily odor with hypocrisy—because clouds of it rolled out of my brother's room, and no one in our family ever talked about it.

As Dreux escalated up the drug scale, so did his anger, and when he erupted in a rage—which was often—he would clobber anyone or anything in his path. For some reason, that usually ended up being me, and not my sister, perhaps because I reminded him of our mother since I inherited her dark French looks, and Sally takes after the blond and blue-eyed German side of the family.

By the time he was a teenager, Dreux stood six feet tall and weighed more than two hundred pounds. Until I hit a growth spurt at fifteen, I was five foot three and weighed a hundred pounds. It was no contest.

One afternoon when I was twelve and he was sixteen, Dreux confronted me as I carried a stack of clean laundry into Roger's upstairs bedroom.

"What are you doing in here? This isn't your room."

"I was just putting laundry away," I retorted sharply, "and it's not your room, either."

The blow came so fast that I only had time to choke out a short scream before his fist slammed into the side of my head. Knocked into the wall with a resounding thud, I slid down it, blinking my eyes rapidly as I struggled to stay conscious. The only other thing I remember from that day is my sister shrieking at Dreux to stop.

Years later while living in Tampa, I took kickboxing lessons to work through those memories and confront my fear. No one likes being hit, but because of growing up with Dreux, I was afraid that if physically confronted by someone during a story, I would freeze like a rabbit instead of defending myself. Becoming frozen with shock was often a reaction I had with Dreux, who, in between delivering the real thing, delighted in throwing mock blows close to my face just to see me flinch.

"Don't hold back," I told the instructor, a fiery Latino named Manny who had the solid, heavy build of a refrigerator, but of course he did. Time after time, week after week, he and I would circle each other in his small, simple dojo, both of us wearing weighted gloves and no other padding, and spar. Although Manny would pull his punches, he'd also taunt me. He had to, because during the first several sessions, every time his gloved fist came near my face, I would instinctively jump back, then realize it was just him and giggle. I guess I was releasing nervous energy. Still, I hated myself for it.

"C'mon, c'mon, you hit like a girl!" he would yell at me in an attempt to get a rise of anger, and it usually worked. The turning point came one day near the end of a particularly tough sparring session when suddenly neither of us was holding back. In the midst of delivering a flurry of hammer-like blows to my midsection, Manny unexpectedly and firmly threw both gloved hands against my shoulders and slammed me against the wall.

I panicked. I couldn't move, couldn't breathe. I was twelve again, cornered by someone stronger than me.

But he was *not* fiercer. Not anymore.

The pain of being hit snapped me back to the present.

"Get out of it, get out of it!" Manny yelled as he resumed pounding me, his arms working like speeding pistons into my stomach as he bent over with intent. In that instant, something clicked inside my head. Instead of giggling or crying, I clenched my jaw, drove myself up and over the crouching Manny, hooked my left arm around his head, and pounded my right elbow between his shoulder blades as hard as I could—*wham wham wham wham wham.* His breath exhaled in a sharp gasp and he broke free, turning away. "Good job," he said, his voice full of pride, and although I was sorry I hurt him, I was proud too.

After that, whenever a frightening memory of Dreux surfaced, I was able to shrug it away. "You are no longer that helpless little girl," I would remind myself. Still, I resented that he had any impact at all on my life.

So when I got a call on my cell phone from my mother one breezy afternoon in May 2004 as I drove to King Soopers, I rolled up the windows and simply sat in my car in the parking lot for a while, digesting it.

Dreux, the tormentor of my childhood and the threatening presence inside too many sleep-twisted dreams, was found dead after his ex-wife and son didn't hear from him for a few days. The coroner would later determine that his heart had stopped, but we all knew he had drunk himself to death. He was only forty-five.

I hadn't seen or talked to him in nearly twenty years—by choice. The last time I had seen him, I took a loaded gun out of his hands as he sat, cross-legged and stinking, swaying drunk, on the floor of his apartment. I was there because of a frantic call from his estranged wife that he had been threatening suicide, and other than feeling resentful that I had to suddenly leave work, I realized I felt nothing for this pathetic figure of a man. By that time, he had been stuck in the same pattern for several years: binge, enter a rehab center (paid for by my parents), and leave said rehab center halfway through treatment.

In that moment in his apartment, I decided I was done. "You won't see me again," I told him.

And I kept my word. I maintained an unlisted number and refused repeated requests from my family to give it to him, a stance reinforced when they would occasionally give me the latest report on Dreux's life, a consistent litany of binges and rehab centers and outbursts of rage.

Still, my cold dismissal of our sibling angered my sister. "He keeps calling me and asking for your number, and it's not fair that I have to deal with him about it," she said to me once on the phone, and I could tell she was fuming.

"So, let me get this straight—you want me to call him just to tell him that I don't want to ever talk to him again?" I replied. "Nope, I'm not gonna do it. I don't want to have *any* contact with him, ever again." And so I didn't.

Now, as I sat in the car, I searched for an inkling of regret and found none.

"How do I feel about Dreux's death?" I wrote in my journal later that night. "Relief—the boogeyman is gone. Sad that he died alone. Sad that we never really had a relationship. Sad that I couldn't help him. Is that what spurs me to go back to work? I couldn't save my brother?"

The Little People and I flew to Missouri, where my parents now lived, and we caravanned with Sally, her husband, and their kids on the drive to Kentucky for the funeral. The day before the service, I accompanied my parents to the funeral home so they could pick up my brother's ashes as well as choose caskets for their own future burials. Struck with the sad reality of this act for these now elderly, frail people—my father had Parkinson's and my mother's health never improved—I pulled up my protective reporter wall to walk through the afternoon in as stoic a manner as possible.

After I drove them back to the hotel, my father carefully holding the urn in his lap, he handed me the container for safekeeping. Then my parents immediately escaped to their room, and I was left with the distasteful decision of where to keep the bronze urn with my brother's ashes until the next day's service. What to do? Minutes later, I found Sally and my oldest brother, Roger, sitting next to the indoor hotel pool, watching all our children happily splash under a chlorine cloud.

"Dreux is in Mom and Dad's car, in the trunk," I told them.

The next day at the funeral at St. Thomas Moore Church, I sat in a honey-colored wooden pew and watched my sister step up to the podium for the eulogy. She has a master's degree in theology, and I was sure that if anyone could deliver an inspiring, articulate talk on a subject so difficult, she could.

Sally searched out with her deep blue eyes our parents and my brother and me, and flashed us a smile that can only be described as brilliant in its warmth. Once she started speaking, I was mesmerized by her words. What she was saying was not academic. It came, as the best art does, from the heart.

"Part of my relationship with Dreux was colored by hope—hope and longing that I could get to the real Dreux, and sadness when that wasn't possible," my sister began. "Every once in a while I got—we all got—glimpses of the real Dreux, the parts that I would like to think were most truly him: his generosity, his sense of humor, his compassion, his brilliance. But so many other times our relationships with him were marked by sadness, by disappointment that the real Dreux couldn't show himself. I don't understand what all kept him from displaying what I'd like to think of as the truest parts of who he was, but I know those parts were there."

I sat motionless, thoughts tumbling in my head as I struggled to identify with her perception of our brother, and I tried hard to find a good memory of him. Instead, I could only recall mean scenes: Dreux screaming and stamping his foot in rage on the thin floor upstairs because he ran out of hot water in the shower. Dreux slamming his fist on the thick black metal grate on top of our gas stove so hard it broke, then snarling at our mother, "Better the stove than you." Dreux discovering I was leaving out food next to the alley for a scared, stray, brown-and-white spotted pointer dog and telling me, "If you feed it again, I'll kill it." Dreux coming home to find me alone because our parents were at the Mayo Clinic in Minnesota and, twitching from the chemicals coursing through his system, staring at me with hooded eyes and asking if he could see me naked. Wordlessly, I backed away from him and then turned and bolted for the safety of my room.

No, I didn't know any other part of him other than a hateful one.

With a sigh, I turned my attention back to my sister.

"This is a time for facing the truth, and the truth is that none of us can control another's destiny," Sally was saying. "Many of us, at one time or another, tried to help Dreux, reach out to him, help him find healing and hope. It is our agony that we were unable to do so, but the responsibility lay with him. So many times we all waited with baited breath as we watched and prayed for Dreux to climb out of the valley of darkness, and so many times life and hope and healing were just around the corner for Dreux, but ultimately out of reach.

"And why was this so? Human suffering and weakness and illness are a mystery. Who among us can judge the interior of the human heart?"

Who among us can judge? That thought resonated with me. By holding on to my anger and contempt for my brother, wasn't I also continuing to judge him? I didn't know the secrets of his childhood, what heartbreak he might have felt before replacing it with rage. Still, could I forgive him?

I didn't think I had it in me.

Yet I had seen, up close and personal, the devastating effects of hanging on to anger, hate, disappointment, and despair. I saw it in my mother, in Dreux, in the countless crime victims I interviewed over the years, in myself. I knew it was toxic, and I'd be healthier without it. But *how* do you forgive?

Later, I would ask my sister that question. "Well, it takes time," she told me. "Forgiveness is a process."

Aha, I thought. As a long-distance runner, I understood about *process*. I understood settling in and learning to breathe and being patient and malleable and enduring, even when parts of you balked with pain or fear.

So on my next run, I decided to conduct an experiment.

I waited until I was well into my fourth mile, the air flowing readily in and out of my lungs, legs easily striding, and my feet pounding out a familiar rhythm on the dirt trail that was as comforting to me as the sound of a mother's heartbeat to her baby.

It was time. But the words stuck in my throat—I could barely get them out. Nevertheless, I was determined to try, and determined to keep saying them, even if it took years, until they rang with truth.

"Dreux," I said out loud, almost wincing at his name, "I forgive you."

Brents is NOT considered a management problem. He has been polite and courteous to staff and peers alike, and gets along well with everyone. He admits he was difficult to handle before, but has learned that it is better to do his own time and move on than to be a troublemaker.

—From Brent Brents' Colorado Department of Correction Progress Assessment Summary, February, 14, 2004, five months before his release from prison

FIVE

A Man in My Life

Strangely, Colorado now seemed like home. On the return trip from Missouri, I found myself smiling at the Front Range mountains from my plane window. And cold and snow notwithstanding, I was determined to try to be happy there. I scraped together some money and bought a small, gray house in Boulder County with a large, flower-filled yard, perfect for one woman, two boys, and a rapidly growing dog. I returned to work at the *Post* in the beginning of August 2004, rested, wiser, and determined to put in practice the new boundaries I'd learned to balance my demanding career and the rest of my life. From now on, I vowed, I would be more aware.

I tried to no longer plow through each day at breakneck speed. Instead, I slowed down, focused, and tried to pay attention to the details. Especially warning signs.

But without Robot from *Lost in Space* to wave his metal arms and shout to me, "Danger, danger, Will Robinson!" I still missed a lot.

Because the *Post* building was in the middle of downtown Denver, which held an interesting mix of business people, students, homeless persons, and thugs, I was always careful at night when I walked the five blocks from work to the cheap place where I parked my car. I would pass several alleys along the way, each with the strong ammonia stench of urine, and empty stretches of desolate-looking parking lots.

Although security guards were available to escort us out, they either had heavy bellies lapping over their belted uniform pants or white hair and twig-like bones. The joke among the reporters was that the guards looked so un-guard-like that *we* would have to protect *them*.

So I always walked briskly and alone, head held high, keys in one hand and my cell phone in the other, and as soon as I climbed inside my Jeep, I'd lock the doors. One late night in September 2004, a month after I'd returned to work, my steps were slower than usual. It had been a particularly grueling day of writing about the death of Gordie Bailey, a freshman at the University of Colorado who tragically died of alcohol poisoning after an absurd fraternity hazing that involved guzzling wine and liquor. His fraternity "brothers" had then used markers to write slurs on Gordie as he lay passed out in the frat house, including the word "bitch," one letter for each finger of his right hand. He never woke up. I had two teenage boys at home close to Gordie's age, and the senselessness of his death hurt my heart.

Once inside my car, I put down my cell phone and the pen I always kept tucked behind my ear at work. It was time to transition to home, time to try to shake off the sadness of the story.

It was peaceful in that spot, quiet. I closed my eyes and breathed deeply, trying to clear my mind of work and let go of thoughts of death for the night.

As I always do after a story that reminds me of mortality, I asked the universe to look after my boys. I pictured their young faces, one after the other, and prayed they'd stay safe. And as it always does when I think of them, my heart began to fill with lightness.

I felt no sense of danger.

I should have.

Because I didn't know it then, but I wasn't alone.

He sat on top of a brick wall that bordered a downtown Denver parking lot and waited. It was a perfect vantage point—high enough to give him a bird's eye view of every direction and yet shielded by the shadows of nearby buildings to prevent any glint of streetlight reflecting off his wire-rimmed glasses. As a hunter of humans, he knew the importance of those things. Ever the patient wolf, he flexed his thick forearms while he waited for a sheep to appear.

And then he saw her and had instant recognition. He knew he had seen her before—he never forgot a face—and it only took him a moment to remember where: first on TV months ago, talking about some story dealing with rape in the military, and then later on the *Denver Post* elevator. A reporter. He'd still been in prison when those military rape stories ran, and watched her on the news. She was sharp and earnest, and had a fierce energy to her that had caught his attention. She reminded him of that social worker he once knew, the modern-day crusader. She also had long brown hair, like Teresa.

Now she was within his sights, and he sized her up: Wearing a dark suit, she was tall and athletic-looking, but he had brute strength and the element of surprise. And it would be so easy—just a hop off the wall and a few quick strides, and he could cut her off before she reached her car. No one was around to hear if she tried to scream.

Just then, she passed under a street light, and through the curtain of her long, straight brown hair, he caught a glimpse of her face. She looked so . . . sad. Heavily burdened, as if any moment, she would dissolve into tears. He sat rooted as she unlocked her car and got inside and then did something unexpected: Laying her cell phone on the dash, she pulled out a pen from behind her right ear, tucked her hair back in its place, closed her eyes, and just sat there.

Minutes passed, and he stared, feeling unable to move. He found himself scanning the street, not wanting anyone to disturb her. Then she sighed deeply, started the Jeep's engine, and drove away.

Still seated on the wall, the man stared after the car. He would see her again. He'd make a point of it.

For the most part, life at the *Post* went smoothly that fall. In fact, my life overall was firmly in place. Only one thing had been missing.

Back at the end of August, on a morning when the bright light of the high-desert summer streamed across my mahogany queen-sized bed—where I lay smack-dab in the middle—I acknowledged the small voice that had been nagging at me.

You are alone, it whispered.

Yes, I'm alone, I agreed with the voice, but what's wrong with that? I'm reasonably happy.

You could be . . . happier, it persisted.

So I made it a deal. "Fine," I said out loud to no one in particular and the universe in general. "If I am meant to be alone, then tell that whisper to shut the hell up. If not, and I'm supposed to be with somebody, then give me a sign. And make it *today*."

Later that afternoon, standing on a pile of concrete rubble at a practice for canine urban search and rescue, I glanced up and saw a tall, lean, tanned man with blond hair, strong features, and kind blue eyes who was evaluating the exercise. He smiled at me, I smiled back, and something deep within my heart shifted.

He was a Boulder park ranger named Matt. The best thing about him is his inherent goodness—you can see it in his eyes. He's also wise, funny, independent, sexy as hell, and brave—an essential quality. I know it's not easy to be with me. It's not for the faint of heart.

The boys became crazy about him, and even though he initially took Matt's arm in his teeth, Pike warmed to him. So I surrendered my heart. On New Year's Eve, witnessed by our families, Matt and I married. I was in love and happy, pinching myself over my good fortune and smiling every morning as I drove toward downtown Denver to go to work.

Once back in the newsroom, however, I soon shed the cloak of my home life as I always had and became the same relentless reporter. I may have surrendered my heart, but my inner cat-with-claws still existed, and I could call upon her at will. Part of it was the demands of the job. The rest of it was my competitive spirit—evident in all facets of my life, a remnant from a childhood spent struggling for attention and approval. So I didn't simply jog for recreation, I ran marathons; I couldn't take one self-defense class, I learned kickboxing until it was second nature; and when I focused on a story, I refused to be bested.

In February, as the reports of a rapist striking in Denver began to have familiar circumstances, officials confirmed my suspicions that a serial sex offender appeared to be responsible. Once police identified the man as Brent Brents, *Denver Post* reporters, like others all over the city, scrambled to develop a profile of him.

And now that the name was public, the shocking truths began.

On Thursday, February 17, after being deluged with calls from the media, Aurora Police Chief Ricky Bennett held a news conference to defend one of his detectives who in November heard a graphic confession from Brents about molesting the eight-year-old son of his girlfriend—yet never arrested him.

Earlier that day, the Arapahoe County District Attorney's office released details of the confession in an affidavit that accompanied the warrant for Brents' arrest in the case, and reporters immediately picked up on the discrepancy of two dates: Brents' confession on November 23, and the fact a warrant for his arrest wasn't issued until January 26.

What happened?

"I called the police in October about my son," the boy's mother told reporters. "They didn't file charges until the middle of January. It shouldn't take that long for anything, particularly when children are involved."

The woman said she met Brent Brents in July 2004, shortly after he moved in across the street with Derrick West, the man he met the day he was released from prison. She was pregnant, going through a divorce, and vulnerable.

Within a few weeks, she and Brents became lovers. At times, the woman told police, they let her eight-year-old sleep in their bed because he seemed to crave the security.

Yet to the woman's family, something about Brents was off, and soon a background check revealed their worst fear: He was a convicted pedophile. Brents had told the woman he'd gone to prison at seventeen for beating a girlfriend.

The mother questioned her son, who revealed that Brents had indeed molested him in their bed. After the boy repeated his story to social workers and police, a detective asked Brents to come in for an interview on November 23—and surprisingly, he did. Once there, he admitted to using his hands to molest the boy, including anal penetration.

The entire interview was recorded by digital camera.

"She's not a liar," Brents told officers during the interview about the mother's claims. "I freaked out because I had done that and I was scared to death."

Why didn't they arrest him—a convicted pedophile who just confessed to what amounted to sexual assault on a child?

The officers allowed Brents to leave because they needed to do more investigating, their chief later said.

"All I can tell you is statements were made," Bennett told reporters. "This person has a right to a fair trial."

After receiving the police report two weeks later, on December 9, the Arapahoe County DA's office drew up charges. Yet emails sent by an assistant DA to the detective on the case, Del Matticks, went unanswered—because they were being sent to a nonexistent email address.

An assistant DA finally called Matticks on January 3, and a week later, he went to their office to sign the affidavit for the warrant. The paperwork couldn't be found. On January 18, on his day off, Matticks again went to the DA's office, but a sign on the door said to return the next day, so he did, and finally signed the paperwork.

A week later, on January 26, a judge signed the warrant for Brent's arrest, but by then, he was long gone, and his victim count had been stacking up ever since.

Who *was* this man?

When you really want to learn about someone, you go to their family. A quick scan of databases by *Post* researcher Barbara Hudson revealed several potential relatives in Fort Smith, Arkansas, and we reporters began to bombard them with phone calls. For the most part, they would not talk.

A tenacious reporter with the *Rocky Mountain News*, our competitor, managed to get a few seconds on the phone Thursday night with a young woman who would only identify herself as Brents' sister. Upon being told of the allegations against him, she began to sob. "I had no clue," she cried. "Oh fucking God, he deserves whatever he gets."

An edited version of the quote ran in the Friday morning edition of the *Rocky*, and three blocks away at the *Denver Post*, editors read it and frowned. No fewer than five reporters at the *Post* had been making those same calls, yet the *Rocky* had scored a dreaded coup. I had been one of those reporters dialing and redialing that number, leaving pleading messages when the machine was not too full to record them, but I had also been on deadline the day before with the story of how Brents had been allowed to walk after confessing to molesting the eight-year-old boy. As I talked to one of the editors, my frustration showed.

"If we want to get these people to talk to us, we're not going to get them from a newsroom in Denver," I told him in my typical blunt fashion. "Someone needs to show up on their doorstep in Fort Smith." A few minutes later, two of the editors walked up to me. "Great idea," one of them said. "We want you to go."

I balked. I didn't want to leave Matt, who did not have children of his own and was still learning the ropes of fatherhood, to play "Mr. Mom" while I spent the next few nights in Arkansas. "Can't someone else do it?" I asked, glancing around the newsroom. "No," Editor #1 said. "We want you to go."

It was noon. In turns cursing and apologetic, I called Matt to break the news, and he took it well. "Do what you have to do, honey, then come on home," he said in his cheerful fashion. I then booked a $1,200 3 p.m. flight on American Airlines using my *Post* credit card, ran the three blocks to my aging green Jeep Cherokee, and drove the twenty-seven miles from downtown Denver to home in twenty minutes. I threw a few things in my blue duffel bag, drove the forty-five minutes to Denver International Airport as fast as I dared and made it with time to kill.

The trip took nearly four hours and the last leg was on a "commuter plane," a polite term for puddle jumper. They always make me nauseated. The car rentals were closed at the tiny airport in Fort Smith, so I took a cab to the Residence Inn down the road, checked in, and began to scout the area for a decent place to eat.

Sure theres a good guy in here. One whose kind and sensitive, Caring, understanding Outgoing athletic, funny. A Man Who Loves Life. An man who enjoys the beauty of the world, Art, history, places, people. Yet I can't get past my brain.

Like I said Karma is a motherfucker and Its Lookin me full in the face.

Now I only have one true regret. I never gave anyone the chance to love the real me. Had I done that and been courageous years ago maybe Just maybe Tiffany would have found an empty apartment. And the countless others would never have suffered my destruction.

—**From Brent's journal**

SIX

Manhunt

Back in Denver, Aida Bergfeld could not sit still. Before becoming a prostitute, her mother, Kim, had once earned a living as a fortune-teller, and Aida had her own sixth sense, she told Brent. She was filled with such a terrible sense of dread, she said, and begged him to leave the city with her, to walk right out of that building at 1057 Marion Street.

"Baby, bad shit's gonna happen," Aida said to him now. "I'm scared."

Friday, February 18, 2005

Late Afternoon
From Brent's journal:

> I had $2,300 in cash. She asked me if we could go see Hunter Thompson. I said yeah we'd leave after dark. I went to King Soopers and bought her cookies and Big K soda . . . someone saw me and called the cops. I was back in the apartment, Aida was riding me and arranging cookies on my chest and stomach when she saw the cops through the window. They were looking for me I was sure. But they left. I smoked a bowl and relaxed. Later that evening we were laying there when

Aida again noticed someone coming only this time it was Tiffany and she was coming in.

With her strawberry blond hair, high cheekbones, and small, turned-up nose, the slender thirty-three-year-old Tiffany Engle resembled a tall, real-life pixie.

Yet her schedule and work ethic belied that waifish appearance. Engle, who was single, put in a full week as a brokerage assistant at Marcus & Millichap, a Denver investment services firm, and managed two apartment buildings on the side.

One of those buildings was at 1057 Marion Street.

Near Cheesman Park, much of Marion Street is a nod to Denver's past. According to records, after a fire in 1863 devastated the city, a Brick Ordinance requiring all new buildings be constructed of brick or stone was put into place that same year and stayed in effect until the 1940s. Rows of historic, stately redbrick bungalows line nearby neighborhoods. The apartment building at 1057 Marion Street, however, was built in the 1950s, and its squatty, rectangular shape didn't fit.

On Friday, February 18, although she had already put in a full day, Engle, wearing a skirt, blouse, and tall, high-heeled boots, parked her car on Marion Street and headed toward the building to check on vacant unit number 4.

She had no way of knowing who was inside.

5:30 p.m.
From Brent's journal:

I told Aida to hide in the little room, while I hid behind the bedroom door. Tiffany came in and said what the fuck noticing our stuff piled on the wall. She walked to the kitchen. Then I heard her go into the bathroom and finally she came to the bedroom door and hesitated. Then came in and saw me.

I was neckade and sweating from Adrenalyn then Aida came out also necked. Tiffany put up her hands and backed up. I told her I didn't want to hurt her, Just go in the bathroom Lady I said and we'll split. But she freaked and moved backward and tripped over the 2 x 4 on the floor just outside the door. She fell backward Landing with a thump. Instinctively I went to help her up. She flipped I guess thinking I was going to attack her. She kicked me a couple of times and stabbed me in my right hand with her keys. I got control of her arms and pushed her up against the wall in the hallway opposite the bedroom. I told Aida to get the knife and go cut the string off the window blinds. As Aida came around me Tiffany kicked out catching Aida in the chin with her boot. Aida screamed in pain and I lost it.

I picked Tiffany up by her throat and slammed her into the wall and then down to the floor. I started choking her and blacked out when I came to I had one hand (left) on Tiffany's throat and pushed myself up, Standing over her. She was purple she was quiet until she caught her wind and then started to cry and scream and moan. There is a pool of blood under her head Sometime during my blackout I hit her with the 2 x 4. She wouldn't stop screaming and I was pissed because she fought me. All I wanted her to do was go in the bathroom. She wouldn't shut up and I was like you fuckin bitch you'll shut the fuck up. I picked up a 2 x 4 and hit her in the head again. She stopped screaming but kept moaning. So I got down and started choking her. You fuckin cunt you'll die.

AIDA is beating me on my back Come on baby Let's go! Shes screaming at me. Then I could see Tiffany like a slow motion movie she was dying. There was blood in her eyes.

> She was purple, her lips are blue. The light is not in her eyes now. She knows and I know she's going to die.
> Somehow, she reaches up with her right hand and touches my cheek and mouths the word Please. No sound comes out but the word is plain. She's looking me dead in the eyes. Please. Her hand is flat against my cheek. Then it falls slack and I let go of her throat. I got off her chest. Her skirt was hicked so her panties were showing . . . her hose were all screwed up from struggling. It just did not seem right to leave her like that so I fixed her hose and her shirt and her skirt. I brushed the wisp of hair out of her face. Aida was standing there she's pretty huh. Yeah I told. Aida had packed all of our stuff got my cloths for me. I tied Tiffany pretty loosely. I wasn't sure she would live. Aida handed me a cigarette. I took a couple hits where's my vodka Aida.

As Brent drank, Aida took a hit of heroin before packing their belongings in Tiffany's Mazda at his instruction. He took the driver's seat and they left Denver, speeding west on I-70. They were headed toward Aspen, near the home of the noted writer Hunter S. Thompson, to whom Aida felt strongly connected. In a strange twist, two days later, on February 20, Thompson would fatally shoot himself.

Along the way, Brent pulled over and gave Aida another hit of heroin, as most of her veins had collapsed. They had sex for the last time, he would later write, and then he walked away from the car, heavy in thought.

―――――

9 p.m.
From Brent's journal:

> The whole Tiffany scene going round and round. Worrying about what to do with Aida I didn't want her to go to jail.

When I returned to the car she had hit again. Aida what the fuck baby. I need it baby she tells me. Shit I think to myself. I had stopped earlier to get her cinnamon jellied sweetrolls the ones with the white frosting and jelly centers. She always liked those. When I was in the bathroom at that gas station I noticed Tiffany's blood all over my hands. I couldn't seem to get rid of it.

I am looking at Tiffany's blood on my hands and I don't know me. I am everything I hate. I am my father, my mother, sick, evil, twisted, confused, angry, sad, lonely.

Shortly before 6 p.m. in Denver, a bloodied and screaming Tiffany Engle staggered out of the Marion Street apartment, flagged down two motorists, and then collapsed. Paramedics from the Denver Medical Center found her lying on the ground but conscious. Before being transported, she was able to tell them she had been attacked by two people who stole her wallet and car keys.

As police cordoned off an area of several blocks, officers began searching it by foot. The K-9 unit was called, and the department's helicopter, Air One.

Detective Martin Vigil, a veteran of Denver's Crimes Against Persons Unit, was called to the scene. Like the numerous other officers and detectives already there, he followed the blood trail left by Tiffany from the street to apartment number 4. The scene inside the vacant apartment told a grim tale: Blood stained the living room floor, and a knife, a bottle, and a mini-blind cord littered the room. More blood spatter flecked the hallway.

At the hospital in critical condition, Tiffany was able to remember a few more details, telling a detective how she had gone to check on an empty apartment and was attacked by a man inside. A woman there helped hold her down and tie her, Tiffany said. The man then stole her purse, which contained her car keys and cell phone.

Those details proved to be crucial.

As officers ran a registration query, they found that Tiffany owned a 2004 gray Mazda, tag number 980 KLS. They issued an alert for the car, and then detectives called Tiffany's cell phone company.

Within minutes, technicians with Cingular/AT&T Wireless were able to use a GPS satellite to locate the phone. It was near Aspen, Colorado, they told the detectives.

The officers issued a statewide alert for the car.

———

On Interstate 70, Brents pushed the Mazda up to speeds of 120 miles an hour, chain smoking a pack of Marlboro cigarettes. Aida kept nodding off. At one point she asked for donuts, so he stopped to buy her cherry-filled cinnamon rolls, but she couldn't eat them, and they now lay scattered on the seat. Thirty miles outside of Aspen, Aida began to lose color, telling him, "I don't feel good."

They pulled over, but she couldn't vomit. Handing her a liter of the soda, Brent commanded her to drink. Finally, he pulled Aida out of the car, put his own index finger down her throat, and forced her to wretch.

———

10:30 p.m.
From Brent's journal:

> Either Aida has done too much or it's bad shit. I figured it was both. I saw the cell phone in the center divider of the car. Fuck Aida, you brought the damn phone. She was supposed to put it in the dumpster. Oh well I thought they know where I'm going now it won't be long. Back on the road I told Aida I was going to stop at the first gas station in Glenwood Springs get gas then head to Hunter Thompson's place and wait for

daylight. So I get to Glenwood Springs get gas. As I'm filling up I see the first Glenwood cop he doesn't see me. It's got to be the cell phone. Two more cops go by. I get in Aida's not doing good at all. Fuck. I get out on the freeway and I've got to get to the next exit. I do I get into a secluded area and get her to puke again. Back on the freeway I pass another Glenwood cop. I'm behind a semi and its between us. I think he sees me. He does and its on. I know I can't outrun the Crown Vics of the state police on the freeway. None of them can keep up with me in the city and I make it to the city and they can't keep up. I can corner back and out run them in the shorts. I get away for a while. But another Glenwood cop comes out of nowhere and the chase is on in earnest. By this time theres damn near every cop in town and the state police. I blow there doors off down the service road. At some point I hit a patch of snow and ice at an Entersection 130 miles an hour I manage to save the car. And because of the slide and traffic I turn up into the mountains to avoid hitting another car. Wrong turn. During the slide out of control and saving it I somehow jumped a ditch on the side of the road and fucked up the car. So going up the mountain I am easily outrunning them. I don't know it's a dead end. I don't care. I'm doing 50 60 miles an hour up an ice and snow and mud caked dirt road that has a shit load of 130 & 90 degree turns and no guard rails. Aida screaming go baby one minute, don't kill us the next. All thru the chase she somehow managed to get the fuckin seat belt stuck. Then the drive line or gears or something break and I feel the car desentagrating and I lose forward momentum I can't go forward so fuck it I go reverse here they come.

    I push Aida's head into the seat headrest. Blam. I hit the sheriff's Bronco and bury my foot in the gas. I tell Aida she'd better start screaming for help. I'd swear I heard a shot even Aida said whats that. So I stopped I didn't want her to get hurt. I lit a cigarette and sat. I couldn't hear anything but my own heart beat roaring in my head. Aida tells me she loves me gives me a kiss thank god for dark tinted windows. She opens the door and screams like I'm murdering her.

SATURDAY, FEBRUARY 19, 2005

In Fort Smith, I was oblivious to the outside world. I woke at 6:45 to run the treadmill in the Resident Inn's exercise room, because when you have a family history of chemical imbalance and addiction, a regular release of endorphins is a good way to stay in check. Still, I was grumpy. A fifty-something-year-old man on the exercise bicycle had gotten there first, and I'd been forced to watch ESPN on the single television. And now, back in my room, I didn't have time for my usual ritual of CNN and breakfast. Instead, I had to rush to be in the lobby by 9:00 sharp to meet the freelance photographer the *Post* had lined up for me, a broad, burly man who reminded me of the television character Grizzly Adams.

He opted to drive since I was unfamiliar with the city, and we began checking addresses provided by Barbara the researcher of anyone listed as Brents—no luck. Finally, we drove down a wide street with modest homes to a white wood ranch with peeling paint surrounded by a chain-link fence. It was listed to a woman named Brents, identified in records as Brent Brents' mother.

I hopped out to knock on the front door, and a glance at the mailbox reassured me: The name "Brents" was hand painted, along with a simple drawing of a church, on one side, a cross on the other. Purple plastic flowers were stapled above the door, pink plastic flowers adorned the flower boxes, and blinds and black fabric covered all the windows. A long wooden plank propped on concrete blocks sat in the front yard.

The photographer snapped several photos. No one appeared to be home, so we walked back to his car to wait. When it became apparent

I meant to stay there until a sign of life showed at the home, no matter how long it took, he shifted in his seat and began making calls on his cell phone.

An hour later, he quit, while offering to help me find another freelancer to be on standby. Since I was nervous that his sheer size would intimidate a potential interview, I readily agreed. He dropped me off to get my rental car shortly past one, and I drove to a nearby Panera Bread restaurant, ordering a tuna sandwich on wheat to go.

I drove back to the Brents' home and parked across the street half a block away. I was on the last bite of my sandwich when a young blonde wearing jeans and a sweatshirt walked through the yard's gate, opened the front door, and hurried inside. I nearly choked as I took a swig from my water bottle and, praying I didn't have lettuce in my teeth, grabbed my notebook and ran across the street. The keys were still dangling in the lock of the inside door as I opened the screen door, leaned in, and knocked.

From the back, a dog began a deep-throated bark, and the young woman appeared, eyeing me suspiciously, taking in my black wool suit and black Cole Haan penny loafers. Behind her, an older woman peeked around the door. As I introduced myself, the young woman erupted in a fury. "GET THE FUCK OUT OF HERE, YOU FUCKING REPORTER!" She advanced on me, and I instinctively braced myself. Years of knocking on doors as a reporter had taught me to never back up.

The older woman began to cry, which seemed to inflame the other, so I looked past the younger one and tried to speak soothingly to the woman I took to be Brents' mother. "Look, Mom," I told her in a low voice, "no one is trying to judge you. We're just trying to figure out who he is and what he was like for you growing up. Please, if you could just help us paint that picture. No one blames you. Please."

We locked eyes as I focused on her, ignoring the protests of the angry young woman in front of me who was yelling something about calling the police and turning her pit bull loose on me. Slowly, Brents' mother, a plump woman with carefully coiffed blond hair, stepped toward me. "We done the best raising him we could," she said, her tears lessening. "I know you did, Mom," I told her. "Every family has their share of heartbreak, of someone they can't help. I had a brother the same way. He drank himself to death."

As the words came out of my mouth, I froze, momentarily flabbergasted. Since Dreux's death nine months before, I hadn't talked about him, let alone to strangers I was trying to interview. But it was the truth, and she recognized it as such. "Come on in," she said to me, as the young woman, who I later learned was her twenty-five-year-old daughter, threw up her hands and followed me into their dimly lit living room. As I walked in, I noticed a long steel bar leaning against the wall near the front door, and the daughter caught my questioning look. "That's in case Brent comes home," she said.

As I settled on a worn couch, the daughter sat across the room from me, watching my face. The mother sat on a recliner to my left, folding her legs beneath her.

How do you sum up someone's life in an hour? They were guarded, and generally in such a situation, I would engage in light conversation before bringing out my notebook, but I needed to have my story written by 6 p.m. My mind tucked away questions as I jotted down their descriptions: The oldest of three, Brent was an intelligent child, his mother said, and willful. His father, who died of heart failure the previous May, was an oil field worker, so the family moved often (a sign of instability?). Brent loved sports and the outdoors, and was adept at hunting and fishing. His mother left the room and reappeared with a photo album, filled with pages of sports ribbons for track, wrestling, and boxing. There were a handful of photos of a young Brent, and I stared hard at the rounded, smiling face of a freckled young boy with a mop of brown hair.

What had gone wrong?

Problems began in school, his mother said, because Brent had a learning disorder, and he soon became frustrated and then angry. Around the age of ten, he began to drink and smoke marijuana. That was also when he began to beat his mother (why the rage at her?).

His sister, the youngest, had hardly known her oldest brother, she said. She was three when he was thirteen and sent away to juvenile detention, for what his mother described as a prank of pulling a switch on a railroad track. No one was hurt, but the accident caused thousands of dollars in damage. After that, Brent remained in juvenile detention for the next several years because he kept reoffending, but his mother was not clear as to why he was held. "They never told us what he did," she said vaguely. "They just said it was better if we didn't know."

A few minutes later, as I pressed, she offered more details. "They just said he had a lot of mental problems, and they were assessing him, and he kept abusing other inmates. One time they did say something about a sexual abuse thing." (Wouldn't she as a mother want to know more about those alarming allegations?)

It seemed as though the two were the only family Brents had left. Neither of them thought he had maintained contact with his younger brother, Brandy, because Brandy had been adopted out as a child. "He had needs we couldn't help him with," the mother said of her middle child, and I mentally pictured some type of extreme medical condition that a financially struggling family could not afford.

I didn't have time to pursue that thread. The sunlight was fading, and the living room where we sat, lit by only a single lamp, became even darker. If I was going to file my story on time, I needed to hurry, so I moved on.

The last either of them heard from Brents was when he called home three weeks before and talked to his sister, telling her he had a girlfriend. He and his sister also talked about their father. "Brent had a lot of anger in his heart toward Dad," she said. The warning bell sounded in my mind.

I turned to the mother. "I'm sorry to ask, but it's a standard question when someone sexually abuses others," I said carefully. "Was Brent ever abused in any way as a child?"

She looked down and picked a speck from the comforter on her lap, pausing for several beats before answering. "Brent makes up all kinds of lies," she finally said.

The answer didn't sound honest. So I tried again, leaning forward.

"I'm sorry to ask, but could that be why Brent was so angry at his father? What about abuse?"

"My husband was a Christian," she replied. "He never abused Brent." As she spoke, she stared at the wall.

It was time to go, and I gathered the family photos of Brent that they offered for the photographer to transmit to the *Post*.

Back at the Residence Inn, I called the new freelancer, a woman, and arranged to meet her. Then I put in a quick call to my editor before settling at the desk in my room to write on my laptop. "By the way, he was caught last night," he said, and since I only had one hour to write, I didn't ask for any details. Good, I thought as I began to type on the blank screen, feeling unsettled by the interview. This awful story is almost over.

But I was mistaken. It was only just beginning.

I would cruz at night stalking one hooker or another or case houses or follow teenage girls home from school. Drinking smoking. Waiting for the right time. What realy sucks is That I could not break myself away from it 90% of the time. I would get the urge and literaly start to itch with anticipation.

—**From Brent's journal**

SEVEN

The Interview

Friday, February 18, 2005

Midnight

Homicide detectives are used to their phones ringing at all hours—murderers rarely kill on a polite nine-to-five schedule.

But this late-night call to Denver police detective Jon Priest was different—there was no corpse, at least not yet. And Priest knew this criminal from more than fifteen years before, when he had helped his wife, Carrolyn, a sex crimes detective, with her case against a young rapist named Brent Brents.

Now Brents sat in jail in Glenwood Springs, and a young woman named Tiffany Engle lay in a Denver hospital, fighting for her life. The Denver district attorney needed Priest to use his wits and his experience of Brents to gather a solid case, so the detective tuned his car's radio to a classical station to clear his head and began the three-plus-hour drive through the winding canyons of Interstate 70 to a charming mountain town that now housed someone he knew to be a monster.

At age forty-nine, Priest had been with the Denver police for more than twenty-five years and couldn't imagine being anything other than a cop and, as such, nothing less than a detective.

He loved pitting his brain against a criminal mind. He almost always won. And now, while driving, he pulled from his memory what he knew about the old adversary he'd soon face.

The eighteen-year-old Brents Priest had known had shown signs of being a psychopath. He was controlling and manipulative, yet could be charming—like Ted Bundy. Once a victim was in his web, Brents liked to inflict his pain in an up-close and personal way, which is why the knife was his weapon of choice. Second choice: his hands—for strangulation.

Now that Brents was thirty-five, how much more proficient of a predator had he become? Priest knew that most serial sexual offenders had the capacity to become serial killers, because eventually their satisfaction wasn't reached by leaving the victim alive.

He also knew a crack in Brents' armor: being asked about his childhood. At that, Brents became vulnerable. It was clear from the way he reacted that there'd been abuse. And like most offenders from broken homes, that uncertainty and fear led to a deep need for control.

Brents knew what he was doing through the rapes. Priest was convinced of it. Being a psychopath is not a mental illness—it's a behavior disorder. He'd made a decision that in order to be fulfilled in life, this is what he had to do.

He likes forcing his will on other people, Priest reminded himself, so don't give him any control.

Striding into the Glenwood police department shortly after three on Saturday morning, he was ready.

The Brents he saw when he opened the door to the interview room sat hunched over. He looked up and said hi in a small, sheepish voice.

Experience told Priest what the man was thinking: I can't control the situation, so I'll let you dominate me.

Priest's six-foot-two frame would easily tower over the five-foot-eight prisoner, so the detective sat quickly and slid down in the metal chair. Be smaller, give him some level of empowerment, he thought.

Flatter his ego. Be personable. Don't interrogate.

"My name's Jon Priest," he said. "I don't know if you remember me."

Glenwood Springs police officers drove a drugged and dazed Aida Bergfeld to the hospital, where she was given a rape exam and treated for an overdose. The plan was to wait for a rape victim advocate before they tried to question Aida further, but the entire department was in an uproar with news of the high-profile capture. As the hours passed and officers ducked in and out of the hospital room where Aida lay, one of them returned to a surprise: Her bed was empty. She was nowhere to be found.

Brents had been read his rights—and signed them—and then he and Priest settled into an easy conversation.

"What I'd like to do is just kind of open this up to you," the detective said at the start in a low, almost pleading voice, consciously trying to soften his baritone voice. "Tell me in your words what happened."

And Brents talked, in graphic, rambling detail. He told Priest he hadn't slept in days, but his level of exhaustion had clearly not affected his memory. He described attacking the two women on February 11—and the grandmother and her two granddaughters on February 14—kidnapping and raping Aida and beating Tiffany. He made a point of telling Priest over and over that Aida was a victim, not an accomplice.

He talked about the knives he'd used—a yellow-handled butterfly knife, a black-handled stainless steel kitchen knife, and a large serrated hunting knife—and explained where he'd stashed them as well as a black bag of extra clothes, some of which were still bloodied from cutting one of his victim's hands when she struggled.

After more than an hour of questioning, as early dawn approached, Brents was becoming frustrated in trying to explain the "why":

Priest: You thought you were better—it just didn't work out. Is that right?

Brents: No, it's not even . . . there's something fucked up in my brain, you know.

Priest: OK.

Brents: I, I thought maybe I was better, but I knew from the day I got out—first day I fucking got out—I had sex with a goddamn prostitute that I raped about three weeks ago.

Priest: OK.

Brents: First fucking day.

Priest: Hmm.

Brents: And I thought I tried, I tried my fucking hardest to stay out of trouble. Couldn't get a fucking driver's license, because Social Security wouldn't give me a goddamn card because they said that the number I've always known my entire life was bullshit . . . And I asked them and I asked them and I asked them, and they wouldn't, they really didn't motherfucking help me, so, you know, it's fuck it as far as I was concerned . . . Because I had to earn money somehow, I couldn't get a decent job without a driver's license. So I fucking hocked my ass for a sorry motherfucker.

Brents went on to tell Priest about how he earned money other than prostituting himself. Men who frequented strip clubs made the easiest marks because they weren't going to report being robbed there. So Brents would lurk at ATMs near the strip clubs and bars, and when a buzzed customer stumbled up to withdraw cash to tuck into a dancer's taut garter belt, he'd scare the bejeezus out of the guy and take his wallet. Like taking candy from a baby.

Priest took it all in matter-of-factly, which is how Brents recited the details. And when he was done describing the most recent half-dozen cases, Brents casually mentioned a larger number: There were at least twenty-eight prostitutes he had raped within the past six months, in addition to all the other cases.

"I can't give you specific dates or names," Brents said, "but if you bring a photo lineup of the women that have been arrested for prostitution, I can probably pick every one I've done—that's about the best I can do for you."

Not exactly. There was one prostitute whose name Brents did know, and he wanted to talk about the case now. Her name would soon become painfully memorable to Denver police because she had reported her attack the day it happened, way back in October 2004, months before the final, brutal crime spree of February 2005. DNA evidence had been collected in her case that could have identified Brents and led to his immediate arrest. Yet somehow it had been overlooked. So Brents had gone on and on.

"Tracy," he told Priest.

This is what investigators later pieced together.

Twenty-five-year-old Tracy Seidel lived however and wherever she could, and depended on an occasional hit of heroin or cocaine to numb the pain. At five foot five and 120 pounds and sporting short, spiky blond hair, she sold sex to get by.

Brents claimed that he had known Tracy before he raped her and that the attack was revenge for her ripping him off. He had given her money to buy heroin for him at a drug house and instead she'd hot-footed it out the backdoor.

Whatever the reason for his rage, Brents and Tracy both gave the same version of what he had done to her.

On October 20, 2004, shortly after 9 p.m., Tracy was dumpster diving in the alley behind 15th and Emerson streets when a man with thick arms, close-cut brown hair, and oval wire-rimmed glasses asked if she was hungry. After she said no and refused to go home with him, she walked away from the man, she told police.

Moments later he ran up behind her.

"He put his left arm around my neck and a knife to my throat," Tracy said. "Then he forced me to the ground and made me undo my pants. He kept threatening me: 'I'll kill you! I'll cut your throat! Do what I say, bitch!'"

Her attacker forced her to perform oral sex, then raped her vaginally, all the while holding a butterfly knife with a white-and-silver handle and four-inch blade. He then took a bottle of Steel Reserve beer and poured it into her vagina.

Later, Seidel would say to a detective, "Yeah, like he had to dump this forty ounces in me! It's not really going to do much for DNA, but it will give me a yeast infection."

The man then collected his glasses and jacket, which he had taken off, and walked hurriedly away, jumping a gate to get back onto Emerson Street.

Shortly after 9:30 p.m., Tracy ran into the lobby of the Denver police substation at 15th and Washington streets, walked up to the officer behind the window, and said simply, "I was just raped."

She gave police painstaking details of her attacker: He wore jeans, a red T-shirt, and a jean jacket trimmed with white fur; he smelled like strong cologne; his eyes were brown and closely set; he had a possible scar on his penis. An officer drove Tracy back to the scene where she pointed out the exact location of her attack, as well as the presence of semen on some leaves, before an ambulance was called and she was transported to Denver Health Medical Center where nurses gave her a rape exam.

Two days later, when Tracy failed to appear for more questioning, a detective pulled her criminal history and saw that she'd been arrested twenty-four times in Colorado. The arrests included prostitution, obstructing police, false statements, resisting an officer and shoplifting. Police began to have doubts about her credibility as a victim.

Then a nearby store clerk told police he remembered seeing Tracy the day of her alleged rape at the 7-11 with a guy he assumed was her boyfriend, who police later identified as a Denver man named Nick. The clerk described Nick as six foot one and Goth in that he usually wore black and said that day he'd been wearing black baggy pants with zippers and a black or gray sweatshirt.

One officer noted in his report that the clerk's description of Nick was "similar" to the description Tracy had given for her attacker, despite the fact she'd described her rapist as wearing jeans, a red T-shirt, and a jean jacket trimmed in white.

Later, Tracy would tell police that she hadn't shown up for questioning because she had fallen into a deep depression. For the next several weeks after her attack, as she made her way among the businesses on Colfax, she kept seeing the face of her rapist.

Only it wasn't an illusion.

In a bizarre twist, Brents kept running into Tracy and would try to befriend her, telling her, "You need to be taken care of." He started buying her food and giving her money and even brought her to his roommate's house once to give her a place to stay.

She struggled to reconcile these Good Samaritan gestures of a man she suspected of raping her.

"Maybe he just did it to me and I'll just keep it kosher," she said to herself.

Even so, every once in a while she would say to him, "I still think you're the guy that raped me!" And he would tell her, "No, I'm really not!"

Days and then weeks passed. Tracy's case meandered its way slowly through the system, taking months, when later, high-priority rape cases would be processed within hours.

On October 27—a week after the attack—a detective completed a lab request and delivered it to the crime lab.

On November 16, the lab reported that Tracy's rape kit results contained semen taken from her as well as from leaves collected at the scene.

On December 17, a male DNA profile was completed based on the results of the rape kit, and the ensuing report said the profile would be submitted to CODIS, or Combined DNA Indexing System, for a possible match.

But it wasn't.

Authorities would later say that due to a computer glitch—the state database was down for maintenance on the exact day the DNA from Tracy's rape kit was submitted—the male DNA profile that would have identified Brent Brents was not put into the system.

For the rest of October and all of November, December, January, and February, Brents was free to walk. During that time, he would later tell investigators, he estimated he raped more than two dozen women and children.

He attacked a lot of prostitutes, Brents told Priest, because he knew he'd get away with it.

"Most cops aren't going to prosecute a motherfucker for raping a prostitute because it's a prostitute's word against his. I start stacking them up maybe," he said.

Priest didn't respond.

"I mean, look at Tracy—how long it's taken you guys. You could've arrested me a long time ago, you know, but she's a known prostitute. And she's out there turning seven-dollar tricks for food. Are you really going to try to waste the taxpayer's money and prosecute me for that? You know, I knew that."

Nothing would surprise me, Priest thought.

"Anything else that we haven't discussed in relation to this?" the detective asked him after a while.

"Probably not."

And then Brents *did* surprise him.

"How's the lady doing that I hit tonight?" he asked, referring to Tiffany Engle.

"Well, she's in the hospital," Priest said. "She's being looked at. I don't know how she's going to be. She was hurt pretty bad."

"That's the kind of shit I'm talking about, man . . . I just flip out . . . I didn't mean to fuck her up. I really didn't."

When Margaret fought back I became almost overjoyed. I literally could feel my Blood rushing into my head it sound like a train roaring through my head . . . it was hitting her in the back of the head that was getting me off . . . remember seeing a meat cleaver on the counter and thought it would realy feel good to smash her skull. Then I like woke up and was totally different . . . how fucked up is that.

—From Brent's journal

EIGHT

Finding a Victim

SATURDAY, FEBRUARY 19, 2005

Noon

The black Dodge Neon had been reported stolen in a carjacking the day before, but the driver, a twenty-three-year-old female who said her name was Kari, kept insisting to her arresting officer she hadn't done anything wrong. As he escorted her to the main headquarters for Denver police to process her arrest, she asked why there was such a large crowd of media.

"They're probably trying to get a picture of someone we're bringing in," he told her.

"Is it that man who was on TV?" Kari asked.

"Yes."

"Good," she said. "He raped two of my friends."

"Did they report the assaults?"

"No, because they were scared."

A few moments later, as the officer and Kari arrived at the elevator, detectives walked up escorting Brents. Kari and Brents stared at each other, and she froze as the officer accompanying her said they'd take the next one.

As Brents stepped into the elevator, Kari finally spoke to him just before the doors closed.

"You get what you deserve," she said.

Inside the elevator, Brents turned to Priest. "Her name is Kari, and she was one of my victims."

The portable video equipment the Denver police brought to Glenwood Springs for the interview did not pick up good audio—the subject was speaking too softly.

So they packed up and drove Brents to Denver. Laser-focused to get on with his questioning, Priest didn't even stop to change his shirt after spilling coffee all over it during the return trip.

They had enough from Brents to ensure dozens of felony charges so far, including attempted murder, kidnapping, and several counts of rape. One of those cases was a woman in Aurora he said he attacked as brutal retaliation to Aurora police who had been calling him and telling him to turn himself in for molesting the eight-year-old boy.

"It's just the way that one cop talked to me," Brents told Priest. "He kind of treated me like shit so I'm like, well, fuck you. You know, I told you I was going to turn myself in on Monday, and if they'd let me, then it would have all been good. I would have just done that."

So far that was the only Aurora case. As the charges piled up, prosecutors at the Denver DA's office set bond at $25 million. Now they needed to fine-tune the details.

At the Denver police department, Priest was upping his control. On the way to the interview room, Brents asked him to take off his handcuffs so he could eat lunch, but Priest had someone else do it and walked away. They had ordered McDonalds—a Big N' Tasty for Priest and two Quarter Pounders with cheese, French fries, and a Coke for Brents. Now as officers walked him into the interview room, Brents paused and looked around for the familiar face.

"Where's Priest?" he asked.

Outside the room, watching through the one-way glass, Priest waited as Brents shifted in his seat and became clearly more uncomfortable. Detectives and members of the DA's office continued to gather, so there was more of an audience now. Brents was aware of it, and Priest didn't want him to start showboating to them. Don't let him think he's in control, he thought, or he'll start to lie.

This Brents was very different from the young man Priest knew before. Children no longer excited him, and only hours before he had admitted to choking many of his victims while raping them.

To get the feelings he wants, he hurts people—but the pain isn't what he's after. The control is. Pain and struggle and fear are starting to excite him.

That thought logically led to the pressing question: Did he kill anyone?

Not that they knew of—yet. Tiffany Engle was still alive, although reports indicated the bleeding inside her brain was steadily increasing.

It was time to get back to it. As Priest stepped into the interview room, Brents looked up at him, his food as yet untouched.

"I really want you to sit and eat with me," Brents said.

The pressure in Tiffany Engle's brain continued to climb, and over the weekend, she became less and less responsive. Shortly before midnight on Sunday, February 20, surgeons became alarmed and performed an emergency craniotomy, removing a piece of her skull and a section of her bruised brain before putting her in a medically induced coma.

There was no way of knowing when she would wake up, hospital officials told Priest.

Or if.

Monday morning found me at my desk in the newsroom at the *Post*, staring at a blank sheet of white copy paper in deep thought.

Brents sat in a Denver jail, the object of an obsessed media that fought for every new detail about his case like a school of frenzied piranhas.

What was he like? What did he have for breakfast? What about medical tests—was he HIV positive? Was he talking? What else had he confessed to?

And it wasn't just the media that was interested. One psychiatrist, a man with an impressive list of accomplishments, peremptorily scheduled a weekend symposium, all about Brents. In the description for it, he promised to reveal the secrets of Brents' mind.

Full of optimism and ego, he showed up at the jail. Hours later, dejected and empty-handed, he left.

The head of the public defender's office also made it clear that their client wasn't going to talk. Undaunted, reporters and photographers continued to troop to the jail throughout the day in hopes of gaining access to Brents. Those with recognizable faces used different last names on the visiting log request form, but to no avail.

I didn't bother to drive to the jail, figuring it was a waste of time—I would be just another desperate reporter. What I needed to do was set myself apart, and I decided to send him a handwritten letter—typing was too impersonal—but not on *Denver Post* stationery, because he was surely being bombarded by media requests from around the country and would probably just throw another one onto the already-burgeoning pile.

If you're a serial rapist, the object of so much hatred and also morbid interest, I asked myself, what would grab your attention?

So I turned to the one advantage I had over everyone else and referred to it straight away.

> Dear Brent,
>   I went to Fort Smith, Arkansas, where I talked to your mom and your sister. If you were to ask them, they would say I treated them with dignity and respect, and I will do the same for you.

Short and simple.

I then gave him the 800 number to the newsroom and asked him to call collect anytime.

I signed the letter and sealed it in a plain envelope with just the initial "A" as the name on the return address, which I listed as the street address of the *Post*. As a last-minute thought, I wrote on the outside of the envelope, "Please don't be afraid to open."

Maybe that would reassure someone who was no doubt getting tons of hate mail, I thought. At the very least, it would get his attention.

What I didn't know then was that I already had.

Tuesday, February 22, 2005

Forty-year-old Georgia Wood was on the small, grassy lot in front of her Aurora condominium playing fetch with her black lab, Lexi, when a petite woman with dark hair she'd never seen before walked up to her and began to talk.

"It makes me nervous that you left your garage door open," the woman told Wood. "I accidentally locked myself out of my house because I keep my door locked all the time now—because I was raped by Brent Brents."

From *Rocky Mountain News*, published February 23, 2005, at midnight:

> Aurora will revamp its arrest procedures after coming under heavy criticism for not locking up Brent J. Brents before he allegedly committed a series of rapes in Denver.
>
> Mayor Ed Tauer said Tuesday that it's too early to release specifics of the overhaul, but he did say that city leaders are

making "forward and backward" changes so arrests can be made without undue delays.

The list of revisions will be completed in 10 days, with most going into effect immediately and others possibly taking a bit longer, he said.

"We don't want this to happen again," said Tauer, who has been critical of procedures that resulted in an arrest warrant not being issued for Brents until more than two months after Aurora police questioned him on molestation allegations.

Thursday, February 24, 2005

My job as a criminal justice reporter at the *Denver Post* was to dig deeper behind the headlines of stories dealing with crime or the courts. Once the police had arrested Brents, the unfolding of his case throughout the system reverted back to the veteran court reporter.

The list of his charges, released by the Denver DA's office, was staggering:

Charges Filed Against Brents
Denver District Attorney Mitch Morrissey has formally charged a suspected serial rapist with 80 felony counts today, including sexual assault, kidnapping, and robbery.

Brent J. Brents (DOB: 05-12-69) is charged with:
24 counts of *sexual assault* (F2)
7 counts of *second-degree kidnapping* (F2)
1 count of *attempted first-degree murder* (F2)
3 counts of *sexual assault on a child* (F3)
2 counts of *child abuse resulting in serious bodily injury* (F3)
1 count of *second-degree assault* (F3)

4 counts of *first-degree burglary* (F3)
4 counts of *aggravated robbery* (F3)
1 count of *aggravated motor vehicle theft* (F3)
8 counts of *menacing* (F5)
1 count of *vehicular eluding* (F5)
1 count of *false imprisonment* (F5)
5 counts of *habitual sexual offender against children* (Sentence enhancer)
18 counts of *crime of violence* (Sentence enhancer)

The charges reflect allegations against Brents involving attacks on eight people in five different incidents.

Brents will be formally advised of the charges TOMORROW, Friday, February 25, 2005, at 9 a.m. in Denver County Court, room 12T. He remains in custody in the Denver County Jail. His bond is $25 million. The investigation is continuing and additional charges are possible at a later date.

That afternoon I was eating a green apple at my desk in the newsroom when an editor called out to me. Aurora Mayor Ed Tauer had just issued a statement that there was another confirmed victim of Brents in his city, which is just east of Denver.

Since authorities will protect the identity of a victim of sexual assault, they will only release the cross streets of where it happened, which is the cryptic description Tauer made public: 1st and Nome.

"We want you and a photographer to go to the location and try to find the woman," the editor told me.

A few minutes later, as I stood near the door of the newsroom, I was joined by photojournalist Kathryn Scott Osler, a petite, energetic brunette with a musical voice. Kathryn and I looked at each other and grinned. We had been paired up for the military series "Betrayal in the Ranks," and the many grueling hours that we'd spent together at different locations around the county for the project had bonded us and solidified a confidence in each other's work.

She had been with me the day of that awful first interview with Sharon Mixon in St. Petersburg. Afterward, as Kathryn and I walked dazed and silent into our air-conditioned hotel room, still stunned by the magnitude of Sharon's trauma, Kathryn flopped her thin, wiry frame flat onto one of the double beds in the room, and stared up at the ceiling. "Holy shit, this is tough," she said. "But we'll get through it."

Now this task—first of finding a victim at a vague location and then convincing her to talk—seemed almost as formidable. It was 1:30 p.m.

"Well, let's go!" Kathryn said cheerfully. She was always upbeat. It was disgusting.

Four hours later, even Kathryn's optimism was wearing thin.

After going to what we finally figured was the wrong neighborhood because it was in an area that looked too commercial, I managed to snag Ed Tauer's cell phone number from another reporter and called him directly to clarify the location. He seemed surprised, almost amused, that we were actually going there and was very friendly and polite.

Once in the actual confirmed neighborhood, Kathryn and I stood on a street corner and collectively sighed: We were facing a small city of condominiums. They lined the street like giant Legos, six rows deep, in alphabetical order: A, B, C, D, E, F.

We opted to each take a side and started knocking on doors.

As darkness fell and the editors at the *Post* changed shifts, they would occasionally call my cell phone to check in: any luck?

Finally, shortly before 7 p.m., I started to feel hope. We had skipped dinner, canvassing the area for hours, asking folks, "Have you seen any crime scene tape here lately? Police? Did you hear of anyone being attacked by the serial rapist Brent Brents?" Finally, we found a nurse, who knew the neighborhood handyman, who said he knew the victim, and lo and behold, he had a name and a door number: Margaret at 18B.

It was exhilarating to finally be this close. I ignored the fact that it was dark and nearly 7:30 when we finally walked up to the door, arranging a hasty game plan. Kathryn and her off-putting camera would stay a few feet back from the door, and I would do my best to get us inside. I knocked firmly, confidently, three times.

There was a stirring on the other side of it, and a full minute passed before I heard locks tumble. When the door opened, I found myself staring at a nervous-looking man. He ran his hands through his hair as I introduced myself. Behind him, a tiny woman cautiously peered around a doorway, her fingers clenched to the door jam.

"You scared us," the man said accusingly, and I was taken aback—in my single-minded pursuit of the story, I hadn't expected that.

But it wasn't going to put me off.

"I'm so sorry. I know it's late," I told him. "We've been trying to find Margaret for hours. We're really hoping to hear from her about what happened. "And," I added in what I hoped would be the winning argument, "it may help other victims step forward."

The man looked at me dubiously and said, "Give us a minute." He stepped back inside and shut the door. I stood stock-still on the dim porch step, trying hard not to tap my foot impatiently while muffled voices went back and forth.

After what seemed like an eternity but was only a few moments, the door swung open and the petite woman stepped into the hallway and nodded. "OK, I'll talk to you," she said, and I gave a silent and hasty thank-you to the universe.

I've been to all sorts of crime scenes—thickly tangled woods; hot, dusty streets; lavish, layered homes; crowded, shabby duplexes—and every one of them share the same feeling: a somewhat painful, palpable negative energy that remains of the violence that happened there, like a dark mist too fine to be seen hanging in the air.

Margaret's home was the same way. As she showed us where Brents had rushed her at the very front door where we now stood, she stepped into the living room and gestured to the couch.

"There," she said, pointing to a large, bare patch in the upholstery. "He raped me there. The police cut part of it away for evidence."

Oh. I stared transfixed at the spot, suddenly feeling nauseated, and finally with effort managed to drag my eyes away.

You are on deadline, I told myself firmly. Get a grip. Shrug it off.

I turned and nodded encouragingly at Margaret as she continued to talk in a frantic rush, her words pouring out in what seemed like relief.

The attack had happened almost three weeks before, yet fading yellow and brown bruises remained on her cheek and throat.

And like many victims I've interviewed over the years, Margaret had felt a premonition before the attack that something awful was going to happen.

She had seen the man she now knew was Brents on a Wednesday while out for her daily walk. He was bundled against the cold, but even beyond the layers, he looked intimidating, walking slowly and staring intently. Instantly unnerved, she had hurried home, and the next day, still feeling unsettled, she decided to skip her walk.

That night she had a nightmare, a distressing dream she couldn't remember but one that woke her up with a start.

On Friday, with her car in the shop being repaired, Margaret rode the bus to run errands, fastening her bag securely around her waist to keep from getting pick-pocketed.

Once she stepped off the bus for home, the same heavyset man she had seen earlier in the week appeared, walking past her in an apparent hurry. Then he suddenly turned and began walking briskly back toward her. Her heart pounding, Margaret darted into the nearby street, dodging heavy traffic. When she turned, he was gone.

Relaxing a little, she again headed home. As she opened her front door, the man suddenly charged out of nowhere.

"His eyes, they were big," she told me. She had one thought, "Oh my God, an animal."

He was out of breath. "I started screaming," Margaret said. "I tried to shut the door, and he pushed it. I started screaming, 'Somebody help!' and then I saw a fist coming."

As if the attack hadn't been awful enough, the rest of her story was also distressing. Aurora police told her it would take two months to process the DNA from her rape kit and gave her no hope the case would be solved. Then two things happened back-to-back: Margaret saw a photo of the now-captured Brents on TV, and during his interview with Priest, Brents gave details of his attack on her that enabled investigators to put two and two together.

Deadline for the front page was 9 p.m. It was now 8:15. Kathryn, who works swiftly and unobtrusively, had already finished taking photos, none of which would show Margaret's face. As she drove us back to the newsroom, I popped in the cinnamon gum I always chew when writing and scribbled asterisks next to important details in my notebook.

After grabbing a quick gulp of water at the fountain, I sat down at my desk to the familiar pounding rush of trying to do someone's story justice on deadline.

-PUBL-   DENVER POST
-SLUG-   CD25VICTIM
-DATE-   Fri, 25 Feb 2005
-EDIT-   FRI FINAL
-SECT-   A
-PAGE-   A-01
-TYPE-   INTERVIEW
-SUBJ-   rape; sex crimes; victims; metro
-HEAD-   Victim recounts horror

An Aurora woman tells how the man identified as Brent J. Brents beat, choked and raped her on February 4.

-BYLN-   Amy Herdy, Denver Post Staff Writer
-CUTL-   PHOTO: Kathryn Scott Osler | The Denver Post

An Aurora woman who was assaulted February 4 by a man police have identified as Brent J. Brents holds the beads from a necklace her attacker was wearing as well as one of her fingernail tips that broke when she tried to fight him off.

–**TEXT**–

Aurora—She'll never forget his eyes.

"They were big and so angry," she said. "To me, he looked like the devil."

And, like a predator, the man stalked her for two days before he beat her and raped her on February 4, she said. During the attack, she said, one thought pressed in her mind: "Oh, my God, this animal's going to kill me."

She said she recognized her attacker as Brent J. Brents when she saw his face on TV nearly two weeks later. On Thursday, Aurora police called the woman and said Brents had told Denver police about her case.

Arriving at her home on Nome Street in Aurora after running errands, the 49-year-old unlocked her front door. From nowhere, the attacker charged. "He was out of breath," the woman said. "I tried to shut the door, and he pushed it open."

It was 3:50 p.m.

He swung his right fist into her left eye, knocking her 5-foot-2, 112-pound frame into the wall. "We fought," the woman recalled, bruises still evident on her face, throat and neck. "I scratched him, bringing blood behind his ears. . . . I thought, If I'm gonna die, I'm going to fight till the end."

"What do you want?" she screamed. She realized she had seen him before, while out walking two days earlier.

The attacker grabbed her foot, she said, and dragged her back into her living room, telling her, "I'm going to rape you, bitch."

Her eye swollen shut, she began having trouble seeing, and begged him, "Take anything you want; just leave me alone." He pinned her to the floor, she said, telling her, "I'll kill you," as he choked her. As she began to lose consciousness, she finally nodded her head. He then grabbed her by the hair and dragged her back to the front door, which he locked.

Taking her back to the living room, he put a pillow over her face, she said, and raped her. When it was over, he asked her if she was married and what time her husband would be home.

It was 4:10 p.m. "I lied and told him my husband got off work at 4."

The attacker then asked, "Where's the money?" she said. She gave him what was in her purse—about $20—and he got dressed.

Before he walked out the door, she said, he told her, "See? All you had to do was be nice." As he walked away, he picked up her underwear and froze.

"He stood there for a full minute," she said, "staring at it." He then hung the underwear on her front door and left.

She locked the door. "I immediately called 911," she said. "I was so scared."

Aurora police responded and drove her to the hospital, where nurses performed a rape exam.

At the hospital, her husband told the Denver Post, "I almost collapsed at the way her face looked. Black and blue, and all swollen . . . A cop pulled me into the hall and told me I had to calm down."

Both he and his wife fault Aurora police for how her case has been handled and the fact that an Aurora detective allowed Brents to leave after an interview in November in which he admitted to molesting a child.

"What gets me is these stupid people had this guy, for molesting an 8-year-old," the woman said. "If they had kept him in there, then I wouldn't have gotten almost killed and raped."

The detective, she said, told her it would take two months to process the DNA taken from her rape exam.

"They gave us no hope," her husband said. "Not long after the rape, they said the case will probably go inactive."

On February 16, the woman said, the detective in the case brought her eight photos of bald men with mustaches. None looked like her attacker.

On the 17th, she was watching the news when a current photo of Brents flashed on the screen. "I said, 'Oh, my God, that's him,'" the woman said.

Her husband called Aurora police the next day, February 18, and a detective told her he would bring her a form identifying Brents for her to sign.

"But he never came," she said.

Thursday, the detective called her and told her Brents had made a statement regarding her case, she said.

She has trouble eating and sleeping and becomes nervous around 4 p.m., or if she hears a man's voice. The victim advocate for the Aurora police department told her to contact a charity for help, she said, and the woman at the charity told her it had little money to pay for somewhere else for her to live until she overcame her fear of returning home.

The woman said, "I told the charity worker, 'I was raped and almost killed.' She said, 'Been there, done that.' I was crying."

Larry Martinez, a spokesman for the Aurora Police Department, said he had never heard of a charity being recommended by a victim advocate. He could not explore the victim's complaints against the detective, he said, until he could reach the detective today.

As for the case being labeled "inactive," he said, "When something goes on what you call 'inactive,' it doesn't mean the case is closed. We're waiting for other leads to come in."

Of Brents, the woman said, "I hate him, and yet I still feel sorry for him. An animal, poor creature. . . . Maybe it's the only way I can comfort myself."

Denver's ABC 7
KMGH-TV

February 21, 2005

Dear Mr. Brents,

I believe you have an incredible story to tell. My name is Tony Kovaleski and I am an Investigative Reporter at KMGH-TV in Denver. In my position as a broadcast journalist I want to offer you the opportunity to tell your story in detail. In my three decades of work as a reporter I have learned there are always two sides to every story. Colorado wants to hear your side of this story and I am sure there are significant details that have not yet been reported.

You are probably wondering if you will receive fair treatment in an interview with a journalist you have never before met. I am willing to promise you, here in writing, the opportunity to air the key issues and pieces of information you want the public to understand about you and your life.

It is highly likely I will not be the only journalist offering you this opportunity. The question then becomes, "Why should I do the interview with Tony Kovaleski instead of another journalist?" My answer to this question is simple: I believe no other journalist will provide you the opportunity to tell this story from your perspective and detailing your life experiences. Simply stated, I want to tell the Brent J. Brents story and I believe my experience as an award-winning journalist offers you a unique platform for a highly informative and compelling story.

I would like to sit down and meet you before you make your decision. This would provide an opportunity to answer any questions you may still have and look me in the eye to see I am sincere in offering you this opportunity to tell your story.

Kindest Regards,
Tony Kovaleski
Investigative Journalist
KMGH-TV

NINE

A Phone Call

If you want a hard, fast way to detox, get thrown in jail.

The days since his capture were passing in a fog for Brents. He slept, paced, and alternated between curling up into a ball on the floor and lying on the rock-hard mattress in his cell, soaked in sweat laden with chemicals seeping out of his pores.

Methamphetamine. Cocaine. Heroin. He'd done it all, adding bottle after bottle of Grey Goose vodka chasers to boot. Now as the hours passed, he started to hallucinate. The walls of his cell dissolved, becoming the windows and doors of home. He would stand up and grasp his hand on a doorknob that suddenly didn't exist, or go to pet his dog, Georgia, who sat nearby yet would evaporate when he reached toward her.

He was losing his mind, what little was left of it.

The only thing that kept him in the here and now were the letters. They poured in every day by the dozens—some damning him to hell, others offering to pray for him, and reporters trying to beg or manipulate him into doing a story. He divided them into three categories: Crazy People, Media, and Crazy Media.

One letter had caught his attention, and he'd carefully set it aside.

"Don't be afraid to open this," the envelope said, which surprised him. How did the writer know of the hatred that constantly came at him, like giant vultures with fangs and deadly claws? It matched the self-loathing he felt deep in his brain, the disgust and shame that constantly circled and gnawed.

One afternoon, after being escorted to the shower, where he could still smell the lingering skunkish body odor of the inmate before him, he stood in the filthy tile-and-concrete cubicle as the lukewarm water trickled down and poised a razor in his right hand over the femoral artery in his thigh.

Do it already, his brain urged. End this misery. You're a monster. Everyone wants you dead. Nobody cares.

And then he thought of the envelope and the promise for dignity written inside, and in that instant, he made a decision.

After being escorted back to his cell, he pulled out the letter and studied the phone number handwritten at the bottom of the page. "Hey," he called to the nearby guard for the first time, "can I have the phone?"

The *Denver Post* and the *Rocky Mountain News* had a "joint operating agreement" to share business costs, but to us reporters, there was nothing joint about it. The two newsrooms were embroiled in a fierce war for survival that the *Rocky* would sadly eventually lose in 2009.

But in 2005 the competition was still in full swing, as it had been for more than a century. As a result, the atmosphere in the *Denver Post* newsroom alternated between desperation, triumph, and despair, depending on how well we competed with the *Rocky* on any given day. Once after popping into an editor's office to tell him that our rival might possibly have caught wind of an exclusive story we'd been feverishly pursuing, I watched as the man folded his arms across his stomach, doubled over in his chair, and began to rock, all the while moaning like someone who had just been told he was going to die by torture very, very soon. I stood for a few moments in horror and then hurried away. It was embarrassing.

The process of entering contests for highly prized awards became rigidly formal, and editors spent hours poring over forms to make *Post* entries as attractive as possible. In general, the *Rocky* won more contests than we did, and *Post* staffers often griped that it wasn't because they had better writers and photographers but because *Rocky* editors could write prettier story descriptions on the entry forms.

Over time, this fervor to win prizes colored every major editorial decision at the *Post*. Despite the accolades we received for "Betrayal in the Ranks"—and despite the fact it actually spurred reforms in the U.S. military, the most powerful institution in the world—I always got the impression it was a resounding disappointment to *Post* editors because although our work had been nominated and made it to the top ten finalists, it didn't win the Pulitzer. After the series ended and we were receiving tips on new military abuse cases both nationally and internationally, editors at the *Post* eventually gave a tired shrug.

"No more military rape stories," one of them told Miles and me dismissively, and the implication was clear: That kind of story didn't win, so let's try something else.

So it was under this pressure on the first Thursday in March that I was trying to come up with a scoop for the Sunday paper regarding crime's latest hot topic: Brent Brents.

I had been shaking the branches of the law enforcement grapevine hard and heard some tales of Brents showing detectives the locations of his assaults, as well as where he'd stashed weapons and clothes. I was at my desk busily trying to verify the information when suddenly a shout erupted from across the newsroom.

One of the editorial assistants, a man we all knew simply as Dutch, was standing up, his hand clutched over the receiver of his blocky black desk phone, his eyebrows skyrocketing upward on his face.

"Amy!" he shouted, and I stood up and started toward him, unsure of what was happening. "It's Brent Brents calling collect for you!"

"Accept the charges!" I immediately shouted back, afraid that any delay on our end would drop the call.

"OK, I've got him!" In the middle of the floor, I hesitated. Our phone system was notorious for losing transferred calls, and I was afraid that asking Dutch to send the call to my desk phone would torpedo it.

As if reading my mind, Dutch waved me over. I ran to his desk and sat down as he shoved the phone toward me with one hand and a green steno pad with the other, complete with doodles that resembled daggers. Flipping to a clean page, I pulled out the ever-present blue pen from behind my right ear, parked the phone on my left shoulder, and breathlessly said, "This is Amy."

"So you saw my mom and sister," a male voice said with false joviality, as if working really hard to drum up a measure of friendliness. "That's why you're the only one I called."

An exclusive! I gave myself a mental high five.

"I'll be straight with you," he said. "I'm not going to give you anything. My attorneys don't want me to. Don't get me wrong—I'm not the nicest guy in the world. Obviously I'm fucked up in the head."

Obviously.

"But I read your stuff, and I'd rather tell somebody like you my story. Eventually I want to print a public apology to some people, eventually tell my story the right way, without any bullshit."

But first, he said to me, he had a make-or-break question, and he wanted the truth.

I inwardly braced.

"Everybody says they hate me, that I'm a monster," he said. "Do you think so?"

I was shaking my head even as I spoke. "No, I don't," I told him honestly. "I think you've done monstrous things, but I don't consider you a monster. It's not my place to judge anybody."

And that's how it began.

For the next hour, Brents rambled and I probed, playing a slow game of cat and mouse. He was incredibly soft spoken, so much so that at times I plugged my finger in my other ear and frowned angrily at the curious coworkers who talked as they hovered nearby, trying to listen in.

He begged me not to write about his cases, and I reluctantly agreed.

He would start to tell me a detail and then stop, repeatedly saying, "My attorney's gonna kick my ass."

Finally I became impatient. "What's your attorney's name?"

"Carrie Thompson."

Hmm. A woman. Clever strategy. The next time he said he couldn't answer my question because of his attorney, I decided to sting him.

"Really?" I asked. One of my hovering coworkers widened her eyes at the confrontational tone. "You're gonna let a woman make your decisions for you?"

Bingo. After that, he talked.

"I want people to understand there's an animal there," he said, and I drew an asterisk next to the quote in my notes. "But there's so much more to the man."

At one point in the conversation, I realized I needed to double-check that it was indeed Brents. What if another inmate was playing a sick joke? Anything's possible.

"Tell me about your brother," I said, and without hesitation, he said, "His name is Brandy, and his middle name is Lee. He was taken away when he was little."

OK, it's him.

He also tried to turn the tables.

"I want to know who you are—what you're about."

Searching for common ground without revealing anything too personal, I remembered him mentioning his dog, a German Shepherd mix named Georgia. "I have a German Shepherd too," I told him. "His name is Pike."

"I'm worried about Georgia," he said. "I have no idea where she is now. I had to leave her at the place I was staying. I hope my roommate is taking care of her."

"I'm sure he is." I had to get back on track.

"What are your earliest memories of your dad?" I asked, changing the topic abruptly.

"Trying to follow his footsteps in the snow." His memories, he said, "weren't always bad things . . ." He fell silent.

"Did he rape you?"

"Yes."

"What about other sexual abuse?"

"She knows," he said wearily.

"Your mom? Dad?" I pressed.

"Yeah, both of them." And almost imperceptibly, he sighed. It sounded real.

"I'm sorry," I said almost automatically, then realized I meant it.

"You're the only one who did the right thing," he said. "There was a lady at the *Rocky* who sent me a questionnaire, asking shallow-ass questions. I want the *whole* truth out there."

And the only way to do that, Brents told me, was for me to work on something long term, like a book. He would give me every detail, he said, if I promised to hold the story until he was sentenced. Meanwhile, I should go to all his court appearances to learn the facts.

"I'll think about it." I promised to ask my editors. If I did do a long-term project, I told Brents, I didn't want him to talk to any other media.

"No other media," he repeated.

"By the way, if I do go to your court appearances," I said as an afterthought, "I'll sit up front, and you'll know it's me because I have long brown hair and I always wear black."

"Oh, I know who you are." The phone went dead.

No! I wasn't done, and it wasn't clear what I could use. Since I knew the number to the jail by heart, I dialed it and asked the sergeant on duty if there was any chance someone could please ask Brent Brents to call me back again?

The answer was no.

Glancing at the large digital deadline clock on the wall, I cursed. It was 4 p.m., which meant that I had barely an hour to try to catch people in their offices for comments about what Brents had said.

But first . . .

In some respects, we reporters are childlike in that we're always looking to please our parents, the editors. And since most ranking editors are male, I guess we're especially trying to please our fathers.

I danced into the office of one of the head editors, leaned against the door frame, and grinned.

"Hey," he said distractedly, glancing up from his computer screen. "How's that weekender coming about Brents giving police a tour?"

"Oh, sorry, that's dead," I said to him breezily as I realized he'd been holed up in his office the whole time I'd been on the phone—and didn't know.

"But I have something better," I offered, and waited impatiently until he looked up again before I broke the news: "Brents just called me. I got a great interview!"

A newsroom that has snatched up a big fat scoop is a fun place to be. There's an expectant feeling of joy, like knowing you're going to get that shiny new bicycle you've wanted, only this is an anticipation of the readers who will gather at the watercooler the next morning and say, "Didja see that story in the *Post*?!"

At the same time, there's a certain smug satisfaction in knowing your competition will take one look at the story and feel crushed.

It was 4:05. I had fifty-five minutes to contact Brent's attorney, call the jail to try to reach him again one more time and at least confirm that he had indeed been on the phone, alert as many of his victims as possible there'd be a story, call his mother, and coax Aurora police officials into responding to something he had told me: that a detective mouthing off to Brents had triggered his final crime spree.

Another reporter, Felisa Cardona, was given the task of heading to a coffee shop Brents had told me about in an effort to find folks who knew him.

At 5 p.m., my cutoff time, I sat at my desk to sift through my notes and start to write, but soon realized I was stuck. Brents had rambled a great deal, going back and forth between "on the record"—usable information—and "off the record"—which means information for background only and not to be attributed to the person.

While he hadn't used those exact words, he had been quite specific in what I could and could not use, cautioning me repeatedly not to write anything about his cases. Yet in the next breath, he'd answer another question about them. I wanted to honor the age-old agreement between a reporter and a subject, but the lines on this one were blurry.

I hurried back to the editor's office, only this time I sat heavily in the chair next to his door while I explained my dilemma, all the while flipping through the green notebook of scrawled notes. "I gave him my word I wouldn't write about his cases, but then he'd offer up details about them. Since I can't call him back," I told him, "I'm not sure what to do."

The editor looked at me sharply in surprise, like I had suddenly sprouted pig ears.

"Use everything he said," he told me firmly and with great emphasis. "He's a piece of shit—the last person in the world who would ever sue."

I stared back, too dumbfounded to speak. Wordlessly, I stood up and walked back to my desk. My gut knotted in disappointment and then I felt naive and stupid. What the fuck? I said to myself as I started to write. Is this how everybody works? And as I often did when on deadline, I put the discomforting feelings away to deal with later.

There are different deadlines for the different editions, and after each one, I would dive into the story again in an attempt to make the next version better. As it sailed through the process of being edited at various levels, I accompanied it on its electronic journey from computer to computer, standing behind the editor who had the latest edition, trying to guard every word.

-PUBL-	DENVER POST
-SLUG-	CD04BRENTS
-DATE-	Fri, 4 Mar 2005
-EDIT-	FRI FINAL
-SECT-	A
-PAGE-	A-01
-TYPE-	INTERVIEW

-SUBJ-   sex crimes; injuries; police; arrests; prisoners; metro; Denver

-HEAD-   "There's an animal there"
Brents claims more than 30 rapes, asks his victims for forgiveness

JAILHOUSE INTERVIEW WITH BRENT J. BRENTS BLAMES SPREE ON COPS

An officer called him "punk" on the phone, touching off his final rampage, Brents claims. He says he's sure he'll be killed in prison.

-BYLN-   Amy Herdy, Denver Post Staff Writer

-TEXT-

As he sat in a Denver coffee shop trying to negotiate his surrender for molesting an 8-year-old boy, the phone conversation Brent J. Brents was having with the Aurora police officer turned ugly and Brents snapped, he said.

"He called me a little punk. 'Tell me where you're at. I'll come get you, you little punk,'" Brents said Thursday in a telephone conversation from jail. "I said, '[expletive] you. Come get me.'"

Turning to the owner of the coffee shop, whom he considered a friend, Brents told her, "I love you. Thanks for everything. Goodbye."

Then, he said, "I worked myself into this rage, walked out of the coffee shop . . . [thinking] 'You wanna play games? I can play games, too.'"

That February 11 exchange started his final rampage. "The number's gonna climb, I'm not gonna [expletive] you," Brents said. "It's over 30."

In a rambling, hour-long interview from jail, Brents, 35, told the Denver Post he wants to apologize to his victims, family and friends. Sobbing at times, angry at others, he mostly sounded tired and defeated. He misses his dog, Georgia. He knows he will die in prison, he said, most likely at the hands of other inmates, and he wants his story to be heard before that happens.

"I want to do this before it's too late. . . . Just tell 'em, to all my victims, and to my friends, whether they believe me or not, that I am sorry," he said. "And somehow I'll make it right. Somehow, some way, I'll make all this right."

Having been in prison before, he said, he knows the reality of the violence he'll encounter from other inmates because of the nature of his charges. "I'm probably gonna die within a year of being in prison. I'm not afraid of dying; that's not even a problem," Brents said. "I want people to understand there's an animal there but there's so much more to the man."

"I don't feel sorry for myself," he added. "I deserve everything I get.

"If you really want to know [me], outside of one crazy little bastard," he told a Post reporter, "go to the coffee shop and just hang out. These are my closest friends and family, and I'm sure they're hurt and torn up."

In the days before his arrest, Brents said, he met someone that he fell in love with. "I always meet these people at inappropriate times," he said. "I spent the weekend with this woman, made me feel like I was 16 again."

Yet, he said, "How do you tell somebody, 'I attacked someone earlier today' or, 'By the way, I'm a [expletive] monster and an animal? I did have a girlfriend, someone I loved for the first time in my life," Brents said. "She really blew me away." By virtue of having had contact with her, he said, "I made her a victim."

The trigger to his final rampage, he said, was not his roommate West asking him to leave but "an Aurora cop, talking [expletive] to me on the phone," he said.

Aurora officials said Thursday that they would investigate Brents' contact with any of their officers.

"Clearly, this is very serious, and we are going to look into this immediately," said city spokeswoman Kim Stuart.

Kaewyn Kulsar, 28, said she remembers the day Brents was on the phone in her coffee shop but did not know he was talking with Aurora police. When he hung up, she recalled, he said a strange goodbye. "He told me, 'Thank you so much for everything.' There was something not quite right, and he left," she said.

Kulsar said he gave her the impression that he was going to hurt himself in some way. "Just the energy behind it, I thought it was extremely strange. He sounded like he was going to do something to himself."

About an hour later, Kulsar said, an Aurora police officer came to the shop and said he was looking for Brents. The officer told her Brents was wanted for molesting a child and told her not to tell Brents they were looking for him.

Kulsar said she knew Brents had been in prison, but he told her and others that it was for assaulting his ex-wife's boyfriend. Brents had been in the coffee shop numerous times and connected himself with several members of the tight-knit community there. Kulsar herself had been alone with him, she said. Brents had briefly been to her home. "He had a creepy vibe, but he did nothing disrespectful or caused us to have concern."

Now, his apology isn't making a difference to her, she said. "We're over it. He's not worth it. We have given him enough time and energy. We are not the ones he needs to be apologizing to. We are not victims."

Brents said he was having trouble remembering details and faces after he left the coffee shop. Denver police would later charge Brents with sexually assaulting five people over the next four days.

"Sometimes things that happen . . . some of them, I barely

remember," he said. "I was so, God, I was drunk and on a rampage. I didn't do drugs. I was drinking like a fish."

Of many of his victims, he said, "I don't remember what they looked like. I don't know what else to tell people."

On February 11, police say, Brents sexually assaulted two women in Denver. That night, he said, he met a woman at The Church nightclub on Lincoln Street. "She did not look her age at all," he said. "We spent a wonderful weekend together."

On February 14, police said, Brents sexually assaulted a 67-year-old woman and her two 11-year-old granddaughters in the family home near Cheesman Park.

On February 18, police said, a woman who managed an apartment building in the 1000 block of Marion Street was beaten nearly to death by Brents. Later, police would say that Brents had held a woman captive in a vacant apartment in that building, raping her more than a dozen times. That night, Glenwood Springs police captured him as he drove the woman's car, tracking him by her cell phone.

Of all his victims, Brents said, he remembers the property manager the most. He declined to say why he nearly killed her. "It was just bad timing," he said. "But at the same time, it triggered something, too. She didn't confront me. Poor lady, she didn't have a chance."

Now, Brents said, he wanted to send his love—and apologies—to his family in Arkansas.

"Yeah, he's my brother, but do I care about what happens to him, about his sob story, or believe it? No," said his sister, who asked not to be identified. "It's a little late for apologies, don't you think?"

Brents' mother said she does not put stock in his repentance. "Whether it's a 'jailhouse sorry' or a truthful sorry, who knows," she said. "I've been through it so many times before with him."

Of allegations by Brents that both his mother and father molested him as he was growing up, it never happened, she said.

"He's proficient at lying," she said.

For his part, Brents promised a darker tale still to unfold. "There's things I could tell," he said. "It's sad, and it's sickening, and it's violent."

Staff writer Felisa Cardona contributed to this report.
Staff writer Amy Herdy can be reached at 303-820-1752 or aherdy@denverpost.com.

Handwritten on a plain envelope:

Christine Chang
Channel 7
123 Speer Blvd.
Denver, CO 80203-3417

>Denver County Jail
>Attn: Brent Brents
>10500 East Smith Rd.
>Denver, CO 80239

Handwritten on plain paper:

3-4-05

Dear Mr. Brents,

I just read your interview from the Denver Post and must admit, I was not surprised to hear about your love experience before you were caught. I've always believed that every human being has multiple sides to them and that when love hits, you just know. Guess I'm a romantic that way.

I was one of the reporters at the Denver Police Station that day when you were taken in. You never looked up, so it's hard to really read a person without seeing them eye to eye. All I know of you is what I've read, what police are saying and what our station has reported. I guess I would really like to talk to you myself to hear the real story.

Besides, you had mentioned you want to get your story out, and as you know, television can have a stronger impact with <u>your</u> face and <u>your</u> words. If you don't feel comfortable talking to me, I can understand. ~~But~~ And to say that writing to an accused rapist is something I've done before, would be a lie. But what you said in the Denver Post intrigued me enough, that I hope you'll share more.

So, think about it. We'd like to sit down and talk to you for an exclusive television interview. You can call collect (was going to give you a calling card, but someone told me you wouldn't get it) on Thursday, March 10, around 9 a.m. if possible.

Thank you for your time,
Christine

TEN

Fallout

All too often I've trashed my health on deadline.

There was the time I raced away from a divey fast-food drive-through, wolfing down a lukewarm, stale bean burrito en route to a *St. Petersburg Times* story, only to break out in a cold sweat during the interview as my gut began to rumble with the first signs of food poisoning. I barely made it back to the newsroom in time, yelling "I'm sorry!" as I scrambled for the bathroom.

Then there was the time that same paper sent me to Orlando for three days to do a story about a couple who had let their two-year-old son die from hundreds of wasp stings because they didn't believe in medical treatment. I rushed around frantically and became dehydrated on that trip and ended up in the emergency room in Tampa with a kidney infection so painful I couldn't sit up.

While working on the military series at the *Denver Post*, Miles and I maintained a brutal pace of little sleep or food for several months, trying to make a September publication deadline (that was eventually pushed back until November). We would give ourselves only one break for forty-five minutes every afternoon, when we were fried from staring at our computers or poring over files or notes, and we'd power walk down the 16th Street Mall in Denver to the local smoothie shop for lunch. We'd get our protein smoothies to go and brainstorm as we raced back.

In the midst of this liquid diet, I splurged on an immense tub of popcorn during a movie one night, and some errant kernels became lodged in my gut, which then promptly twisted and became infected. While meeting with editors two days later, I sat doubled over in pain, my face hot with a high fever. One of them looked over at me and remarked with a knowing smile, "I had that stomach flu."

After the meeting, Miles threw a caring friend's fit: "Go to the hospital!" So I agreed.

Still single at that time, I called the babysitter to say I'd be late and somehow drove myself to the emergency room in nearby Lafayette that night straight from work. I remember writhing in pain on a table as the doctor insisted to me that I needed to be admitted because my entire stomach lining was infected. "No," I gasped. "I have to be there when my kids get up in the morning, or they'll be scared." After that, I made a note to self: Never eat popcorn on an empty stomach.

Missed meals are a way of life for a journalist. I learned to squirrel away food in my purse, car, and desk drawers, and once I became extremely angry with an editor who, while I was on the phone, casually took an apple off my desk and ate it.

The night I got the jailhouse interview of Brents, I came home a mess after being on deadline for six hours. Light-headed and shaking with hunger, I was also ramped up from the adrenaline rush of pushing a complicated story through in a short amount of time.

My mind was still reeling with the implications of the conversation, and while I had not yet begun to process the actual interview itself, it had left me feeling upset and sick at heart. It's not every day you press someone for the harsh details of why he molested an eight-year-old boy or raped and choked a middle-age woman or nearly beat a young woman to death with a two-by-four. In the moment, I could be clinical. Later, I would relive every part of the conversation and cringe at the details I wish I didn't know.

I wasn't used to trying to explain any of this to someone after work, but now that Matt and I were married, things were very different. That night, the boys were asleep once I arrived home shortly before eleven, but Matt had kept a plate of spaghetti for me, which I demolished without even really tasting it. I changed my clothes, and with both of us wearing sweatpants and T-shirts, we lay on the couch on opposite ends, intertwining our legs in the middle.

I sipped a glass of garnet-colored merlot and tried to will my body to let go of the ramped-up feeling of being on deadline. Since I rarely imbibe, I'm a cheap drunk. At half a glass, I could feel a heaviness start to descend through my arms and legs, but my brain still refused to quiet, and the wine did nothing for my heart.

"What's wrong?" Matt kept asking me, and I kept shaking my head, unable to pinpoint it exactly. I felt like I had brushed up against something cold and evil, and somehow, a scaly, chilling tendril of it had wrapped around me and wasn't letting go.

"He wants me to work on a long-term project with him, like a series of stories or a book," I finally told him, and Matt frowned. My husband looks a lot like Kevin Bacon, with a slight upturn to his nose, hollowed-out cheekbones, intense blue eyes, and a lean build. When he smiles, he can illuminate a room. When he frowns, though, his whole countenance turns dark and he can absolutely ooze irritation.

As a park ranger for nearly twenty years, he is also a commissioned law enforcement officer. So Matt's first reaction to the idea of my regularly interviewing Brents was as a cop: no, because it will put you, and possibly our family, at risk.

"Anyone with his background is going to have prison gang ties in order to survive," he said. "What if you write something that angers him? How do you know he won't have someone come after you, or the boys?"

I contemplated that for a bit, turning it over in my mind. "Good point," I finally acknowledged.

"And why would you want to spend any time talking with someone like that?" His frown deepened. "He's as bad as they come. Don't subject yourself to this, because the details of what he's done will break your heart. It wasn't that long ago you had your fill of trauma. Why put yourself through something like that again?"

I nodded. Dammit, he was right. Matt knew about the toll the military series had taken on me, and he also knew firsthand the damage of a steady diet of witnessing destruction. As a park ranger, he was first to arrive on more than one scene entailing human injury or death, and then when 9/11 happened, he was deployed to Ground Zero with other FEMA Urban Search and Rescue teams. He worked a search dog during the night shift on "the pile." At one point, he gave an interview to *Good Morning America*, and I have since used the tape as a teaching example of a trauma interview.

At the time, Matt had been going for two days straight, and minutes before leaving Ground Zero to go to the ABC studios for the interview, he'd just finished a search that uncovered more human remains. On the show he was articulate and appeared to be relaxed, when actually he was numb. It hurts me every time I look at that tape and see the pained, faraway look in his eyes. It took him years to come to terms with those tragic events. So yeah, like me, Matt knew about trauma. I'm sure when our psyches met, they sighed in recognition.

"It's not worth it, sweetie," he said to me now, softening his tone.

I shook my head. "I don't know about that. I'm a journalist. This is not just what I do—it's who I am. And this is a huge opportunity to try to understand what makes someone like that tick."

"Who cares what makes him tick? He's a sick, twisted son of a bitch," Matt said, almost spitting out the words, and I knew this was the cop in him talking again.

"And darlin'," he continued with a much gentler tone, and now he was my husband, "I don't want there to be any chance of you getting hurt. Or having any of that story rub off on you."

Once again, I nodded. He was right. His logic made perfect sense. So why did doubt gnaw at me?

That night in bed, curled on Matt's chest under the nook of his left arm, I could feel the heaviness in my heart finally bubble up. I started to cry, and once the tears began, it was like a dam breaking—they became gulping sobs.

"What are you crying for?" Matt asked me again softly, rubbing my back, and wordlessly, I shook my head. It was too much to try to explain. I was crying for the pain of what Brents had done to his victims, I was crying for his wasted, awful life, and I was crying for what was yet to come.

Because I knew what Matt had not yet realized: I wasn't going to walk away from the story of Brents. The thought of it chafed against every fiber of my being. I had never backed down from any challenge, and I wasn't going to start now. Not for him, not for me, not even for our marriage and the cost of my loving husband's eventual anger and disappointment when he didn't understand.

I was crying tears of dread.

While I was still in college, a sensitive reporter friend for the *Courier Journal* newspaper in Kentucky once tried to explain to me the angst of turning over a meaningful story to editors who could then chop it up at will.

"You labor and labor over it, like a child, and then suddenly, it's gone, out of your hands, off your computer screen and poof! into the atmosphere," she said, making a flinging motion above her head with long, delicate fingers. "And you're left to just worry over it. It's awful."

That's a bit extreme, I thought.

Early in my career, I lucked out with dedicated and deft editors at the *St. Petersburg Times*, one of the more memorable being Tampa's hard-charging and passionate city editor, Tom Scherberger. Contrary to the stereotypical image of a mousy print editor, Tom was a force of nature who blew into the newsroom each morning like his own hurricane, his thick salt-and-pepper hair askew every which way, his colorful tie hanging like an afterthought on his dress shirt, the sleeves shoved up his arms.

For all his fervor in pushing us reporters to cover news—and Tom was evangelical in that regard—he held us to even higher standards when it came to editing. When I screwed up, Tom didn't preach. When I turned in bad copy, he didn't shame me or dismissively rewrite me.

He would call me to his desk, briskly point out in blunt terms what was wrong with the story, and issue the confident command, "Now go fix it." Then he'd move on to the next crisis.

I worked hard in those early days to get better, because compliments from him were like gold. Over time, I did get better, and we developed confidence in each other.

I once snuck into a Tampa hospital to see a teenage girl whose parents had been accused by police of severe neglect. The parents were charged with ignoring the grapefruit-sized tumor in their daughter's chest and letting her slowly waste away on their living room couch, surrounded by clutter and filth. One night her heart stopped, and her younger brother drove her to the emergency room in a frantic attempt to save her. The police said it was one of the more horrific cases of neglect they'd ever seen, while the girl's father insisted that she didn't look that bad.

I had to see her myself to know the truth, but sneaking into a hospital intensive care unit is like trying to break into Fort Knox. So early one morning, a *St. Petersburg Times* photographer and I stepped off the elevator at the hospital's ICU unit and immediately took off in opposite directions down the ward. I knew the camera around his neck would attract instant attention, giving me only a matter of seconds.

As a crowd of outraged nurses and security guards surrounded the photographer, I found the girl's room and stood, transfixed, at her doorway. I didn't know a human being could look so gaunt and still be alive, if that was indeed what she was. She stared at the ceiling, unseeing, while her claw-like hands curved toward each other on her chest and her breaths rattled inside an increasingly empty shell.

The next day, when my story appeared with the exact physical description of the girl in the lead paragraph and it became clear to hospital officials I had violated every policy they had, Tom fielded a call from the very angry hospital spokesman. I could hear the man shouting at my boss through the phone from ten feet away, where I hovered, a knot in my stomach over his accusations that I had irreparably harmed the newspaper's reputation. Tom said very little during the call, then hung up and turned toward me with an emphatic nod as he uttered two words.

"Good job."

They don't make editors like that anymore.

Later at the *Denver Post*, after I started to turn in worthwhile stories only to have them butchered by some uncaring editor, I came to understand exactly what my reporter friend had meant about fear of abandoning your story. You immerse yourself in an assignment, trying to answer every question on behalf of the readers, driving here and there, knocking on doors, making phone call after phone call, pressing and challenging and sometimes even begging for details—and all to find the missing piece to the puzzle that is your story. Once it's whole, there's an immense satisfaction, as if by leaving this account of accurately documented history, you have now justified your place in this world.

Then some guy who had a fight with his wife that morning and never gets out of the newsroom sits at his desk littered with empty soda cans and pink coconut snowball wrappers, pulls your story up on his screen, decides that your creative narrative lead is just too damn poetic for his tastes—who do you think you are, anyway, Rumi?—and proceeds to take out his frustrations on your hapless story like a linguistic Jack the Ripper.

As a result, I never wanted to see my stories once they ran in the paper. I didn't want to know if my labor of love had been bastardized, if precise wording I had sweated over now resembled something a fourth grader could spit out the night before it was due.

So the next morning when I went into work and saw issues of that day's *Denver Post* lying around the newsroom, I glanced at the front page and cringed.

My vigilance with every editor the night before had ensured that the words in the story were, indeed, what I had written. It had not been butchered.

What I hadn't counted on was how the story would be pimped.

THERE'S AN ANIMAL THERE the headline screamed in large

bold type, and elements of the story-related photos and quotes sprawled across the entire front page. His picture alone—the recent mug shot—spanned three columns wide and five columns deep, with this caption above it: **JAILHOUSE INTERVIEW WITH BRENT J. BRENTS**.

The phrase above the story, a "blurb," proclaimed, "Blames spree on cops," and I cringed again. That line certainly wouldn't make me popular with anyone in law enforcement. The general public doesn't realize that reporters don't write headlines or blurbs.

I called the public defender and spent a few minutes on the phone with the man, who sputtered with anger and hung up on me, but not before telling me that no way was I ever, ever going to be able to talk to Thompson, Brents' attorney. I later learned that they had been considering an insanity defense until my story ran, quoting someone who sounded cold, deliberate, and very much in control of his faculties.

I called the jail to see about visiting Brents, and the captain on the other end of the phone guffawed at my request. Evidently the place was in chaos because of the story: Dozens of reporters had shown up clamoring for interviews.

"You can send Brents a letter," he said, "but you'll have to get his permission to see him."

That afternoon, Aurora police officials angrily denounced my story at a news conference. The day before, the Aurora City Council had suspended the city manager and the deputy city manager for two weeks because of the mishandling of Brents' case. The chief of police, Ricky Bennett, had been placed under "administrative and legal review."

The day the "jailhouse interview" ran was Bennett's last day as Aurora's police chief in a decision that Mayor Ed Tauer called voluntary.

The entire situation was painful, and the newly appointed acting chief lashed out.

"We don't understand the credence that they would be giving to a convicted sex offender who has a propensity to lie anyway [to] gain people's confidence," said Aurora Deputy Police Chief Terry Jones at the Friday afternoon press conference. "And to boot, he's a con man."

Con man or no, I wondered what Brents' reaction was to the piece, if he had indeed caught hell from his attorney, and if he felt that I had betrayed him by revealing more than he intended. And then there was the sheer sensationalism of the piece. Not knowing if he would have access to the newspaper, I carefully cut out the story, minus the headline and blurbs and all the added hype, and folded it into an envelope along with a letter.

> Hi Brent,
> Well, the stuff must have hit the fan for you. I called the jail today (Friday) to ask how I could be put on your visiting list and a captain told me that by late afternoon, reporters were lining up at the jail and your attorney was on the way.
> I tried to say what you wanted—to apologize and to let everyone know how the Aurora PD handled it (the city says they are investigating the incident) and, for the most part, to shy away from your cases. My editors asked if you talked about them, and I was honest and said some, but you had asked me not to print some parts and I was going to honor that. I tried to walk that line, of being your voice and giving my editors enough detail so that they would be happy and allow me to take the time away to work on something long term (in keeping with your idea). They agreed. I've been cleared to attend all of your court hearings and maintain talking to you without writing about it anymore for now.
> As you will read in the story, I called your mom and your sister for their response, and what I could not say in the story was that when your sister first talked about you, her voice was warm and kind. Then she put her tough girl self on—I know you know the one I'm talking about. As for asking your mom about any possible abuse—well, I feel it's necessary, and an issue that shouldn't be swept under a rug. I wanted people to get an idea of how things were for you.
> So, I'm sending you some blank paper, if you still want to write. And I will try to get on a visitor list, and I'm

planning on being at your next court appearance. I have no idea if all of that is still what you want. Could you let me know? I can't call you—I tried frantically to have someone relay a message to you to call me back on Thursday so I could run some things by you, but the jail won't deliver messages. I guess you can try to call me collect again—my direct line, so no one else has to pick up, is 303-820-1752. If you can't reach me there, try the 1201 extension, but I would hate to see the buzz then sweep around the newsroom that it's you on the phone, and get back to your attorney and get you in more hot water with her. I called and left a message for her but she has not yet called me back. She's probably pretty mad at me for simply talking to you.

    I have to tell you, that was tough—trying to write just a small part of what you wanted to say. I want you to know, whether you hate the piece or not, that I struggled with it and did my best. When I was done, I hovered over it as editors worked on it, trying to protect every word.

    By the time I got home, it was late, and my head was still buzzing with our conversation, and the things you said, and all the things you can't say yet that I could feel there, under the surface.

    So, as you say, no bullshit. If you do decide to meet me, face-to-face, and talk about the possibility of working on something long term, I know it's going to be hard on me. And that probably sounds selfish to you—you're the one in prison, going through this, facing all of those charges. But I am affected in spirit by every person I interview.

    So let me know what you think. But if nothing else, please know I tried my best to do right by you.

    Regards,
    Amy

April 6, 2005
Amy,

    Hi, It's me . . . I have to tell you that every reporter so far has tried to either bribe me, manipulate me, Make me out to be a monster. Every one has only showed Thier greed, selfishness, bitterness and hatred. Amy I don't care if your a greedy self centered bitch. What I do care about is This. I am going to put me, my story Into your hands . . . I am going to tell you my story truthfuly and I hope you will not screw me over in the Long run like every woman I've ever felt I could trust has . . . If your sincere then you'll know That we have to develop a sincere trust. A Relationship of Trust . . . I am sure you have an opinion and probably some deep feelings about what I did. If you would please tell me what you think and feel about me and all the stuff I have done. Get This Amy, The truth please no matter how harsh or painful it may sound . . . You've been pretty superficial so far . . . Show me the real you and show me I can trust your heart and I'll give you my story . . . Sencerely wanting to believe.
    Brent.

ELEVEN

Down the Rabbit Hole

Psychologists say we are prone to choose partners who have the same traits we couldn't stand in our parents or caregivers in order to rework that relationship. It's as though we're constantly trying to hit the reset button.

For me, the worst thing is physical or emotional abandonment. It flashes me back to the pain of my childhood, as if I'm once again a baby left in her crib, making hopeful noises for hours to get someone to pay attention to me. The family joke was how I learned to climb out of that crib before I could walk, and eventually I'd fall asleep on a rug somewhere or at the foot of one of my sibling's beds, like a dog. I guess I was trying to get what I needed. A few short years after that, I discovered I could get a positive reaction—and attention—by becoming the tiny responsible adult who would scrub the bathroom and clean up the kitchen and fold a half-dozen loads of laundry after school. Knowing this, I have to struggle to not revert back to being twelve when those buttons are pushed, when someone shuts me out emotionally—like my depressed mother—or simply is not available—like my workaholic father.

So I took the weekend to think about it. When I broke the difficult news to Matt on Monday, March 7, that against his strong objections, I was going to work on a long-term project about Brent Brents after all, his reaction could not have been worse.

"Really?" Matt asked incredulously, his blue eyes looking at me in shocked surprise for what felt like a long time, and I could only nod. We were standing in the kitchen, cleaning up after a taco-night dinner.

"I'm going to see how it goes," I said. "I won't share anything personal with him. He won't know I have a family." I leaned against the kitchen counter and watched him closely. He broke eye contact and turned away.

Methodically, Matt began to wash and rinse the navy-blue-and-green dinner plates in the sink—our house was too old and too tiny to have a dishwasher. From my sideways view, his face was a careful screen that hid his thoughts. When he was done, he turned to me without expression and said one word: "OK." Then he walked out of the room.

I didn't follow. That night, I went to bed alone while he stayed up and watched television. And over the days and weeks that followed, a slow anger roiled between us, like a pot of water set at low heat. He resented me for choosing the Brents project over his wishes. And I resented him for not understanding I had done so because it was that important.

Eight days later on March 15, I got my first letter from Brents, sent back to me in the plain, self-addressed, stamped envelope I had sent the jail. And my whole conversation with Matt seemed like a waste of time and energy.

> Amy,
>   I am Disapointed yes. However I do understand. At this time I am Not going to write anymore to you or anyone Else; on advice of my councel. She is a smart woman and only has my best enterest at heart. When all is said and done you and I may continue.
>   Sincerely
>   Brent Brents

One of the elements of newsworthiness is timeliness. My editors weren't going to care about a story being done after "all is said and done." I wanted to be able to gather details of his story *now*. So I wrote Brents back, asking if he still wanted me to attend his court hearings and if I could meet with him in person, but mostly, just trying to keep a dialogue going.

A week later, on March 22, the reply came to the *Post*, in the cream-colored Hallmark stationery I had sent him.

> *Amy,*
> *Yes I still want you to Attend my court hearings. As for meeting me. Not now. I have to trust Carrie. She's my attorney. She's The only person I realy can believe in right now so I'm doing As she asks. I will keep my word to you. Eventualy we will meet and you'll get your story ok. There are Things going on that I can not discuss with anyone. Please have a little faith in me. I know There are other Front page news stories out There. I don't want you to use me and I feel a Little Like That after The Phone deal. Please be patient and show me this isn't Just about a story.*
> *Thank you*
> *Sincerely*
> *Brent*

I reread that letter several times. Had I used him? Exploited him for the story?

I didn't like my own answer: Yes, I had.

Well, is that going to make you stop pressing him for another one?

No, it's not, I admitted. So I wrote him again and enclosed a recent story I had done about prostitution in Denver. I pursued that story for two months because it fascinated me so.

Every January the National Western Stock Show comes to Denver for a few weeks, featuring events such as heifer judging, bull riding, and reining horse contests. Cowboys from around the country flock to Denver for the event—and so do prostitutes. After hearing talk from some police officers about the annual influx of working girls, I got permission to ride around with some undercover vice detectives one bitterly cold January night to see for myself about these "circuit girls." We were at the police station preparing to leave when I noticed a large black binder on one detective's desk and asked about it.

He flipped it open to some words typed on the first page: "Look at this and ask yourself if prostitution is really a victimless crime."

Inside the book, he had placed arrest photo after arrest photo of a dozen street prostitutes, each one in sequence, so the viewer could appreciate the ravages of that lifestyle over time.

The photos were riveting, such as four of a young blond girl. In the first one, she is smiling and fresh-faced, looking like someone's kid sister. In the second, her hair is disheveled and she appears angry. By the third photo, her right eye is swollen shut, her left eye sports a dark bruise, and her jaw is wired shut. In the fourth and final photo, her hair looks filthy and uncombed, her mouth is agape, and her eyes are half-closed in some drug-induced zombie state.

"It's all because they don't care," the detective said. "Well, I care."

The art was compelling. The detective's motivation and compassionate spirit were inspiring. I vowed on the spot to do a story on the book, and after the detective told me I needed to go through proper channels and ask, I did so.

After being put off for a week, I was told no. Release of the contents of the book would violate those women's privacy, police officials said to me. Besides, the detective used it as a training tool to raise awareness—for example, he had made a copy for a judge who presided over prostitution arrests—and as such, it was not public record.

Baloney! I told the officials over the phone at my desk as we argued back and forth. Those mug shots are all public record. And the fact the book had been given out showed it wasn't confidential. Wait a minute, I thought. The book had been given out!

The vice detective gave me the name of the judge, a tall, slender, velvet-voiced man with jet black hair and distinguished gray at the temples named John Marcucci, and I immediately called him to see if I could borrow his book, crossing my fingers that he knew nothing of the bitter fight between me and the police officials.

"Sure," Marcucci said to me, and I hung up the phone and ran the five blocks from the *Denver Post* newsroom to the courthouse, grabbed the book from his secretary, and smiled all the way back. I still needed the names and details of the women the detective had written in his original version, but at least now I had the photos. I then called the police officials and asked for a negotiation meeting, which they agreed to do that night. On the way there, I ordered cheese pizza to take some of the sting out of their defeat. They laughed when it was delivered, and during the meeting, the detective handed me a neatly typed list of the names of the prostitutes featured in his book. One of those names would later become very familiar to me: Aida Bergfeld.

I did both stories—the stock show "circuit girls" as well as the book, which was called *Faces of Prostitution*. In the story, Marcucci gave me an amazing quote about the women he saw appear before him on prostitution charges nearly every day: "They're victims and they're defendants and they're perpetrators and they're drug addicts and they're sociopaths—all rolled into one."

Until then, I guess I had always viewed prostitution in more black-and-white terms, as simply a crime, and didn't take into account that most of these women are traumatized and have a history of sexual abuse. For them, there are few other ways to survive.

I was also aware that most of Brents' victims were prostitutes. I wondered if it were possible at all for him to view them in another way as well.

"I'm sorry you feel used," I wrote him in my letter. "Here's a story I did that you may find interesting. What other stories are out there that I should be reporting on?"

As for his phrase "show me this isn't Just about a story," I decided that it was a plea of some kind, for sympathy perhaps, and that he must be feeling very alone. While I didn't respond to it directly, I did shoot for a kinder, less demanding tone. And oh, I had one question:

"Right before we got disconnected from that phone call, you said you knew what I looked like. Have we met?" And I enclosed more cream-colored stationery.

On April 8, I received his reply.

Amy,

Thank you for your understanding. Yes There is a whole Lot I cannot discuss with anyone. Eventualy I will with you.

As for Knowing what you Look Like. Don't trip I've Actualy stood 2 feet from you in The Elevator At the post . . .

Anyway yes I have known who you were from the beginning. I can safely say This about you, so far I've Loved you and hated you all at the same Time. When I first saw you I thought you were very beautiful. But when the story came out I thought of you as another She Devil. I loved you because you remind me of my first girlfriend when I was 17 . . . Tall, forceful, beautiful. Anyway I liked your story and I will give you more to help you with it if you want.

For the next two pages, he described places on Colfax Avenue and other areas where I could find drug dealers and prostitutes if I wanted the real inside story.

He signed off with words of caution.

This Letter is between us. Please don't say Shit to anyone about it. If you do then I'll not give you my story when I am finally able. I promise Amy I'll do you right If you do me right. I think you're a real Kind person But also Ambitious Like A Gambler. Hold The cards for now and you'll get the Royal flush eventualy, I promise.

Brents

Sitting at home at my mahogany dining room table as I read this letter, I felt a flash of anger. What was this crap—"Ambitious Like A

Gambler"? He didn't know me. He didn't know anything about me. And clearly he was lying about standing two feet from me in the elevator at the *Post* in an effort to have some kind of commonality. Such bullshit.

I tore off a sheet from a notebook and wrote, "Please don't try to manipulate me into giving you personal information. It won't work. And more important: You have to always tell me the truth, because otherwise, I won't waste my time—I'll walk away. No deal."

And then I stopped, because from some corner of my brain, I suddenly realized we *had* seen each other on the elevator: Brents had been the man in the rumpled gray suit who gave me the creeps when I first returned to work. That incident had unsettled me so much that I even told Matt about it the night it happened.

Telling him of this latest development didn't make him feel any better about the whole thing. "Great," Matt said. "He stalked you."

I decided to chalk it up to coincidence, not stalking. As for the rest of the letter, especially the way he would toss in personal questions, such as "Tell me about your marriage"—I just ignored it all. I hadn't told Brents I was married, so he was making assumptions.

One common theme I didn't ignore: In every letter, he asked me to "be real." So I tried to reassure him. I wasn't going to lie to him, I wrote, and I wasn't going to break our deal. I wouldn't use anything he sent me until he was sentenced.

"I realy believe you are capable of humanity," Brents wrote in his next letter, and it struck me as more of a plea than a statement. When I admitted I'd mistakenly thought he had lied about seeing me on the elevator, he seemed offended. "I would not lie to you about something so trivial," he retorted.

That letter, postmarked April 19, sat unopened in my mail slot at the *Denver Post* newsroom because I was happily on vacation. I had been invited to do some guest teaching on trauma journalism at the University of Washington, so Matt and I had the gift of a free week in Seattle.

We had been looking forward to this trip for a while, and I secretly hoped it would bring us closer as a couple again. Since I had started corresponding with Brents, there was a definite tension between us. Talking about it didn't seem to help, because I wasn't going to stop working on the story. So neither one of us brought it up. And unresolved anger is one of the worst corrosives there is—it will eat away at a person, at a marriage. And clearly that was happening to us; although we didn't argue, we didn't check in with each other anymore. We stopped having early morning coffees and late-night couch conversations. We greeted each other with a polite smile after work instead of a warm hug and kiss.

As it turned out, spending a springtime, rain-soaked week alone in Seattle was just what we needed to reconnect. We stayed in an elegant suite at the Inn at the Market, a gorgeous boutique hotel a half block from Seattle's historic open-air Pike Place Market and, in between my teaching, spent hours there browsing, shopping, and sampling creamy and rich clam chowder. We strolled. We slept in. We made love. We drove to Lake Union and kayaked, then had nachos and margaritas afterward. We laughed. It was if we had called a truce to our private, unspoken war on the Brents situation, which was easy to do because we were a thousand miles away from it.

I hadn't thought of work, until late one afternoon when my cell phone rang and I saw that it was coming from the newsroom. Matt was in the shower getting ready for our evening out, so I picked up.

"Sorry to bother you," one of the editors said, sounding rushed and nervous, "but I wanted to tell you two things."

"OK," I said, looking out the window of our hotel room at the sight of a cheerful red-and-white tugboat chugging along Elliot Bay. It was near sunset, and the water reflected orange. In the background, the majestic Olympic Mountains jutted upward in a dark purple outline. This was heaven. I was in a bubble of tranquility nothing could break.

"Um, first, I thought you would want to know that Aida Bergfeld died," he said, and I had to take a moment to get back into work mode to remember who that was. "She was Brents' last victim," he reminded me. "The woman who was with him when he was caught. She overdosed."

"That's too bad," I waited, thinking, You're calling me in Seattle to tell me this?

"Also, you got another letter from Brents," he continued, starting to speak faster now, "and since you weren't here, I opened it for you. I thought you should know."

That took a moment to register too. "You opened my mail?" My voice cracked in surprise on the last word.

"Well, yeah, but even though it's addressed to you, it's sent to the *Denver Post*, so technically, any mail that you get here is not really yours," he said, sounding defensive. "And I decided to open it to see if there was anything newsworthy in there."

I felt the bubble of my tranquility start to crack. "Wait a minute," I said quickly, feeling incredulous. "To see if anything newsworthy was in there? You know we have an agreement with him not to publish what he's sending until he's sentenced."

"Yeah, but if he sends something worth printing, all bets are off," he said, and just like that, the bubble burst.

"So you would have blown the whole deal, made me out to be a liar, and jeopardized any future information we could have gotten from him *in case* you found something you thought was worth one little story?" My voice was rising with every word.

Out of the shower now, Matt peered around the corner in curiosity, a thick white towel wrapped around his waist, shaving cream on his face, a razor in one hand. I waved him away.

"Hey, if you don't like it, you can appeal it when you get back," he said.

I suddenly didn't care that he was my boss and that if I fell out of favor, I could be writing obituaries for the remainder of my time at the *Post*. Red-hot anger took control of my tongue.

"Oh, I *will* appeal it," I said through clenched teeth. "Meanwhile, keep your *fucking* hands off my mail."

Silence. Then, "Whatever," he said, and I hung up, still livid. I grabbed some hotel stationery from the desk of our room and immediately sat and wrote Brents a letter.

"Don't send any more letters to the *Denver Post* newsroom," I warned him. "The editors there can't be trusted. As soon as I get back home, I'll open up a post office box for you to write to."

My first day back, I tried to talk to the editor about opening the letter. He shrugged and pointed me toward another editor, who shrugged and sent me to yet another.

"Do the words 'federal offense' mean nothing here?" I asked one of them inside his office. "This is bullshit. He can't just open my mail."

"I'll talk to him," he said, sounding like a weary parent, so I left.

I immediately went to my car and drove to a post office in Boulder, where I opened up a box just for the purpose of corresponding with Brents. I didn't want him writing to me at home because I didn't want him knowing where I lived, and besides, Matt would go ballistic if his letters started to arrive at our house. But evidently I needed to keep them out of the newsroom.

The irony wasn't lost on me: I was protecting a serial rapist from my editors.

I just didn't trust them anymore.

April 22, 2005
Amy,
    Time after time from the age of 5 until I was in my 20s I was betrayed by men and women, family and so-called friends. Around the age of 10 I became them and I've been trying to hurt Them ever since I think.
    —Brent

TWELVE

A Question

Of all the incredibly useful things I learned during my four-month hiatus from the *Denver Post*, one of the best was how to protect myself emotionally from someone's negative energy.

So anytime I step into what promises to be a wrenching or combative interview, I take a few moments to visualize strapping a virtual safety harness over my shoulders, just like the kind you find on a roller coaster. If the story is particularly awful, I wear a thin silver chain with a black onyx pendent, since onyx is said to have protective qualities and helps ground the wearer, giving him or her better focus.

Of course when it came to Brents, I figured the more protection I had, the better.

Sally thought so as well. Like Matt, she had tried to no avail to talk me out of the project on Brents. My sister and I have the same cell phone plan, and despite living in separate states, we often talk several times a day. Lately, she had been fixated on one topic: Brents. She wanted me to run, not just walk, away from anything having to do with him.

She was worried, she said, that Brents would stain my psyche, that he would scar my soul.

"Is this about Dreux?" she asked unexpectedly at one point, and I immediately scoffed.

"No, it is not. This is about a story, nothing else. I know what I'm doing." I tried not to sound defensive. "And it's an amazing opportunity. I'll do the story and walk away. I'll be fine."

"Still, to be exposed to so much *darkness* is *not* healthy. I know you don't really pray," she said, "but will you at least try while you're working on this?"

I hadn't stepped foot inside a church since my brother's funeral, and before that, it had been years. I object to the political structure of most organized religions, and as a lapsed Catholic, I cannot abide the church's patriarchal stance that using birth control is a sin. My grandmother followed that ridiculous rule and gave birth to nine children, creating a household of dysfunction and despair into which my mother was born. After the ninth child, my grandmother apparently put her foot down and said No More, which prompted my grandfather to move into another bedroom.

After marrying at twenty-two, my mother gave birth to four children within six years and suffered a debilitating miscarriage in between each child, so she was steadily pregnant until I came along. After that, she used birth control until having a hysterectomy. Yes, I am grateful for being alive, but it's not fair that it was at the expense of my mother's own quality of life. The cost to her, and her mother before her, was enormous. How does anyone, let alone a church, mandate another person's reproduction? I don't believe either my mother or my grandmother was physically or emotionally capable of bearing so many children without it crippling their well-being. Somewhere along the way, they lost part of themselves. To this day, my mother bitterly denounces the Catholic church's ban on birth control, because the rhythm method of trying to time sex to avoid ovulation is laughingly ineffective.

"Let the pope have babies, and see how long that lasts," she says.

So over time my beliefs have evolved. If pressed to define them, I would say they are a cross between Buddhism and Wicca, and meditating while running is the closest thing I do to consistent prayer.

"I don't formally pray, but I do talk to the universe," I explained to my sister, wanting to reassure her, "and I do believe in a higher power."

"I don't know if that'll be enough."

"I'll make a point of protecting my energy, I swear."

Finally, Sally relented, after making me promise that whenever I was going to be in the vicinity of Brents, I would first surround myself with white light.

This is a type of spiritual protection that involves visualizing a protective barrier of shining white light from head to toe, with the intention of keeping darker, more sinister forces at bay. Since I hadn't yet been in the same room as Brents, so far I hadn't needed to, but I did intend to keep my word. I love my sister and was touched by her concern.

What's that saying about the best-laid plans of mice and men?

While in Seattle, I had sent Brents some of the cheerful sage-green-and-cream stationery from our hotel, so he could write me another letter.

It would be the last letter from Brents I'd receive at the *Denver Post*, and after pulling it—unopened!—from my mailbox in the newsroom, I tucked it into the middle pocket of my large black suitcase of a purse for safekeeping until I could read it at home.

Once there, and blissfully alone—Matt was still at work and the babysitter had taken the Little People to a skateboard park—I took the letter from my purse and smiled at the hotel's clever teal and sage logo featuring a mask, a guitar, a fish, and a pear imprinted on their thick stationery. I then opened the envelope and pulled out the two-page letter. I looked it over fondly, remembering how I found the stationery inside the dark cherry wood desk in our elegant hotel room. It was lovely to be reminded of Seattle. That had been such a great trip.

Seated at our dining room table, I started reading, and almost immediately, my smile faded. A feeling of horror seeped into my head like poison and trailed, black and cold and foreboding, down into my chest and then to my stomach, leaving me nauseated.

There had been no warning. I was not prepared. All his letters prior to this had contained only surface, cursory conversation. Now, with each line, Brents words leaped off the page and struck me like the desperate slap of a drowning man pulling his rescuer under.

4-22-05
Amy,

    Some days I just want to give up. I won't because I gave you my word. Some of my betrayal hurts so badly, There are no words to describe it. I got a letter today from someone who I didn't believe would be able to forgive me. I can't tell you how terrible the hurt is for both of us. Mine is not a selfish hurt it is for her. She was a Rape Victim years ago and she Told me how I made her feel it all over again having done this Thing That I have done. For this woman to express any emotion is amazing but for her to forgive me and tell me she still cares is unbelievable. Carrie told This would all get worse and She was right. Hell it hurts to sit in a courtroom and have a realy good woman defend me to the absolute best of her ability, To see her Raw emotions and pain when she goes over a case with me, Reading the details, The pain is on her face yet she drives on. Fighting a losing battle. I wish I were that brave. I would Tell you to do a story on her sometime but she hates The press because of the hype. Besides your editors would never allow you to do her Justice.

    You asked me what happened to that Little happy Boy, I remember that picture. I wasn't 13 I was 12 and far from happy. Shortly after That Photo my Dad Raped my 12 year old girlfriend and beat me so badly I literally could not get out of bed for 3 weeks. When I was finaly able to get out of bed and had no Bruses for people to see I went Into the hospital with a fractured cheek, a blow out fracture in my orbital Bone and a torn Retna.

    Rarely was I happy. I was happy when they put me in my first foster home because I finally grew enough balls to tell on my dad. What did the state do oh yeah, your dad went to church we're going to send you home. The minute I got home he hit me with a belt on my ass so many times it bled and I had to sleep on my stomach for a week. I was only happy

A Question

when I wasn't home. Oh yeah well I had one happy Thing at home, I got to screw my mom whenever I wanted! Happy HAPPY was waking up in the morning and having him find my sheets dry and not getting beat for wetting the bed, which was rare. Happy was having him away for a week on business (out fucking some woman) I didn't get hit or called names or fucked in my ass. Happy was giving him head rather than him fucking me because no matter how often it happened he always found a way to make it hurt. Happy was coming home and finding him passed out or too drunk to catch me. Happy was having him fuck or get his dick sucked by one of the nieghbor kids so I didn't have to. Happy Amy was him being drunk enough to point a gun at my head and pull the trigger, unfortunately, he missed. I realy wish he would not have missed. Happy was the rare occations Mom stepped in between us so he would not kill me, although it was me who took most of her beatings. Did she ever say thank you. No Amy I was not a happy kid no matter what those photos say.

If that kid existed then I don't know him. I lied to alot of people and said I forgave them for what they did to me. The truth is I never have never will, because they made me what I despise most in life, "Them."

You know, I hate my mom's guts for being such a coward and denying The Life that we led. But I would give my Life for her without hesitation. But where was she when I needed her, worshiping him. Here's sick for you. When I was first in Juvee, The first Time I got Raped in There a guy held a knife made from a piece of rusted steel to my throat. Spit on my ass and fucked me. That's not the sick part; I got a hard-on, thats sick. You have no idea of my shame and Guilt. Nothing changed from home. I was still a weak bitch, having sex for protection, sucking dick for cigarettes. I remember the first guy I thought was a nice guy. He was a staff member. I realy trusted him. I gave myself to him and when he pushed his cock in my ass His exact words were, "I knew you'd be a good bitch!"

I was his good bitch for 2 years.

Time after time from the age of 5 until I was in my 20s I was betrayed by men and women, family and so-called friends. Around the age of 10 I became them and I've been trying to hurt Them ever since I think. There's this voice in my head Thats always telling me to hurt Them. It's There 24 hours A day Amy It Never stops, never goes away.

So now you know why I have trust issues. Funny 2 women who wrote articles in this paper I read lied about some things. Its truly sad that they felt so hurt that they would use a good newspaper to get vengance on me. I hope Amy that your starting to see why I want you to write this book. Its Not about fame or popularity you understand I hope. Theres a Message and I believe you can make people believe.

I'm Tired Im going to close for now. I hope Seattle was at least Dry for a couple of days for you. hope you had fun.

Sincerely

Brent

I know what it's like to trigger someone who is traumatized. I once had a woman end up on the floor in the fetal position during an interview. Another time, one of the female veteran military sexual assault survivors screamed at me—and rightfully so—over the phone because I thoughtlessly left her a question about her case on her answering machine.

"Here I am, going through my day, and I'm fine," she shouted, "and then I hit that button, and there's a goddamned message from you asking some stupid fucking question and just like that, it reminds me of all that shit and my day is ruined!"

If you're not careful—and I thought I had learned over the years to be exceedingly careful—you can take a subject right back to the moment of their debilitating, painful event by a careless question, word, or even gesture.

So when interviewing people who have been the victim of tragedy or a witness to it, I start slowly, establishing a comfort level with them. Like a veteran priest hearing confessions, I try not to appear shocked or upset by anything they say to me—I want them to know they can confidently confide anything in me, no matter how horrific the detail.

"So when you found the baby in the woods," I have asked, "what was the first thing you saw?"

Or, "As he pointed the gun at you and you realized he was going to pull the trigger, what was going through your mind?"

Or, "Where exactly were their bodies lying on the floor?"

I do my homework first, reading reports or talking to others involved in the case so I know what to ask and where my subject may be most vulnerable. I will matter-of-factly approach the topic of the trauma itself, yet closely watch them while doing so, making note of their expressions, their pattern of speech, their breathing, their movement. If any of those things begins to escalate to a point where they appear in danger of spiraling out of control, I'll try to bring them back out of it by changing the line of questions or suggesting a break.

I had never exclusively interviewed someone by letter before. Sure, I had sent letters to people in jails and prisons, but they were always as a means to arrange a face-to-face meeting.

Now, suddenly, on paper, I had clearly triggered Brents. I wracked my brain to recall what I had asked him—I handwrote all my letters and didn't keep copies—and it came to me: "In that picture of you when you were about thirteen, you look rather happy. What was going on when that picture was taken?"

And so he had told me, in candid, horrifying detail. If it was hard to read, well, I'd gotten what I asked for, and I couldn't blame him. Nor could I give in to the tragedy of this and start crying—the boys, and then Matt, would be home soon. I didn't want to distress them.

So instead, I opened the little metal door to the strongbox I keep in the back of my mind to compartmentalize awful things and stuffed the feelings of horror and sadness brought on by his letter deep inside. I then slammed it shut.

Collecting myself, I read his letter over again carefully, dispassionately, looking for anything that smacked of a deliberate ploy for sympathy. But the handwriting was rushed, continuous, as if he had simply sat down and transcribed a stream of consciousness.

Obviously, I had distressed him with my question.

So without hesitation, just as I would have done for any other subject I had inadvertently caused pain, I pulled a sheet of blank paper from the pile by our computer printer and wrote Brents an apology.

"I'm sorry that my question upset you," I told him. "I didn't mean for that to happen. Throughout this process, if something I'm asking triggers you, if it brings back bad memories, then please try to take care of yourself. Take a breath, or take a break, or tell me you don't want to talk about that right now."

I stared at my words after I wrote them, before folding the letter and placing it inside an envelope to later mail. They were certainly familiar enough—I had spoken something like that hundreds of times to various survivors over the years—but this time, I was struck by the twist.

I was delivering those words of caution to a perpetrator, and not just any perpetrator, mind you, but arguably one of the most predatory on the planet—as if he were—there was no other word for it—a *victim*.

Perhaps it was because I was focused on that strange fact that I glazed over another, something I had been quick to lock away.

Something important.

Brents had been triggered.

But so had I.

So is it a need for approval that drives me? Strokes that I don't get anywhere else? Because my parents were distant? Perhaps that's why I do what I do—because I'm good at it, better than most, and I thrive on that recognition.

—From Amy's journal, 2004

THIRTEEN

Excavating

It was 1998, and I was sitting in a small, disheveled apartment near the University of South Florida doing a story for the *St. Petersburg Times* about a twenty-one-year-old freckle-faced heroin addict who was trying to detox on his own.

As the young man scratched his needle-dotted arms compulsively, he described for me what it felt like.

"Your skin crawls," he said, "and then it feels like someone is ripping the muscles out of your back."

I was so struck by what he said that I started the story that way, and his words have stayed with me since. They resonated, I think, because they come close to describing what I feel when I'm emotionally triggered: raw and reactive. Every angry nerve ending in my body lights up like Times Square on New Year's Eve.

If you're great at compartmentalizing, like those of us from dysfunctional homes, then you can submerge your feelings for a while. You won't know why you're walking around anxious or angry or sad until you're finally able to be still and think it through.

In my case, I usually end up lashing out at someone, and we're always at our worst with those we love. For me, that meant blowing up at Matt.

In this instance, the chain of events started one month after we were married, and as usual, it started at work.

In January 2005, a controversy erupted around the country over an essay written by a University of Colorado ethnic studies professor named Ward Churchill in which he said unlawful U.S. foreign policy provoked the 9/11 attacks. Written shortly after 9/11, the essay, "On the Justice of Roosting Chickens," only surfaced years later after Churchill was asked to speak at a New York college, but once it hit, people were furious. In the essay, Churchill said the role of financial workers in the World Trade Center was part of "ongoing genocidal American imperialism" and compared their work to that of Adolph Eichmann, a German Nazi responsible for the logistics of a mass deportation of Jews to death camps.

Within days of the initial January story, Churchill was flooded by thousands of angry calls, emails, and letters, the governor of Colorado demanded he be fired, and CU denounced him. By the first week of February, university officials began investigating the professor to see if he had "crossed" the boundary of free speech. His ethnicity—as Churchill identifies with being American Indian—was called into question.

I had met the fiery activist years before, when I first came to Denver and began reporting on secret files kept by the Denver Police Department on various peaceful advocacy groups that became dubbed "Spy Files." I interviewed him for those stories and found him to be an angry man—fiercely intelligent, outspoken, blunt, and combative—and a chain smoker whose cigarette fumes always gave me a throbbing headache.

So I wasn't thrilled when a *Denver Post* editor called me while Matt and I were on spring-break vacation with the boys in 2005 and asked me to track down Churchill. "He's not doing interviews," the editor said, "but if anyone can get him to talk, you can."

I had heard stories about Churchill's hostility toward reporters, so I decided against showing up at his house, thinking he would simply lump me in the same "loathsome media" category. Instead, I appealed to other fellow activists in the Denver area, reminding them of my tenacious coverage of the Spy Files stories, and asked them to please help me get an interview with Churchill. Once I was able to talk to him, I reminded him of the same thing—that I had a reputation for being fair and painstakingly accurate. It worked, and my first exclusive story featuring an interview with Churchill, "CU Prof Plans Tough Defense," ran March 31, 2005.

The first line read, "Ward Churchill is unapologetic." Further down, it went on to say this:

> In a nearly four-hour interview Wednesday at his home near Boulder, Churchill alternated between his familiar anger and defiance and a more somber, almost melancholy side the public hasn't seen.
>
> He has never backed down from his comments that some of the people who died in the World Trade Center on Sept. 11, 2001 were like Nazis—"little Eichmanns" who brought the events of that day on themselves.
>
> If he has any regrets about the three months since the 3-year-old essay containing his "little Eichmanns" characterization inflamed the public, it is the effect the uproar has had on his family.
>
> "I chose this life; they didn't," he said, referring to his aging mother and stepfather and other family members whose names have been published and who have been relentlessly contacted by reporters and others seeking to verify Churchill's ethnicity.

With that story, the masses had another target: me. As a veteran reporter, I wasn't surprised—people love to blame someone because it makes them feel better, like they're in control. Or perhaps the perpetrator who hurt them is dead or in prison or otherwise unavailable, so they lash out at someone within reach—such as the journalist writing the story—and my email address and phone number at the bottom of stories made it easy. Sometimes, you're a scapegoat for simply being the one who dares to broach topics others consider off-limits.

Soon, my voicemail and email filled up with hateful messages from people telling me what a piece of shit journalist I was because they thought my story sounded sympathetic to Churchill. Others were enraged that I "gave him the chance to speak," as though the decision were mine alone and not controlled by editors.

It's a point of pride with me that I always answer every call and every email regarding a story, and so I did. Sometimes, readers calmed down and came around—realizing that I wasn't going to apologize for firmly believing that everyone is entitled to free speech. Other times, they would scream "You fucking liberal!" to me over the phone, until I would cheerfully say "OK, this isn't productive, so I'm hanging up now" and then do it.

Those incidents never bothered me. Over the years, my skin had become steel plated and nothing could get through—nothing, that is, except for the little areas of raw nerve that popped to the surface whenever I was triggered about my childhood—or someone else's.

So other than the fact that I had received Brent's disturbing letter days before, I wasn't particularly perturbed one afternoon in late April when my office phone rang and the voice on the other end of the line identified himself as Michael Roberts, the media columnist for a popular local alternative weekly called *Westword*. Roberts was highly read among the media and feared by most of them. He had a reputation for being sensationalistic and ruthlessly going for the jugular in an interview. He was rarely known to call reporters about something nice, and that day was no exception.

"What I have to say is not pleasant," he said, "and I would like to get your response."

"OK." My nerve endings waited, flexing in anticipation.

"Sources of mine say," he began, and I sighed impatiently—I hate the anonymous and cowardly "sources say." If you're going to talk smack about someone, back it up with facts and attach your name to it. I do.

". . . that you are dating Ward Churchill."

I was so stunned that I said the first thing that came to my mind.

"No, and I don't know whether to laugh or be ticked that you're actually asking me that." As some of my nearby curious coworkers looked up from their desks—there are no secret conversations in a newsroom—I cupped my hand over the receiver and loudly stage-whispered, "Michael Roberts wants to know if I'm dating Ward Churchill."

Immediately, hoots of laughter erupted. And even though I was highly annoyed at the offensive question and what it implied—that I had used sex to get my exclusive interview with Churchill—I saw the humor in the situation and started laughing too. My nerve endings sank back down.

"So the answer is no?" Roberts said.

"Correct, the answer is no. And the allegation is complete and utter bullshit."

"But, wait, don't you want to know what I've heard?"

Unbelievable, I thought. "What part of 'complete and utter bullshit' do you not understand?"

"But I have good sources who say they've seen you in public with Churchill—with your arms around each other," he said, sounding triumphant.

I snorted. "Who? 'Sources' who couldn't get the interview and are jealous that I did? Still complete and utter bullshit, Mike," I said. "And the only time I've been around Churchill lately has been to interview him in his house, with his wife present. Feel free to check."

Silence.

"So you write whatever you wanna write," I said, "but I will say this: You better *be* right. Because I have worked very hard to establish my professional reputation, and I will go to great legal lengths to protect it. Am I clear?"

"Yes, you are," he said, now sounding crestfallen. He said goodbye, and that was the last I heard from him about it.

That night after the boys had gone to bed, I sought out Matt, who was sitting on the couch in the living room, eating raspberry frozen yogurt and watching a mixed martial arts match on cable. He had recently started working on his black belt in tae kwon do with renewed dedication.

I plopped down on the couch next to him, still feeling unsettled from my day. I needed to grouse to him about the question that Roberts had posed. I needed a sympathetic ear.

"He was implying that I had slept with Ward Churchill, and that is how I got my interview," I griped to my husband with irritation.

My nerves were still raw from being triggered by Brents a few days before.

Matt, who had now flipped to the 10 p.m. news, now turned to me distractedly.

"He asked if you'd slept with Ward Churchill?" he said, obviously trying to catch up. "Well, did you?"

"Ha, ha, very funny."

"Well, did you?" Matt pressed, and I suddenly realized with a sickening lurch that he was serious. He was honestly asking me that outrageously offensive question. Who *was* this man? Did he not know me at all?

I stared at him, my mouth slightly open, incredulous. My neurons fired in anticipation.

"You aren't seriously asking me that question, are you?" I said, my nostrils flaring.

"I don't mean since we've been married, obviously," he said, wading deeper into the quicksand. "But you used to know him, didn't you? And I was just curious, as your husband, if you'd ever slept with him."

"I'm not even gonna answer that question," I said, raising my voice, every fiber of my being starting to fill and swell with anger. "I can't believe you even *asked* me that question. My coworkers knew immediately it was bullshit—why don't you? Do you not understand anything about journalism? Or me?!"

"I just *asked*. Geezus," Matt sounded defensive, and I snapped. Suddenly I was my mother and he was my father, and I hated him for not supporting me and giving me what I needed.

"What the fuck is wrong with you that you would ask me such a stupid fucking question?" I knew I was blowing up out of control and didn't care. At the same time, I scrambled up off the couch, each motion an angry jerk.

I grabbed my purse, ignoring the stunned look on his face. "I don't wanna be anywhere *near* you right now." I stomped out the door, and deep inside my body, my nerve endings gave each other explosive high fives.

My hands shaking, I started my Jeep and quickly drove to the parking lot of our local movie theater, where I debated a late-night movie. But I had already seen *Sin City* and *The Hitchhiker's Guide to the Galaxy*, I wasn't in the mood for a rerun, and nothing else was worth watching.

So I sat in my car and fumed. Red-hot anger still raced through my veins, like molten lava bent on destroying anything—or anyone—in its path.

Eventually, I started to breathe. I recalled the words of my therapist, Michelle.

"If you feel like your buttons are being pushed and you react in an extreme way," she often reminded me, "that probably means it's old."

I had to admit, my reaction had been over the top. So what part of that scene with Matt was old? I asked myself. I thought about it and came up empty. I had no clue.

So stop thinking, I told myself, and *feel*. I closed my eyes and started digging through my emotional layers. The first one was anger. I thought I had worked through a lot of anger with Michelle and was surprised to realize there was still some old anger left. Where did it come from?

Michelle's voice came through my thoughts again. "A common reaction to hurt is anger," she reminded me gently. "The anger protects you."

That was it. I had been hurt by Matt's thoughtless, albeit distracted, question, and had swiftly tapped into anger to cover it up.

And it hurt to think he questioned my integrity, and it hurt because

I had instantly concluded that he didn't have my back, that his first reaction hadn't been unwavering loyalty. I was alone, again, and undefended, just like I was when I was twelve.

Ohhhh.

With that thought, the image of Brents' shockingly graphic last letter came to mind.

> *Time after time from the age of 5 until I was in my 20s I was betrayed by men and women, family and so-called friends. Around the age of 10 I became them and I've been trying to hurt Them ever since I think.*

He'd felt abandoned as a child.

Ohhhh. We had that in common.

Even though I knew my experiences paled in comparison to the horrors Brents endured, they were evidently still lodged in my brain like an old splinter. And Brents' letter about his childhood had brought up the pain of mine.

Ohhhh. I'd been triggered.

The only way to unearth and derail those thoughts—and banish the pain—was to concentrate on staying in the present moment. Breathe, I told myself. Let everything else go.

After several minutes, my thoughts were no longer tapping at the edge of my distressing childhood memories, like someone pressing on a broken bone.

Once the cloud of anger dissolved, everything became clear. I had been an ass.

I drove home, found Matt reading a book on our bed, and flopped down next to him, smiling wanly and apologetically into his eyes.

"I'm sorry," I began. "That was not your fault. It was old."

After carefully marking his place, Matt set his book aside. Then he smiled back. "I know."

Working through a trigger is like clearing out a layer of emotional debris. You don't need that junk anymore, and once you start dumping the old anger and even older hurt, it leaves you more room for the good stuff—like love and compassion and empathy and understanding, not just for yourself, but also for your family, your friends, your coworkers, your child's teacher, a snippy grocery store clerk. Everyone.

When I'm focused on staying in the present moment, I see everything more clearly, as if unawareness is a film that's been peeled from my vision. And so it was with this calmed and heightened sense of reality that I went to the Denver City and County building to cover Brents' preliminary criminal court hearing on May 2, 2005.

May 11, 2005

 This may sound strange but truly there is no motive other than a sincere gratitude when I say This. Having you in court was truly a comfort . . . It brought me some shame too. So now you know there is nothing to hide about what I've done . . . How can you stand to look into my eyes like you do! What do you see? I see it in your eyes Amy, you realy want to know what it is in my mind and heart That makes me who I AM. I'm sure that when you find out though you'll hate me as everyone does . . . More later I'm tired.
 —Brents

FOURTEEN

A Purple Hippo

The courthouse in Denver is also its city hall and holds the offices of the mayor and the meeting chambers of the city council as well as courtrooms for district and county cases. It's an immense building that is a classic example of Beaux-Arts architecture, with ornate Roman columns, richly sculpted details, and marble flooring that tosses up echoes as heels click across it. It's a grand structure that adds seriousness and weight to the proceedings conducted within its walls.

Knowing the courtroom would be packed, I arrived early and sat on the side, only a few rows away from the witness stand so I could catch every detail. I wore a black pantsuit, white blouse, and my onyx necklace.

At the prosecution's table, Denver District Attorney Mitch Morrissey sat with a lead prosecutor in his office, Stephanie Villafuerte, a polished and conservative-looking woman with dark hair and eyes who wore pearls and a rather masculine-looking jacket and severe skirt. Morrissey, whose once-dark hair was now mostly silver, wore a dark gray suit, light blue shirt, and navy tie. He looked grim. I had done a story when he took office, and his coworkers had described him as "competitive and aggressive," a prosecutor who treated the defense as the sworn enemy.

Yet surely, I thought, if any case was a slam dunk for the prosecution, this one was.

As Brents was escorted by deputies to the defense table, he walked with his head bowed, thick chains connecting the shackles that encircled his hands and feet. He had a long handlebar mustache and small growth of beard and was wearing a bright red Denver County Jail jumpsuit and black-and-white Converse sneakers.

I thought the handlebar mustache was odd; it said he was very concerned with his appearance.

His public defender, Carrie Thompson, sat beside him snapping through stacks of paperwork with nervous energy. She wore pearls also, and a black suit and heels. Her nails matched the red shade of the square glasses perched on her nose, and her medium-length hair was perfectly blond and perfectly in place. Her appearance spoke of someone who was meticulous and precise.

I wondered if she put as much care and thought into her case. I wondered how in the world she would be able to defend that man.

After the judge solemnly summarized the eighty charges concerning five separate cases, the first witness was called, a Denver police detective. She testified how Brents had attacked the pet shop owner after entering her store by putting a knife to her neck from behind, and when the woman collapsed on the floor, he said, "Get up, bitch, or I'll hurt you." At some point during the attack, the woman's thumb was badly cut, which seemed to anger him more. Brents then took money from the register before dragging the woman to a bathroom in the back of the store where he repeatedly raped her.

"During that time, he said that she was a Christian bitch . . ." The detective paused, clearly becoming emotional. "He said she knew what she was doing."

Over and over, the detective stated, Brents repeated that to the victim.

Thompson's questions were brief: Did he smell of alcohol? No. Did he seem to be on drugs? No. Was it the victim's opinion he did not intend to cut her? Yes.

The next case was Tracy Seidel's, and a male detective took the stand. After she reported being raped in October 2004, the detective said, he interviewed Tracy in February 2005, and Thompson zeroed in on that date.

"Normally, detectives interview persons closer in time to the crime, correct?" she asked, and he replied yes.

"But your interview followed media attention. And she developed a relationship with the defendant—that included her going home with him? She didn't take a bodyguard, did she?" Thompson said curtly, and I drew a quick breath in surprise. This defense attorney was going after a victim, prostitute or no, and it was shocking. It was also an indication of just how hard Thompson intended to fight for her client.

The next case involved the rape of a woman on Adams Street in Denver and was just as horrific in its details. Brents had assaulted the woman in her home, holding a knife to her throat and choking her until she almost passed out, telling her if she fought back, he would kill her. But fight him she did—in her kitchen, living room, bedroom, finally curling up into a ball in an effort to keep Brents from picking her up.

"Was he using the knife throughout the entire transaction?" Villafuerte asked the detective relaying the story, and I was struck by the use of the clinical term.

I wonder if that's how she hopes to get through this case unscathed, I thought.

And then the proceedings turned to the case of the grandmother and her two eleven-year-old granddaughters. Brents had raped all three, causing serious bodily injury to the two girls. After assaulting the grandmother in the basement, he tied her arms behind her back and her ankles with a scarf, then headed upstairs where her grandchildren slept. A few moments later, she saw the shadow of Brents with her granddaughters walking past, and one of the girls screamed. At that, the grandmother found the strength to struggle out of her ties.

She was free, but naked from the waist down, and terrified.

"She had a horrific decision at that point," the detective on the stand said. "Do I try to save these little girls or do I go for help? She made the right choice, and she intentionally slammed the door as she ran out of the house."

It worked—Brents heard the slamming door and abruptly left.

During their interviews with the little girls, he continued, one of them said she had grabbed a stuffed animal, a purple hippo, and clung to it during the assault.

Oh, God. I didn't want to hear any more. I felt sick, both sick at heart and literally sick to my stomach. My heart ached for those girls and their family. I wondered if they would ever find healing. I hoped they would.

How could someone do such monstrous things, especially to children?

I stared over at Brents, who sat motionless, his head still bowed as if he were in church. And then in the next instant, he raised his head and looked straight at me.

It wasn't a quick glance. It was a stare of recognition, and I realized he knew it was me. And I stared right back, hard, trying to decipher him, allowing my eyes to express what every fiber of my being was crying out, what probably everyone in that courtroom was thinking at that moment: Why? Why, oh, why?

His expression was inscrutable. After a long moment, he looked down. For the rest of the hearing, he didn't raise his head.

Then, the cases of Tiffany Engle and Aida Bergfeld were heard, and Detective Martin Vigil took the stand, a cheerful, confident man with a penchant for bowties.

I liked Vigil, although I didn't know him very well. In passing conversation with him once, he said something that stayed with me: "If you do the righteous thing, you don't ever have to worry." He didn't strike me as a religious zealot, but rather as a man who had firm convictions.

Vigil had been called to Marion Street to process the crime scene investigation of the attack on Tiffany Engle. And the scene spoke volumes.

He found condoms, sugar packets, and a cord with blood on

it, Vigil testified, in addition to a large pool of blood, some two-by-fours, a microwave near the entrance, and cheese and tortillas in the refrigerator.

A pair of sunglasses and some keys were in the hallway, and loose change as well as pieces of paper littered the floor.

After being taken to Denver Health and undergoing surgery, Tiffany had given a brief interview, Vigil said, in which she said a naked man had attacked her and a naked woman had helped hold her down and tie her before the man began choking her.

So her perception, Thompson asked, was that Aida Bergfeld was involved?

When it was her turn, Villafuerte clarified that Aida's version differed from Tiffany's, and that Brents himself had told Jon Priest how Aida was with him against her will.

Then Priest himself took the stand, describing how he interviewed Brents for two hours in Glenwood Springs immediately after his arrest and continued in Denver later that day.

Brents talked readily about all the rapes, Priest said, recalling details such as Brents calling the pet shop owner a "white Christian."

There it was again—"Christian." I flashed back to my interview of Brents' mother. When I asked her if his father had abused Brent, she told me, "My husband was a Christian."

Evidently it was a title Brents now viewed with contempt.

I turned my attention back to the stand, where Priest was saying that Brents had lured Aida Bergfeld with the promise of fifty dollars for sex, then raped her repeatedly. He had just finished raping her when Tiffany Engle walked in.

He began to choke Tiffany until she stopped screaming, Priest said, and then cut a cord from the window blinds to tie her with. When she started screaming again, he hit her in the head with a two-by-four.

"He said he felt she was within seconds of dying, and had it not been for Aida screaming, she probably would have died."

Under questioning by Thompson about his interview with Brents,

Priest said, "He indicated that he had gone seven days straight with no sleep and that he'd been drinking five to six of the last eight days."

He knew it was February, Priest said, but not the day.

Regarding Tiffany, Priest said Brents told him, "There's something fucked up in my head."

"She kicked him and he just flipped out?" Thompson asked.

"Yes, he said he didn't mean to fuck her up. He said he was tired and felt remorse for Tiffany. Brents told me, 'If that lady dies, I'd be grieving for her and her family. But I'm not going to stop—those fuckers won't stop. Then something flips, and it doesn't matter how much I talk to myself—it's just something I've got to do. All I remember is, I know I'm standing butt naked and there's this beautiful woman and she panics, and I don't want to hurt her—all I want to do is just get away.'"

Then Priest moved on to other cases. Regarding the grandmother and the two girls, he said when he asked Brents what happened, he replied, "Well, I lost my fucking mind."

In general, Priest said, Brents talked about his mind a lot.

The detective said he asked Brents if he thought he was insane. "He didn't give me a direct answer. What he did say was, 'There's something fucked up in my brain. I don't want to be that way anymore. It's just my fucking mind is gone. I'm fucking tired. I really am tired, tired of what's going on in my head.'"

Brents told him that the drive was not even sexual. "It's more like animalistic shit," he quoted the defendant as saying.

Then it was Villafuerte's turn to ask questions again, and she led Priest in a line of questioning whose point became clear.

"No, Brents never said he was insane," Priest said. "He was very lucid. He responded to direct questions. He gave lengthy responses to brief, vague questions."

Despite complaining of exhaustion, the detective said, Brents didn't appear that way. And he was able to give very specific narrative details of his crimes. He also went to great lengths to elude police. "He knew his conduct was illegal."

Did he fall asleep? No. Yawn? No. "He never appeared exhausted," Priest said.

In 1988, he had manipulated the system by going to the state hospital. Did he have success at treatment? the prosecutor asked.

"He said it doesn't work," Priest replied. "That sort of treatment wouldn't work on him. He is the kind of sex offender where treatment doesn't work."

Then it was time for Thompson to address the judge, and she began to chip away at some of the charges.

Concerning Tracy Seidel, Thompson said, she asked the court to consider that the alleged victim developed a friendship and relationship with Brents.

As for the pet shop case, Thompson said, it was a business and he walked in freely, so the charge of burglary should be dropped. And the victim's thumb had a risk of tendon damage and scarring, she argued, but the state did not meet the burden for the charge of "serious bodily injury."

Regarding the rape of the grandmother, "Sexual contact was part and parcel for penetration," Thompson said briskly. "It was actually one count and shouldn't be charged as two acts."

As she argued, Thompson was a flurry of motion, striding back and forth between the judge and the defense desk, gesturing passionately with her hands. I was transfixed, as was most of the courtroom. This woman was a fighter. She could have been a gladiator.

On to Tiffany Engle. She said that Brents had no intention of causing her death, pointing out that he had left the woman loosely tied so she was able to get out of the apartment and get help.

Now it was time for the prosecution's response. The district attorney stood and, perhaps sensing the impressed air in the room, took a tone that was just tinged with sarcasm.

"Thank goodness we don't have dead people in this case," Morrissey said. "But his choice to incapacitate them doesn't relieve him from these responsibilities."

He paused just slightly.

"He is extremely violent."

The state was not going to let Brents off the hook for the burglaries, the DA said, and as for the different sexual acts, "We must designate every single sex act that the person engaged in. To do otherwise, is totally absurd, Judge."

Regarding serious bodily injury, Morrissey said, "When little girls get vaginally and anally raped, I think that's sufficient for this hearing."

As far as the pet store, he said, "Brents locked the door. He certainly committed some horrendous crimes after he locked the door. And the loss of the victim's thumb qualifies as serious bodily injury."

Morrissey moved on to Seidel's friendship with Brents. "She's out on the street. She has to live on the streets. The fact is she did things to survive after this man," jerking a thumb toward Brents, "raped her."

He stared hard at the defense table then, his face twisted in disgust.

"The sad thing about this case," Morrissey said, "is that Mr. Brents understands exactly what he is—a predator. In his mind, fucked up and stupid. And that's exactly what this is."

With respect to Tiffany, he said, "He chokes her—something he prefers to do, by the way—then he beats her in the head with a two-by-four, and he doesn't have the mental state to kill her?"

He turned to the judge.

"Bind this predator over," he said.

Thompson was on her feet. "I object to the word 'predator,'" she said sharply. "He's a defendant at this point."

"Sustained," said the judge.

And then he ruled. "Sufficient evidence convinced me that there is probable cause for defendant Brents J. Brents to have committed the offenses he's charged with on counts 1 through 56," he said. Counts 65 through 80 would be transferred to another judge.

Bond was set at $1 million.

The crowd hustled out of the courtroom. Once in the hallway, I looked around for Thompson, but she was gone. Disappointed, I joined the throng of reporters and photographers who flocked around DA Morrissey and pushed my way up to the front to get in a question.

"You made a strong argument against the defense that he's not insane," I said to the prosecutor, "so what do you perceive as the 'why' behind Brents' actions?"

Morrissey scowled. "I didn't say anything about insanity. I said 'mental state.' And I can tell you what I've seen from convicted serial murderers and sex offenders, and it's like you heard in the testimony—it's about animal control, animal power, those kinds of things."

An animal. There it was again. And that seemed almost too easy, too dismissive. And on the face of it, I thought, it didn't make sense. How could Brents be an animal, and yet not insane? It's our ability to reason and to have compassion that separates us from animals, so if you have neither, have you not lost your mind?

If we lose our humanity, are we not insane?

And who gets to decide when, if ever, that line has been crossed, when someone is no longer deemed human?

As if on cue, sheriff's deputies appeared in the hallway, surrounding Brents as they escorted him to the elevator down the hall that would take him to the holding cells on the third floor. From there, he'd be taken to the basement, buckled into a Kevlar-coated bulletproof vest, and then put in a long white sheriff's van to be transported back to jail by armed caravan.

For now, he shuffled slowly, the thick shackles still connecting his hands and feet, surrounded by deputies on both sides, in front and behind.

And then the shouting began.

When a suspect is being "walked"—taken from one location to another—journalists use it as a chance to throw out a quick question or try to spark a reaction. Sometimes you get a memorable quote. Most of the time, it makes for more interesting TV and photos.

In this case, the throng of reporters and photographers who surrounded Morrissey now broke and ran toward Brents, like a school of piranhas. Deflected by the deputies in front of him, they stopped a few feet short and kept that closeness by walking backward as the deputies moved him forward, calling out question after question.

"Why'd you do it?" "Do you feel bad?" "Do you wanna say anything to the victims?"

"How could you hurt those little girls?" "What do you think about Aida Bergfeld dying?"

"Do you think you're an animal?"

I was still standing off to the side, in the same spot where I had spoken to Morrissey. From there, I watched Brents closely. At five foot eight, he was an inch shorter than me, and with his closely cropped hair and oval, wire-rimmed glasses, he hardly looked threatening, let alone evil. Yet he had to be evil to do the things he had done, right?

Right?

Brents peered into the media crowd and never made a sound. What was he looking for? I started walking to get a closer look, and as the movement caught his attention, he glanced my way. In that moment, I saw kid-like bewilderment in his eyes. It confused me. Somehow in the courtroom, he had become a child.

I looked at the faces of the journalists, most of them people I knew from seeing them at the same stories. They were focused and intent on doing their jobs, not recognizing, or perhaps just not caring, that this process was so . . . *obnoxious*. Not too long ago, I had been doing the same thing, pursuing a story with a focus so single-minded that the black and white of everything was all I saw. Now I saw things differently, a shifting spectrum of black, *gray*, and white. When I looked closer at some of the reporters in front of Brents, their eyes gleamed with an odd, fierce light, and I realized they were *enjoying* this, these handsomely packaged men and women in suits and heels confronting a criminal in an orange jumpsuit and chains.

Thronged together, they had taken on a hungry group mentality.

If Brents was before them in a cage, they would poke him with sticks.

Suddenly the entire scene struck me as barbaric, almost an extension of the inhumane and horrific details unveiled in court only minutes before. And in that moment, time slowed. I wasn't feeling reactive; I was very calm and very sure.

I wanted nothing to do with this predatory pack.

My actions deliberate, I turned away from the media crowd milling in front of Brents and stepped abreast of him, on the far side of one of the escorting deputies. If the deputy had not been there, I would have been walking by the prisoner's side. And Brents noticed. He glanced my way, but I simply walked, keeping my eyes forward, my notebook closed in my hand, never saying a word.

There had been enough lack of humanity today.

June 2- 05
Dear Amy,
    You are a woman who has entegrity and self worth. So there is no question of you being fair and honest. I told you I believe in you. You are the only one who hasn't offered money, or as in the case of one woman Reporter for a local TV station wrote me and tried to seduce a story out of me with This. First she used your article, Basically saying Brent I read your story, I find it Romantic that you fell in love with someone YA DA YA DA, I fancy myself a Romantic Soul and would realy Like to get to know you on a more intimate level! I am an Idiot to a degree but damn do I realy come off as Retarded. Carrie laughed so hard She had tears in her eyes. Any way whether you mean to or not you speak volumes with your eyes and Your sincere in this way as well . . .
    Amy I don't think that in the beginning you expected me to be as open and honest and sincere as I am with you. right? Don't stop being yourself with me Amy please. Believe me I can Tell real from not. Without you Amy and your sincereity, I tell no one anything and No good comes from any of this.
    I'll never forget what you did for me in court. I was truly touched. Thank you.
    Sincerely
    Brent

FIFTEEN

The Childhood

At your core, who are you?

I remember sitting on a couch across from my energy therapist, Doug, while he told me that I needed to spend time doing what filled me up. And I remember looking at him blankly, at the time still feeling so lost that just leaving my house was an effort, and saying with true bewilderment, "What is that?" and instead of laughing or shaking his head at me, he answered gently, "You have to find out for yourself."

One thing I knew for certain: Work did not fill me up. It used to, until it took more than I could give. So I began to focus on what did make me happy: playing four square at the elementary school playground with my sons and running near water and sprawling on the couch surrounded by my snoring animals and listening to Freddie Mercury wail on a Queen CD while dancing around my living room. I found a horse stable near my house and began to volunteer my time encouraging wobbly kindergarteners to hold their horse's reins like two ice cream cones. And slowly, I refilled the empty well of my soul.

But now I was asking Brents to look inside, and in return, he was asking me right back. And I froze at responding. First of all, it was a violation of Journalism Rule #1: Thou shalt not get personally involved in thy story.

And I took the rules seriously. I didn't hang out with sources, let them buy me lunch, confide in them, or allow them to lean on me.

"I'm not your friend and I'm not your therapist" was my common refrain. And to the police officers who routinely offered me tantalizing story tips on their criminal cases, I would thank them and offer back an occasional reminder: "Never forget, I'm a reporter. If you screw up, I'll still write about you."

I'm used to being the one who probes for details, not the one who reveals them. Also, I didn't trust Brents. For that matter, I find it difficult to trust anyone.

Most of all, though, I was reluctant to take another look within. Maybe I didn't want to admit I had worked very hard to rebuild myself into a person I liked, but that now, slowly and steadily, I was afraid I was backsliding into an uncaring, reactive work machine. Late-breaking stories were taking an increasing toll on me, and I was missing more dinners at home than I cared to count. When I was at home, too often my cell phone was glued to my ear.

So for the most part, I ignored Brents' questions, whether he posed them in a letter or over the phone. Every few days, my desk line at the *Post* would ring and it would be him. I'd accept the collect call and take as many notes as I could before it was cut off.

And always during the conversation, Brents would bring up that he wanted to die. Maybe he was just trying to garner sympathy or reassurance that someone cared enough to ask him to stay alive. Or maybe he was really looking for some kind of tacit approval for suicide. Whatever the motive, I would always firmly tell him that it wasn't a topic we were going to discuss, that I was never going to tell him that it was OK for him to take his own life. I didn't want that responsibility. Who would?

I've always believed in the potential of life, any life. And now, I had to try to apply those beliefs to Brents as well. Wasn't it possible that he could still accomplish something positive with the time he had left? Would pain and horror be his only legacy?

More than the phone conversations, his letters were what struck me. Despite dropping out of school in the eighth grade, Brents wrote with a certain sense of rhythm and almost poetry. His letters portrayed a man with intelligence and regret whose biggest struggle was within.

6-5-05

Dear Amy,

You know I don't expect you to be a councelor, I tell you my feelings, my thoughts and my state of mind because its the right thing. How can you get to know me otherwise. The Loneliness, the fear, anger, hurt all of it isn't Just since I got arrested. I've been in this emotional Rollercoaster ever since I can Remember Don't Let It eat at you. I will never hurt you emotionaly, physicaly or otherwise . . . Ive always taken from people and myself. All I ever wanted was to be the good guy. I Just Never learned how. I saw a baby picture of me one time and swore it wasn't me. Not because it didn't Look Like me. But because that babies eyes were sparkling with Life. My eyes have not had Life in them since.

Between me and you I have figured it out. I have a plan—You and I are going to do a good thing together. Afterward I am going to do what I should have done a Long time ago. If I can be free to do it, It would be wonderful and I will try. If not I Just want my soul to be free. The Night I was arrested I was thinking about being Able to Take the couple grams of Heroin I had Left and go off into the mountains and find a good spot to go to sleep forever. I feel for AIDA. I hope she did not suffer. We talked about it alot. I will know when the time is right. Its not now, you and I have a lot Left to do and Like you said I can make something good come out of my Life. I want to give people that Knowledge and simple understanding That If you do This to your children, They could very well become Evil.

The IRA has a saying: "Don't fear the men you battle now, Fear Their Children whose Lives you leave empty, for in the war it is They whom you will face." It is often so difficult for me to suppress my Rage and hatred for people. I have Little or no trust, I hate all men. 98% of the women I meet,

Yet I am lonely. I've got some realy screwed-up Ideals

huh! Well I told you I've got mood swings. It realy was good to hear your voice today Amy I do hear you to. Don't Think I don't. I know you trust me and won't give up on me. All things have reason, Even if we can't see it. My Thoughts and wish of peace to you.

Always
Brents

Since I had promised my family and reassured my friends I wasn't going to write or talk about them to Brents, that left me with two safe topics: work and my animals, which consisted of Pike, my German Shepherd, and two cats, Vincent and Callie, both adopted strays. Vincent, named after Vincent van Gogh (but the cat was missing an eye, not an ear), was my beloved companion of many years. I had found him on the street in Florida and moved him with us to Colorado, determinedly lugging him through the airport in his cat carrier along with four boys (one in a wheelchair, because he had broken his leg two weeks before), a guinea pig, and a vast assortment of luggage.

Vincent was short-haired, sleek, solidly black—except for a sprinkle of white hairs on his chest—and the most athletic domestic cat I'd ever seen. Despite having only one eye, he was also the fiercest—he'd sit on the driveway and calmly watch the neighborhood dogs walk by. They all bore the scars of tangling with him. Yet at home, he was constantly at my side, loving nothing more than to sit in my lap or head-butt me at ungodly hours to wake up and give him attention.

The silver tabby Callie, on the other hand, was the result of a spur-of-the-moment visit to the humane society, and one I regretted. She was part Abyssinian but pure bully, and despite promising a docile personality at the shelter, she became a wildcat once we arrived home. She fought with Vincent constantly and loathed Pike, lobbing high-pitched screams at him from her perch high atop the television cabinet.

Since Pike was in training for search and rescue, ill behavior such as killing other animals was strictly forbidden, and he knew it, and it drove him crazy. Every ounce of his ninety-five pounds would quiver with his German Shepherd prey-drive instincts when Callie would pounce on him from her latest hiding place, only to scratch him swiftly and effectively before leaping gracefully out of reach.

Early one Saturday morning in June, I loaded up Pike in my car and drove to the Roosevelt National Forest in Boulder County for a search and rescue exercise. I was supposed to be one of several "victims" who hiked deep in the woods and waited patiently while other search teams tried to find me. I figured Pike would make good company as I waited the two or three hours it took to be discovered. I also figured it would be a good time to write Brents a letter—my life normally ran at a hundred miles an hour, and sitting in the woods was the only time I had to truly slow down and contemplate anything.

Also, I admitted to myself, no need to further irk Matt, who would always frown and then become quietly irritated when he came across evidence of my correspondence with Brents, even though I tried to keep it hidden away. I didn't have time to write him at work, and it created tension when I wrote to him at home. So the woods were safe territory.

As a mountainous area of the rugged Colorado foothills, Roosevelt National Forest reminds me of the Shawnee National Forest in Illinois, where my dad bought property and we often hiked and camped as I grew up. Roosevelt is a combination of lush, thick groves of aspen, spruce, and fir interspersed with the sage green, lichen-covered rock that's a reminder Colorado is part desert. With more than 800,000 acres, the forest is large enough to walk for miles and never see another soul.

As Pike and I huddled deep into our designated hiding spot, I pulled out the notebook and pen I had tucked into my red daypack, next to my water bottles, granola bars, dog treats, a poncho, a flashlight, and a first-aid kit. The pine-scented air smelled like Christmas, and the towering canopy of trees above us formed a silent and majestic cathedral. It was magical. Being in the woods always gave me peace. And then it hit me that Brents would never again have this kind of view.

With that thought, I suddenly felt an urge to give him a gift—of describing what I saw.

And so I wrote to him about the forest and how it was inspiring to sit there in the chilly early-morning mountain air, watching furry black-tailed squirrels scamper, and how it all made me feel alive. I wrote to him about Pike, my cats, my thoughts about the *Post*, and the growing politics of his case.

I asked him more questions, included two that had been in my thoughts: "What drove you to rape? I honestly want to know," I wrote.

"And why do you call it 'sex with my mom?' You were a child, incapable of consent. What she did to you was assault."

When I was done, I had ten thoughtful pages, which I tucked into a large mailing envelope and later dropped off at the post office before I could change my mind.

To me, it was a small gesture, a gift from one human being to another. To Brents, I soon realized, it was much, much more.

6-10-05

Well I got all of my mail finaly. The one Thing I was looking forward to was your long letter. I know I chose right. I sat here and cried. Why? Well because you sat on a stump in my most favorite place in the world Roosevelt Ntl forest, And you wrote to me. On Amy's time, not company time. That my Lady is heart. I can picture you There all bundled up one Leg over the other shivering and yet still managing to write. Amy that says a whole hell of a lot about you and the person you are. I will Never doubt your or your sincerety after that Letter. You have my Loyalty. Any way I love Roosevelt yes I know its huge. I realy love it around Estes park. I want my ashes spread somewhere high in Roosevelt...

I'll try to answer as many Questions as I can from your

letter. Ok you asked about the rapes and what Drives me. Ok as sick as It may seem I'll be honest. Stalking and capturing and hurting and release. The compulsion, The drive, The need is often overwhelming almost and most often to the point of obsesive compulsive insanity . . . Two things feed my sickness and bring mental Release. Watching my penis tear and penitrate and seeing the pain in the womens eyes and feeling them trying to get away from it and eventually ejaculating . . . And yes Its Like doing your very first shot of heroin. Chasing the dragon. I drank because I was trying to mentally cope with a lot of emotions. Raped because That part of me could and truly enjoyed it. Like the wolf or fox or wild dog That found out how easy it is to get at the farm animals. How was it developed? Good question. Abuse-acceptance, Ignorance, Learned, betrayals, hurts, losses. In The End it escalated to the point of oblivion. I was numb to Guilt or right and wrote or care or conscience until Tiffany. Now I want you to think about This. You asked me why I wanted to die? Imagine Pike got away from you one day and for 3 or 4 months he was gone, with no one to care he does what any dog does. Scavenge kills easy prey. Well he comes home, shy of people, but greatful, Then eats the Nieghbors cat. Then another. Bites a nieghbor out of fear gets away with all of it. Pretty soon he's on a roll and after all he's just being a dog. But he can't because In our world there are rules. he can't go on Like this. He doesn't respond to training. So he's caged and day after day you watch the light fade from his eyes until There's no Light and eventualy you know the only solution. Well Amy I'm Pike only I'll never get out of my cage, and I have to Live a thousand other such dogs. Occasionaly you'll see a spark in my eyes, but I don't want to spend the rest of my Life being a dog in a cage. But I want to do it my way on my terms. Not on some Jail house hero's way.

You asked why I called it sex with my mom? Yes I was underage, but I enjoyed it with her how strange I know. My mom taught me alot about women's bodies, sexual desires, need, how to please them. Physicaly, sexualy, emotionaly. She is an A1 manipulator, Between her and my dad They taught me alot but very little good. Brandy wasn't adopted at 6 he was committed to Arizona state Phsyciatric hospital. Shortly after my dad began raping him, entroducing him to my moms sexual sickness and locking him in his window Boarded bedroom and starving him on top of beating The crap out of him. Brandy Broke, I didn't and I wish to hell I had. I had the chance to be adopted when I was 11 and 12, Both times my dad somehow managed to fuck that off and yes I thing I would have been a much better human being...

No I don't think your Paranoid. There are greedy self centered Ego driven people in This world who are not above stealing my Letters to you to get Info. Besides I'm glad you got a P.O. Box for me. Its another sign in many that shows your trust for me. These cops read the mail but I doubt most Them would know you. You don't do enough on TV to be highly recognizable. And I doubt most people remember the name of the reporter who writes the Articles. To me your personal thoughts and feelings and opinions are between us. Amy I will always be fiercly Loyal to you. You've shown me your true self. I don't Think you meant to and you may even feel a little guilt, but don't, I'll never betray your gift. Its 12:00 pm and I usually don't get around to doing anything at 12:00 pm but you have me so worked up. That Letter realy touched me Amy. I realy Liked it That you shared about Pike and training. It is personal and its yours. You did not have to and your wonderful for doing so. I hope I didn't take to much away from Pike. I hope I get to see you soon. I Look forward to A visit From A Long cool woman in a Black Dress. Know that song.

    Peace Always
    Brents

6-17-05
Hello again
    That was a realy good phone conversation we had today. Pretty natural Line of communication between us. I hope to see you when you get back from D.C. I hope your trip will be pleasant and Informational. Wish I was going with you. But Alas someone has to stay here and watch over the Dungeon.
    Amy you realy help me. I know a lot of this is new ground for you and I can only guess at your feelings. Just as I know you can only guess at mine. Its meant to be Amy. I hear it in your voice and Together we'll do something good. After you get these 39 pages so far you'll see how honest and sincere I have been and always will be. I will never hurt or betray you Amy. You've extended yourself personaly and professionaly I will always be grateful to you.
    I know people tell you not to believe in or trust me but you have as I have. You have Listened to your gut and your instincts. I promise you if nothing else if no one benefits you will have simply by doing the right Thing. I know in my heart if it were not for you and your sincerity I would have committed suicide already. I am alone in this world Amy I have no one to blame but myself. So you can understand I think That you are all I have that has any sincere meaning. Your taking the risk on me means more than you'll ever know.
    Somehow some way I hope to give to you the human kindness and decency that you have given to me. Amy you will never know any one more Loyal to you than me. I'll miss you in court this week but That's ok I'll see you next week. You told me today that I had to figure out what There was to

Live for. Thats hard to do when your in a cell thats as wide as a twin bed is Long and only slightly deeper. There is crap on the ceiling flung there by previous tenents, arterial blood splatter high up on the walls from either a suicide or attempt graffiti from floor to ceiling, scratched into the stainless steel toilet. Things on the wall you don't even want to guess at. This is my Luxary suite at the Denver county Ritz. If They could get away with it they would Let the inmates kill me. As it is though they are weary of me for two reasons. They know that physicaly one on one I would beat most of these guys and two They know that any physical altercations I get into means someone failed to do their job properly. See the hardest part about knowing the inmates are going to kill you is not fear of dying. its Them not knowing how to do it right. A good deal of the time the victim ends up brain damaged that is part of the reason Tiffany haunts me. Part of me wishes I would have just knocked her out or even killed her, either would have been far better than what she will have to endure the rest of her Life. It scares me Amy That my mood swings are becoming more violent and extreme, from extreme depression to giddy highs to violent rages with no memories. And the entervals are coming to fast. Well any way I promise a happy Letter will follow this one.

    Loyaly yours
    Brent

P.S. Sometimes when They open your Letters They destroy the envelopes you send to me. So I salvage the stamps and put them on new envelopes.
    Peace.

6-19-05
Dear Amy,
    OK. I promised a happy Letter. I would say my happiest times were at the clubs. Dead beat, church, Gothic, Rock

Island, Dulsenayas, Cervantes. Even the Lesbian bar called No body's business. I've got This Thing for Goth girls and punk girls. I probably spent $50,000 in those clubs in 6 months no joke. I loved to party and watch my girls dance. I spent my time in the clubs between The goth and punk girls and The Hippie girls. Sunday nights was my dungeon night. WOW! I can tell you there are some denver celebs with secrets. I wasn't realy into The big orgies, but I did have a steady dungeon girl and we shared one lover in common on other occasions she and I usually took some woman home with us. When I got here to denver co she tried to see me Like 10x she was so scared I would give her away. But the clubs were cool for me because I could actually unwind and be free. I drank a lot and did a lot of Liquid THC. I had a lot of fun.

Now I have to say the happiest time of my Life was my Time with Sharon my social worker who wanted to adopt me. You and her Look a lot alike. She was beautiful, caring, funny, brave, Loving. She Loved me deeply. I never felt sexual with her. Just Love. She used to take me up to Estes Park almost every weekend.

We would camp, hike, fish. We'd Listen to 80s Rock, air guitared together, sang together, she helped me with my school work. Came to my track meets and school functions. Rode horses together. She was Hippie all the way. We had fun and she really did love me. I hurt pretty badly when my dad threatened to kill her and she Left Colorado. But I Loved her Like a mother and truly felt secure with her.

Amy I have made up my mind as to what I am going to do with my future. I am going to work hard to accomplish our goal. After That I have one more goal. The day will come when I Tell you face to face what that is. The depression and mood swings Are realy Taking A toll on me. So I have to Look at only Positive Things. The next 3 or 4 months Are gonna be very very difficult for me. I will need your support

more than anything else. I do believe in you and That's what is helping The most.
   Always
   Brent

It's very common for someone who has been interviewed by a reporter to feel extremely anxious in the time before the story runs. It's nerve-wracking to have someone else have the power of how you will be presented to the world. I understand that and always try to reassure my subjects that I'll be fair.

In Brents' case, I soon realized, it was more than anxiety. It was deep fear, which he expressed over and over. I found myself trying to reassure him as I would any subject, but it did little good. At times, he presented very much like a child, with a child's fears and insecurities.

Then, in late June, I had to miss one of his court dates to be the keynote speaker at a crime victims' conference in Washington, D.C., and his anxiety started to spiral.

I understood abandonment. And I understood that he was often desperately trying to cement me in his corner. Instead of being repulsed or disgusted with him for it, I only felt empathy for his very human fears. It surprised me—me, the hardened crime reporter, having empathy?

It also alarmed me. I began to wonder what was wrong with me. I began to feel guilty that I didn't hate him, as everyone else apparently did.

Then one random afternoon in late June, Brents' mother called me at the newsroom, as she sometimes did, "just to check in." And during a rambling monologue, she dropped a bombshell: "When I was a child, my father sold me to his friends for sex."

I hung up the phone and closed my eyes. It was hard to hear another brutal confession; it made my gut churn.

But I also felt a measure of relief because her admission verified what Brents had been claiming: There was a pattern of sexual abuse in his family.

When you deal with crime, you learn that patterns repeat. It didn't excuse what he had done, but it did help explain it.

It also made it harder to hate him.

6-23-05
Dear Amy,

I had a long talk with someone today. You came up in the conversation. I was told you were just using me. That you don't give a shits 2 cents about me. I found myself fiercely defending you. to the point of telling one of my attorneys she could go fuck herself. Of course I apologized. I know they are all only trying to do whats best for me. (At least what they think is Best for me.) But I told her then. I said have you seen any more stories on me by her? No. I told them I believed in you. and not just Amy the journalist but Amy the woman. They backed off. Carrie told me later after the others left, she says brent I know your fond of this person just be sure she's sincere. I feel it in my heart Amy just as Georgia wouldn't leave my side when I was sick, I know you'll never hurt me.

I have something to admit to you. I am scared Amy scared like I've never been before. Not one time have I ever had to face my victims. Now I have to sit thier and listen to them during sentencing. I feel like a coward and I am afraid I will break down. I am afraid people will think I am full of shit just faking. I am going to try to not let any thing show. After all that has been written and said about me, Being Branded a Monster or Animal or predator By the media, society So called friends and family why should I care. I do though Amy, tremendously. Its important to me that some people know the love and friendship I shared with them. I am scared no (one) loves me and I'll never be able to love. And

I'm scared to die alone. Not of dying itself just alone. I promised always to be honest and truthful with you. I hate being alone yet I know I brought it all upon myself. I know how I want to die Amy. I don't want to live to be a ripe old age. Living without someone to love and without someone to love me just isn't what I want. I don't want to die in prison by my own hand or that of another but if that is what it comes to, then so be it. I want to die free. I don't want to play death by cop—I want to die peacefully and here in the mountains.

Do you think that is cheating my victims to want to or even to die free. I don't know if you like the Band Boston or not but thier song "More than a feeling" is my all time favorite song when I go that's the song I'll be singing in my head. Teresa and I wore a groove in that album.

I am scared Amy but I'm Ok. Your the first one I've ever been truly honest with. Its embarrassing, but I promised. I am afraid of being alone. I have no one to blame but myself. You know the saying the truth will set you free is a lie. I told you the truth and it still hurts and binds me. And I am still in This Lousy cell ☺ free my ass. So when you tell me not to dispare, It is very near impossible not to. But Alas I try to find positive in every day life. I got two cereals for breakfast today instead of my usual one. I got a letter from some crazy freak who says it's a Government conspiracy against me. I am paranoid but not in this guys league. I got the first shower today which is a good thing because it's the only time the shower is clean. I'll spare you the details. Oh yeah we watched Coach Carter on video Last night good story. And last but not least, the Doppler Radar sized zit on my forehead finaly went away. It's the little things. I know you think I'm looney toones but that's ok. You think you lead a nerdy life. I disagree. I think you enjoy it and you talk and write about it with pride. You asked me if your 10 page letter if I ever wondered whats the purpose of it all? More than you know. Sometimes I think Its just to fuck up every thing and any thing I come in contact with. Maybe this is what it has come to. You and I have some posotive affect on you as you have on me. Maybe in 4 or 5 years if our efforts are successful and some mother whose in an abusive relationship asks you what she should do. Maybe she'll save one of her children from being me, by listening to you. I've spent to much of my life asking that question. Its like trying to pull teeth from a rattle snake. The results are always the same. Painful!

 I know sometimes I find myself angry with you. Here I am telling you my darkest secrets that your going to expose to the world and all the while I don't hardly know jack about you. Unfair. Yet somehow I do know you. Somehow It's meant to be you know it and I know it. This sucks you know Carrie is right. I am fond of you and to lose you and your trust in me would very devastating. If you thought I could or would betray you or hurt you would hurt me deeply. Gabrielle told me in her first of 3 letters that she corresponded with men on death row because she felt safe since they would never get out. Its one of the reasons I chose you. But do you feel this way? Do you think I'm trying to decieve or hurt you. I hope I can send these 50 or so pages I have for you. Ive told more than anyone ever. I've felt from the beginning deep in my heart and soul I could and I have. That makes you the most special person in my life. I feel very vulnerable with you. I guess that's why it feels unfair. Who knows. I can't tell what the purpose of it all is. I hope that you and I can at least find some purpose together. Write me more long letters. You have good things to say and your entertaining.

 So hows D.C. I hope your having fun and getting what you want out of the conference. Did you learn anything new? Summer Solstice was Tuesday and every year on summer

solstice I ask a wish for those close to me as well as myself. For you I asked that you find happiness, love and Success in abundance in your life. For me I asked that I be granted the right to know the right choices. Well I hope that when you get back I'll get to see you soon. There is a lot I want to tell you and ask you and be able to look into your eyes.
   Sincerely your friend
   Brent

Sitting at home in my customary spot at our dining room table, I read that letter and decided what I was going to do. I know how awful it is to feel like a twelve-year-old and be frozen with fear, and as his sentencing date approached, I realized that's where Brents was heading, even though no one else would believe he was sincerely capable.

Was he being sincere? I was *almost* certain he was. Perhaps he was just a psychopath mimicking "normal" behavior and this was all an act. But my gut told me that it was authentic, and that I was getting glimpses of the real man buried beneath the layers of rage and pain.

And I always trust my gut.

Besides, I told myself, if you're wrong, what have you wasted? Compassion. There are worse things to waste your time on in life.

And so I put pen to paper and wrote to Brents, talking to him in the firm way that I talk to my sons when they're facing some wrong they have done. While this was on a much grander scale than any wrong I had ever known anyone to do, the same principles applied.

> June 23, 2005
> Hi, Brent,
>   I got your letter where you say you're scared. And it's understandable. And if you do break down, there is no shame in it.
>   Yes, court is going to be awful. There's no other way to put it. Yes, it's going to be painful to be on the receiving end of your victims' hate, rage and scorn. But that's one of your

consequences. You need to face them and hear them. It's a tiny fraction of what you've done to them, and you owe them that.

Still, I will be there, and I will sit where you can see me in court. And if it gets bad, you can search me out if you want to, and I will keep a steady gaze. I won't look away.

Amy

6-30-05

Sure Amy I could have told any other Reporter my story but sincerely where would I be when it was over. Probably feeling Like I was standing but assed Naked in the middle of Nowhere and the Temperature would be 20 degrees below zero. In other words alone and fucked. I could be wrong Amy Herdy but I don't think you'll Leave me alone and fucked. I think you take your envestments very sincerely and Like me you, for Lack of a better way to say it coming to mind "Love Hard." It means to be honorable sincere and Loyal. I've always loved my friends hard. But I've always had a secret or a whole string of Them which prevented me From being able to remain so. Like I said Amy No more secrets No More Lies I am your friend. Don't trip I can't stalk you, or harras you. ☺ Besides I know you can appreciate a good friend. Any way I hope you Liked my gift to you. I could have had Carrie read it but This is how important you are to me. Kick thier ass Amy and be proud because you got it with your heart.

Brent

SIXTEEN

A Journal

And then just like that, it was about to be over.

"I'm taking a plea, so I'm going to be sentenced next week." Brents spoke fast over the phone on the twenty-seventh, the last Monday in June. "Nobody knows, and it's supposed to be a big secret. I'll send you the paperwork."

And his thoughts and emotions were swirling like an angry tornado, touching down here and there and everywhere.

"Life sucks when you're a sociopath because that's just the way you are.... Once I'm sentenced, do what you need to do with my letters.... We both know I'm a bad person. I'm an asshole. I did some fucked-up things. The media has made me out to be a monster and an animal, and I'm not asking you to save my reputation or whatever. But it's depressing to me to see this only side of me in the paper.... Everybody's my enemy. Everyone."

I briefly considered, then discarded, that he meant me too.

"Why the girls?" I then asked him for probably the hundredth time. I had never gotten much of an answer from him to this question.

"It didn't have anything to do with easy prey," he said.

"Were you replaying your childhood?"

"I don't know. There's so much shit that went through my head that week. It wasn't fun. It wasn't what I expected it was gonna be. In '88 when I raped that boy, I got something out of it. Whatever I got out of it fed my sickness. This time I didn't get anything out of that.

"It didn't feel right. It didn't satisfy whatever it was that I needed to fulfill. None of it, this whole time. That's why Tiffany freaked me out. There was something about death that satisfied me. I was getting to the point where in the end, they were coming really close to death. It wasn't about screwing. It was about watching their eyes roll back in their head and blood vessels pop. I don't know how to explain it—it hits hard right now—it was getting way past sexual."

He was going to be sentenced to at least five consecutive life sentences, he told me, totally roughly 1,100 years.

"Somebody needs to hear the truth," Brents said. "No more lies. That's what I've been about my whole life, is lies. But I'm not all bad. I haven't always been bad. I've never had a life. It's so hard to get out and when a woman's pretty and she's interested in you and wants to hear about your past and you can't tell her because you don't have one other than raping kids and being in prison. Up and down. Depressed one moment, giddy the next, wanting to kill something two seconds later. Driving around and not going to be satisfied until I'd hurt someone, raped someone, robbed someone."

He drank Grey Goose vodka and pineapple juice constantly, he said, and chewed Big Red gum while he robbed people.

And as a boy, he said, "I was in love with my mom. I made love to her. By the time I was thirteen, I'd had more sex than most adult men. When I raped some of those prostitutes, I saw my mom's face, and I was choking them to death because I'm mad as hell at her for not standing by me. . . . I did some really bad shit, and I can't take it back and I can't change it. Helping people learn from this—or not turning out another me—that's important."

And that's why I'm doing this, I thought.

"I'm sorry for the part of me that's fucked up. For once in my entire life, I want to do something that's going to make a difference. What's the point of putting me away for life? Maybe people like me shouldn't be allowed to live. I spent my life in institutions. I've been free a little over a year since I was thirteen. All I know is institution. All I know is violence. I didn't have the tools to cope. I had no fucking clue. I thought I was better—but free life was so fucking overwhelming to me.

"My dad—why was it so easy for him to let go of Brandy, and why did he keep such a stranglehold on me? I had to learn to exist in a freaky little world. Then you cut it off and you expect me to behave. How can I behave? I don't know how to behave. I want people to know I don't like that part of me, and I'm sorry that part of me exists."

Toward that end, he said, he was sending me an apology letter, a scoop that other journalists would not have, his "gift" to me. That apology, he told me, "That's me, that's who I am."

And then he hung up.

I cradled the receiver back onto the phone, already starting to read over the notes I'd just taken. One part in particular made me pause: "When I raped some of those prostitutes, I saw my mom's face, and I was choking them to death because I'm mad as hell at her for not standing by me."

He was angry at her for abandoning him, yet not for the sexual abuse? So abandonment is worse than abuse, at least to Brents? I wondered if that was how other people felt.

And that thought was swiftly followed by another: I wonder if that was how my brother Dreux had felt.

I was starting to understand. *And when you understand someone, it's harder to hate them.*

Then the practical reporter side of me kicked in, nudging everything else away. There was not going to be a trial for one of the most notorious criminals in the state of Colorado. And to top it off, we were going to get the scoop of his apology letter. That was newspaper gold.

If there's one thing that editors like, it's as much advance notice as possible on any kind of big story headed our way. So I walked over to the office of one of them and stuck my head in the door.

"Brents is not going to trial—he's taking a plea," I said. "And he's sending me an apology letter for us to use when he's sentenced, which, by the way, he says is going to be next week."

Silence. He did not look impressed.

"For that matter, remember, I have a bunch of letters from him that would make an interesting piece about his history and how his mind works. We could use them to add heft to the sentencing story." I stopped and waited for his reaction.

"Hmm," he said, barely glancing up from his computer. "I think we'll pass on the letters. But why don't you see if you can get the sentencing confirmed and let's break the story?"

I nodded, then walked away, feeling confused. They didn't want the letters? Why wouldn't they want to know what made him the way he is?

But it was late in the day and I was tired. I didn't feel like arguing. I think part of me felt relieved that this project would be done soon.

First, I needed to tie up some loose ends.

Lynn Kimbrough, the spokeswoman for the Denver DA's office, was a petite woman with honey-colored hair and a calm demeanor. Lynn was easy to talk to and always prompt in trying to answer any legal query a reporter could have.

So back at my desk, I called her office. Yet when I asked her to confirm Brents' sentencing, she hesitated.

"He's sending me the paperwork," I told her, "so if you don't want to go on the record, that's OK. I'll have the documents."

"There's more to it than that . . ." Hearing a strain in her voice, I sat up and listened harder.

"If you do a story that announces the sentencing, you put the whole thing in jeopardy," she said. "There are a lot of factors to consider, and the most important one is the victims, who just want this to be over. Publicity about the sentencing will make it a media circus, and security is already an issue. So then it would have to be rescheduled, which puts a lot of people's lives on hold."

I was quiet as I digested what she'd said.

"Hello?" Lynn asked.

"I'm still here—and I hear you. I get it."

We hung up, and I sat at my desk, chewing the inside of my lip as I made up my mind.

A few minutes later, the editor I'd talked to earlier stopped by my desk.

"Let's plan out that sentencing story," he said.

I arranged my face into a careful mask.

"Oh, sorry, it's a no go," I told him, keeping my voice casual. "I can't get it confirmed."

He stood and looked at me for a long moment, then walked away.

The rest of that week passed in a blur. The boys were in full summer vacation mode, and a joyful, giddy chaos reigned at home, making it harder to extract myself to go to work.

I didn't have time to check the post office box until Saturday of the Fourth of July weekend. Inside was a single letter, as well as a large white mailer packed full. I read the letter first, sitting in my car in the post office parking lot, my cold nature savoring the heat that rolled off the blacktop and into my open windows.

6-30-05
Dear Amy,

Well hello There Long cool woman in a black dress!
Funny Thing after I talked to you on the phone today I heard my all time favorite song on the radio. "More than a feelin" by Boston. I don't know if I told you or not but it is my #1 Most Favorite song of all Time.

Followed by "Stoned in Love" Journey. I think people have Life Ballads or songs that Just fit There true soul. Mine is More than a Feelin. I remember Terressa and the words and the music fit my true soul. Don't worry I won't sing "Amy" to you. I have a sing that makes me think of you someday I'll tell you. I would be nice If I could get into a band in prison. When I was in Territorial I played bass in quite a few bands. If you ever get the chance to Listen to More than a feelin by Boston Listen to it and you'll hear me in the music That's the real me who wants to Live free of heartache and Pain, who wants to soar in the sky and roam the Mtns and speed down the highways and Love so unconditionaly that its euphoric.

 I Like to talk to you on the phone. Your real self moves me . . . No matter what anyone says to you Amy, Just Know that i'll stand by you and will be Loyal from here on out and only to you. I know you work me for info sometimes and its a Little disturbing but I think your starting to believe what I said to you about treating me as a person. I also know That you are as vulnerable as I am. We share the same fears. I know you don't want Those people who Advice you not to believe me, trust me or get to close, to be right. I have people (attorneys) who tell me the same. Amy Herdy I Listened to my heart. Its saying Brent you have nothing to hide any more, Nothing you say can shock This person, she has and will accept you as you are. So I don't need to Lie to you. You Are a warm caring person under your defenses and your Normal self. You'll always find that you can count on me. You more than anyone ever because I have no more barriers to hide behind, no more fears to use as excuses. You have my complete and undevided Loyalty. I have Learned things about you without you having to tell me. And I will tell you, your dedication is nice to see . . .

 After I get sentenced Amy I will need you to stay confident and believe in me . . . Chances are I'm going to have some "accidents" while I'm in DRDC so Don't freak out. I will try to defend myself to the best of my ability. So now I am going to tell you this. If any thing happens to me Amy and I have to be kept Alive by Machines or a surgery of any kind Amy I don't want it. Please don't let them keep me Alive by any artificial means. You are all I have. I know you did not expect to care about me. I know It may feel unfair but it's the Truth. I believe in you. I know I can count on you. I want to be cremated Amy and my Ashes spread in Roosevelt National Forest. I do not want to be buried with my parents *period. Hopefully you won't have to do this but if you do Then I thank you before hand.*

So Tell me Besides The fact its your favorite color, why Black? My favorite colors are Black Emerald Green and Deep Purple. So If you don't watch TV what do you do with your time beside run, write and train Pike and yourself? I know driving to And from work for you has to be a bitch. It sucked for me going from Mississippi and Chambers to Downtown, so I know your trip has got to be hell. Well any way its Late. My Thoughts are with you Amy. Sleep well and take care.

Always
Brents

P.S. Thank the Rocky Mtn News for the stamp on the envelope. So kind of Them. You might have to kick Karen and Carries asses cause they're liable to kick mine for all of this, can I hide behind your skirts? ☹

I knew the song by Boston he referred to. I had listened to it, too, when I was in eighth grade. Still in my car, I sang it softly to myself.

I was twelve the year "More Than a Feeling" came out. Now, that twelve-year-old girl seemed like she had lived in another lifetime. And I realized for Brents, those years of his childhood, the few short ones when he was free of institutions, were forever frozen in time.

He was always going to be twelve.

An enraged twelve-year-old boy inside a thirty-five-year-old man's vengeful body.

As for the large white mailer, I didn't want to open it. I knew what it contained—Brent's journal, a collection of his crimes, his history, his thoughts and motivations. And hopefully his apology letter. But I didn't want to read it right now.

It was a holiday weekend, and I wanted to be in a holiday mood. And so, like a school kid with a term paper due, I put off opening that mailer as long as possible. It wasn't until the evening of Monday, July 4, before I could bring myself to get to it. But now that his sentencing loomed near, I knew I needed to go through Brents' journal and look for any pertinent details that would enrich coverage of the event.

As I settled at the dining room table, Matt walked by and peered curiously over my shoulder.

"Whatcha got?" he asked, followed quickly by "Oh" as he recognized the name on the envelope.

"I need to go through this," I explained with an apologetic tone as I pulled out the thick sheath of paper. "He gets sentenced this week, and I don't know when I'm gonna have time to look at this at work."

"Well, I'm gonna go read too." He retreated into our bedroom, shutting the door firmly behind him.

Sitting at the table, I could see our closed bedroom door, and I looked at it regretfully. That was where I should be, spending time with my husband. Yet at the same time, I felt compelled to finish what I'd started. I was still certain that this project, this uncovering of the layers in a predator's psyche, was worthwhile and important. So I stayed where I was. I would try to make it up to Matt later, I told myself.

I then took a deep breath and started reading.

> 6-29-05
> Amy
>
> My friend it is personal for me now. I trust you and to do that I have to believe that you aren't using me. If you are Then once again I have Judged a person poorly and I will pay as I always have.
>
> In doing this I am going to hurt Carrie deeply, as I know. She will be disappointed in me. And Whatever help she gave me and was going to give me after sentencing will be cut off.
>
> Amy I hear it in your voice when we talk. You are a very competitive and driven woman. I know you want to compete against the News TV and the Rocky Mtn. As you know I am against that, but for you Amy, To show you how much I believe in you I will give to you what No one else will get.
>
> Stop B-sing me. Don't tell me what you think I want to

hear If That's what your doing. I am proud of your will to compete and win. I like you Amy. Treat me as a person and you'll get rewarded with an honest sincere carring person. And That will allow us to accomplish our Goals. Our agendas have to be the same Amy. Your personal agenda is to be successful. Mine is to gain your trust because I have no one else. Our common goal is to help other people. I want to help you do this with my whole heart. I want to help you be successful Amy. Be your stepping stone so to speak. But I don't want you to forget me once you've gotten where you're going.

Don't make me look like a fool. I deserve whatever punishment fate has in store for Amy.

By doing this I am hanging my Ass out on a limb. I am making one Last honest effort, No Lies, No secrets No hidden Agendas, To do The right Thing for everyone I've ever hurt. And Im trying to show you that we can be friends. Please don't screw me. I promise I will now and always be loyal to you and you alone.

I am giving you what No one else has but realy wants. You can go to your editor with Pride Not because you're a Ruthless gold digging non caring, get the story at all costs Reporter. No go to him or her because you got This and This is my way of showing you I care for you and believe in you. Everyone I've hurt deserves This.

Enclosed on the next page is my Apology to All Those I have hurt. It does Not say I'm sorry but the message is clear and it is the only statement I will make and I am making it to you. So now you can go to press or channel 9 or whatever. Whatever you put with it is up to you. If you make me Look Foolish or let your editors do it its on you. As far as the Worlds concerned I am the Lowest piece of shit on earth anyway.

Always your friend
Brent.

Inside was the apology note, written carefully on a lined piece of white notebook paper.

> *To my victims, their families and my own family and those who were my friends. I enterupted each of your lives with violence, pain, hurt, sarrow and lies. None of which any of you deserve. None of you were in any way responsible for my actions. Each of you in your own encounters with me were courageous and brave. Some of you showed me love and kindness which I took advantage of. My options were cowardly and wrong.*
>
> *I chose not to go to trial because each of you deserve to see Justice served without being exploited by the media victimized again with person details of my acts of violence and degradation upon you becoming public knowledge or having your personal lives scrutinized.*
>
> *I will not insult you with pleas of forgiveness. I will accept my fate quietly. I wish each of you never to encounter anything like this again and peace in your lives.*
>
> *Brent Brents*

He included a personal note to me at the bottom:

> *Word for word Amy or don't publish it at all. You'll have to fix my Punctuation of course. I would Like you to do this on Sunday or Monday following sentencing Please Not before. I am Risking Alot by doing all of This Amy. Please do right by me.*

This was the side of Brents that I wrote to: lucid, introspective. It was the part of him, no matter how small, that was capable of some measure of compassion. Remorse. Humanity.

I wondered if anyone else would see it or just think his note was another manipulation.

Thumbing through the pile of pages, I noticed different dates on many of the letters. I decided to just pick up where I had left off. Soon, I found a familiar theme, and I wondered if the tape of these scenes played out in his head every day.

5-13-05
Dear Amy,
   When I was 10 or 11 my Dad left me and my mom in Casper Wyoming supposedly to find a new Job. The real Reason he Left is because He had raped a 14 year old Girl and was very afraid she was Going to tell. At This point I was on probation for Raping a 6 year old Girl.
   I slept with my mother every night in his absence . . . I Liked having sex with my mom. I was never shy about it with her. I Loved her so very Dearly and one day I got into trouble with the cops for accidentally derailing a train. Well a month or two later my mom told the judge to Lock me up. She'll deny it but I was behind That door when he told her she could take me home and That it seemed to be an accident. She told him I needed to be Locked up, to Teach me a lesson. The real Lesson however was not to fuck any other Girls or women.
   She let them put me in the Wyoming Childrens home and Left the very same day to move to Colorado. So here I am In a place thats totally screwed up. I was there a little over 2 days before I got raped. I was Raped Repeatedly for my entire stay there. By at least 4 different teenage boys and 1 staff. AT night in my bed I would cry for my mom. They never wrote and didn't have a phone. All They had to do was drive up and pick me up. Finaly my moms friend Jill comes and asks me If I want to Live with her. I do but only If my parents will tell Wyoming its ok. Well for what seems Like an eternity They fight it out and finaly my parents come and get me. She abandoned me Amy and it wasn't the first time. Once when I was around 5 or 6 she Left. I Realize dad had

beat the crap out of her and probably would have killed If I had not Jumped between him and her and took the rest of the beating for her. We were poor and I can't tell you the fear and Anguish I felt as I watched her walk down the road with a plastic bag of clothes. Begging her not to go away. My Dad did not show up for 2 days Brandy was tiny and I changed him until dad came home. We did not have alot of food and I did not know how to cook so I made sandwiches and cerial. When Dad did come home he sent Brandy some where I don't know. All I know is mom Left me and Brandy and for However Long she was Gone I was his pussy. Its about this time he starts to fuck me Alot and I start wetting the bed . . . Mom and me had been doing sexual shit since I was about four. I don't know what she got from it. Well she Abandoned me several more times Anyway sometime when I hurt them (victims) I would see her face. More Later Im Tired

    I had noticed in his letters that after writing about something difficult, Brents would abruptly stop, an indication that he was becoming distressed. Every time he did, I felt guilt for being the person who was placing him under this scrutinizing microscope, poking and prodding him for detail after detail. I was also struck by the irony of the situation, since I knew many people would say he wasn't capable of feeling distress—or any emotion, for that matter.

    His next letter, I discovered with a bit of relief, was sprinkled with the wry and frank humor that made reading about his history easier to bear.

Sunday May 22 1000 /pm

    Hello, I have news for you. Both DAs agreed to get me out of state . . . Carrie came to see me yesterday. Happier than I've seen her in Awhile. She realy worked hard for this. So in a sense I guess its her victory in an otherwise Total Loss. She and I had a communication issue about you. She's afraid you'll screw me over . . . I don't tell her what you and I discuss, I simply tell her I trust you and believe in you. If in the Long run you make me out to be the Spawn of Satan well hey you know that old saying about opinions! ☺ I realy hate this place. Just because I stick to myself and tell you That I realy feel depressed somedays they send in Mental Health. Well shit what I am supposed to feel. Over Joyed that I am a piece of shit who brutalizes and destroys everything or anything in his path. No one get it. I have no one to sit down and talk with Just about the sun The moon and the stars of every day Life. It sucks but I brought this upon myself. So I have to Live with it. Any way screw that.

    Ok let me tell you some about state hospital prison. I guess you could say Therapy for me sucked. About 90% was group therapy. Well group therapy for a sociopathic sexualy addicted/saddistic Individual Just does Not seem right and Never did. I would sit and Listen to guys tell about there rape cases and get off on it. We had victims come in and tell thier stories. I would wish it was me who fucked them. Hell I fucked a few of my therapists. Bottom Line I was to damn smart for my own good. I could run therapy groups. It realy sucks when you know whats wrong, want to fix whats wrong, yet you can't because your mentaly to far gone. They say being a sociopath is not a mental illness. I disagree. I know I suffer post traumatic stress, and I believe That I have a form of manic deppression which has become severe in the Last 2 years. I've been sociopathic since I was 9 or 10. My Life until I was 16 was Like a war zone. I started having sex with grown adults at the age of four. I start doing drugs at 11 drinking before that. Anyway tthe state hospital. I had one friend thier. Kay. She was special. She knew what I did and made no bones about it. She Looked me in the eye and told me that if I did not Kill someone in my Lifetime that it would be a miracle. She was right. She Never said it to be shitty or viscious. She was kind and loving to me. And guess I Loved her to. I think of her often. Other than Kay it was realy a joke.

I had a thing for a transvestite named Gilbert/Lisa. What a fucking nightmare that was. It was like 99% of my Relationships. It was the worlds Largest mine field. No map, Blindfolded and drunk. Of course I was afraid to be alone so I endured the madness. It didn't help that I couldn't express my feelings Like I can now. Its Like I tell you about being in my cell 24 hours a day. Now hell its easy. Even with the Lonliness and depression. But back then I could not stand it. I fantacized masturbated 24-7 Talked to myself, cried, screamed fought, begged you name it I did anything I could accept behave to stay out of 24 hour confinement. Add to all my behavior that I was a Liar, con artist, Thief, Junky and sex fiend. I did not do so well.

May 24 05 10 05/p

Well I know now for sure I will be sent out of state. New name, new identity. You will be the only person approved by the people Involved who I will be Able to contact . . . I know I should be at least happy about this, but I am not. The shame of who and what I am grows deeper by The day. Add to that I realy believe I am growing more mentaly ill. I have periods of short term memory Loss, I have black outs. I have been living with a Constant Headache. I am having times of extreme paranoia . . . You are my one and only friend Amy Even if your not at Least you and I can do or try to do a good thing. Thats realy all I care about at this point. I have to have something good in my Life or I am going to slip into a darkness that cannot be turned around. You and This are my Grace once this is done and I can hopefully Realize something good out of it. Then I will finish me, because I know what I will do Left unchecked. People say But you can change, You only have to say no, or just don't give in to your thinking or

> *your urges. They don't get it, This is me. Theres no urge or Thinking its me. I know the consequences better than anyone. Sex has little to do with it, Its the control, the domination, The fear, The hurt, The power. When I make Love to a woman, or just consentual sex Its truly enjoyable. But Raping them Its so different. They smell different, some fight, some give in, Believe it or not some even feel pleasure. And Guilt as quick as they feel it. Some beg, some Lie. Some even Talk Reason. It's the same with the guys I would rob. I even raped a guy. Its all the same to me Amy, I am always good to my friends but There is the other side and it will not stay hidden or controlled Its shameful, disgusting, perverted, Brutal, Hateful and sensLess but bottom Line it is who I am.*

I was his Grace? I didn't want to be his Grace. I had a quick mental image of the large pastel-colored statue of the Virgin Mary in the very front of the inside of the Catholic church we attended every Sunday while I was growing up. Dressed in flowing robes, she stood with outstretched arms and open hands, a small maternal smile playing at her lips, as if to say, "Come here, one and all, and I'll give you a big hug." The only thing I seemed to have in common with her was my long dark hair.

I didn't want Brents to consider me his friend, either, and it was something I would regularly remind him about. Despite my admonitions, he apparently still stubbornly clung to the notion.

> 6-3-05
> *I tried to call you today to no Avail. I've put a lot of sincere thinking, heartfelt and brutally honest thinking into my future. You said in your letter dated May 31-05, you said not to dispair That I could still do some good with my Life. After I give you my Life, I'll have nothing. I can never be more honest or sincere than what I am going to tell you now.*

My entire Life has been spent with people who are sociopaths, Rapists, Abusers, Junkies, Liars, selfish Greedy manipulative physcotic, terrified angry vendective murdering souls. I am a Villain in every way. I can never function morally in society or in prison. Yes I have a blood oath type Loyalty to those I call friends. I would kill for them without hesitation. I have four such people in my Life. One is dead, Two are hurt and angry because I hurt them even though I did not entend to. And one doesn't know it but she's the only person of Importance in my Life. You, Amy, are my only true friend. You say you can't be my friend and I understand why you try to Live by this. But its to Late, you know you are. Yet you also know dispite your guilt you'll do the right things. In the end Amy you may betray me, once you have all you need you may just walk away enjoy the fortune and fame and move on to your next project. Driven people are like that. Will I harbor Anger or hut? No! Why? Simple All I have to do is Look in the mirror (not at the physical) But the Life itself.

Amy my pack is small outside of That people are sheep. I've been this way for 25 years. I'm not proud of it. I don't like it, I'm ashamed of it. No matter how good I can be that wolf is Just below the surface, waiting, being patient, watching, ever stalking its next kill I am going back to a cage full of wolves Amy, some worse, some better. I cannot see me trying to stay in that cage very Long. When a psycologist tells you at 11 years old, your going to be a serial predator theres truly a problem. Nobody Addressed it and here we are today.

When I die I want my ashes spread somewhere in the Colorado mountains. I don't want to be buried with my family. I want my soul to go free. Like the wolf. I do believe in Reincarnation. So I wonder who or what I was. I believe that This Life was meant as punishment for a past Life. As for what I will be in the next? Who knows.

Another common theme: his death. In many of his letters, and on the phone, Brents often talked about wanting to die, and wanting me to take his ashes and spread them in the forest for him. I always ignored the request.

What next?

6-6-05

Sometimes I want to tell you about personal things Like relationships. Take Ema Jean. She and I were friends and could have been lovers. But because she was married to Patrick I never violated that. Anyway Ema Jean had cancer and shortly before I was arrested she thought she might be coming out of remision. She was realy sick and she was also pregnant. Guess who stepped up to the plate . . . Brent did. Almost every day I was robbing people at ATMs, Robbing stores, gas stations you name it. The crack dealers were realy keeping me in money.

I guess that's what realy hurts. When they all wanted me to buy Groceries, weed or tickets to concerts or drinks in the Bars or medicine or give them rides to work or buy them gas, call Brent he'll buy it. And he did. They all knew I was doing illegal shit, yet They sure enjoyed it. Any way I am going to describe in detail one particular day in January. It's a Tuesday or Wednesday. I have about $2,000 in cash on me The day before I robbed a man at an ATM. A woman outside a bank and a gas station. So I have money. I got my grey goose at 230 pm I have to take Ema Jean to the Planned Parenthood for an exam. At 830 I pick up a 15 year old hispanic prostitute on West Colfax offer her $40 for a fuck. Are you a cop, No I say and rub her pussy under her dress, and show her my cock. I am about 6 blocks away from a house That has recently burned down the garage and the back of the house Look intact. She has no Idea otherwise. I pull Into the garage and pull the doors shut behind the car.

I open her door pull her out by her hair and put a K-bar military knife to her throat, Push her into the back seat of the car climb in and tell her I'm going to cut her fucking head off if she doesn't give me what I want. She tries to fight she screams even though my hand covers her mouth. I put the knife down on The front seat and reach down and rip her panties off I tell her To spread her Legs she tells me that I'm going to have to kill her. No problem I tell her I start choking her and black out. Some time Later when I come back There is a girl, purple, barely breathing Blood vessels in her eyes are popped Saliva dribbling down her chin and cheeks. Tears flowing and trying to focus on me. I take my cloths off and take hers off. I Light a ciggarrete and finger her while I wait for her to recover Above this garage is an old storage Loft. Once she recovers I take her up to the Loft where I tell her that I am going to murder her if she isn't obediant. I Rape her Repeatedy oraly and vaginaly for a couple of hours. She is bleeding vaginaly because my penis is very long and I can see the pain her eyes and how she flinches when I thrust deep into her, so I position her so that I can hurt her while I rape her. I enjoy causing her pain. I have to go take Ema Jean to the doctor. I choke this girl until she passes out. I gag her and tie her up four point. And go to Ema Jean. Spend 3 hours with her, have diner with Julie. Like nothing happened drop Julie at home, go buy some heroin and go back to the prostitute. Its dark when I do get back. I have a gallon jug of water and some rags I clean her up, give her some Arbys and a soda. I tell her I'm gonna kill her if she gets out of line. She begs me not to kill her. Once she has finished eating I make her suck my dick to hardness. I position her on her knees so I can sodomize her she begs me please not to. I gag her again and then shove my penis into her ass as far as I can get it She screams into the gag and passes out. I pull out my penis and wait for her to come to and do she doesn't pass out but screams. Now I thrust very brutally into her several times and she passes out again. I continue to sodomize her for an hour or so. When I am ready to ejaculate I pull out and pull her gag off and make her suck me until I ejaculate in her mouth which I shove it into her throat because I want her to choke on my semen and penis.

After I rest awhile I shoot her up with heroin. Letting her puke and sweat awhile I start to fondler her gently and she responds. Heroin is good for that. Eventualy she is fucking me on her own. I do her until around sunrise. at sunrise I give her another bump of heroin she nods good. I take her down town give her a gram of H and Let her go. This is just one of the many but it shows how violent and sadistic I had become.

Alot of the time I was doing these things I thought about what had happened between my Dad and Mom and me. When I hurt them I often wished it was my mom I was ripping apart with my penis or choking to death. To this very minute I hate her, Not because of the sex mind you. No I hate her I think because of the denial and betrayl and abandonment. When I was a kid I used to step between her and Dad so she would not get hurt. He'd often say "oh tough guy now that the bitch is given you the pussy huh boy!" Then he'd beat the piss out of me Literaly or fuck me to spite us both. Why I did not do well in school I could no remember my own name much less my math.

I had to stop reading because tears covered the page, and the words had become blurry and impossible to see. I realized I had started crying early on while reading about the torture Brents had inflicted upon that girl. Who was she? Where was she now? Had she ever gotten help? Was she still living on Colfax, battered and broken by her encounter, carrying the pain of it around like a hideous, bloated corpse chained to her ankles?

Clutching the pages in my hand, I stumbled blindly into our bedroom, my eyes swimming with tears. Sitting on our bed, propped up by pillows with a book in his lap, Matt looked up in alarm.

"What's wrong? What happened?" he said urgently, his eyes suddenly wide with concern.

Silently, I handed the pages to him. I needed someone else to know of this horror. I needed to know what, if anything, I could do to find this girl. I needed comfort in the face of the nightmare I had just read.

Matt took the pages from me and quickly began to read. Suddenly, his face twisted, a mixture of extreme disgust and anger, and he crumpled up the pages and threw them back at me in a fury.

"Don't bring that shit in here." The force of his anger made me take a step back. I was so shocked that my tears abruptly stopped.

Still quiet, I picked up the pages and left the room. I felt rejected, ashamed, embarrassed, chastised, heartbroken, and totally alone. Matt and I avoided each other the rest of the evening, and when I settled on the living room couch for the night, he didn't say a word.

But it was no use. I couldn't sleep. The sick feeling in the pit of my stomach would not go away, and I kept seeing those awful words in my mind, describing the torture of that girl.

Please, I begged the universe, please help me deal with this.

Lying on my back, I slung my right arm across my eyes as if that would block out the memory of his letter and started making promises. No more rape stories, I told myself. When this one is over, that's it. They're too heart-wrenching. And I would never write or talk to Brents again, I vowed. Clearly, he was poison, hideously evil to his very core, and I had been ridiculously wrong for thinking there might be some semblance of humanity left inside him worth exploring. How could anyone commit such heinous acts against a fellow human being? Against a girl who was little more than a child?

Unexpectedly at that moment, a thought popped into my head: What he did to her was a reflection of what was done to him as a child.

Bullshit, I told the thought. That's no excuse. Everyone has choices.

Maybe I was wrong. Maybe Brents really was born evil.

You don't really believe that, said the thought that pushed insistently into my mind.

And I knew in my gut I didn't believe it to be true. I had seen enough of the human condition during my lifetime to know we are all born with a clean slate, but pain, loneliness, and fear are harsh molds that can contort us all into monsters.

I thought of my own boys when they were born, their unfocused, gray-colored newborn eyes trying hard to recognize the features of my face when I came into view and how within a few weeks their plump cheeks would break into a blissful smile at the sound of my voice or the feel of my hands as I scooped them up to nestle them against me. Like all babies, they were pure innocence, pure love.

Just like Brents at one time, the voice whispered in my head.

Enough, I told the voice, and squeezed my eyes shut tighter as if that would make the voice go away. Brents is *nothing* like my boys. He's not like anyone else I know. He's by far the most horrible creature who ever existed, and I no longer see the point of caring about how he came to be. Just put him away. Just let him die. Alone.

Well, aren't you being judgmental now, the voice said. What are you so afraid of—the knowledge of just how dark and twisted someone can become? How dark anyone can become? Even you? Even your boys?

By wanting to run away from the manifestation of evil I had just read, was I giving it more power to live on, instead of exposing it by flipping over the rock under which it hid? I became a reporter, a truth-teller because I couldn't stand the hypocrisy of our household during my childhood, yet here I was, reacting the same way as my parents who turned a blind eye to my brother's rage all those years.

I understood Matt's reaction. And now I was slowly able to let go of my feelings of hurt and rejection and forgive him for it.

After a while, I crept softly back into our bedroom and slipped into bed beside him, trying not to disturb him. His sigh told me that he, too, was still awake, and he reached out, wrapped a long arm around my waist, and pulled me into him, keeping his arm draped over me protectively even as we both fell asleep.

That night I dreamed I was sitting at a table with Brents, a rectangular, generic-looking metal table, such as the kind you see in interview rooms in police stations. Brents was wearing his prison uniform and sitting at the end of the table, and I was in a work suit, catty-corner to him on one of the sides. He was looking at me with no expression on his face, both his hands flat on the table, the handcuffs still joining them, waiting. And then I reached out and laid my right hand across the top of his left and smiled at him—a small, sad, understanding smile. His face lit up with joy.

In the next moment, the room, which had been empty save for the table and the two of us, started to fill with men and women. They were agitated and restless, milling about while murmuring angrily, sounding like a stirred-up hive of bees. Soon the murmurs became shouts, and then the people began to grab me, trying to move my hand off Brents' and drag me away from the table. Yet somehow, I was able to remain in my seat, my hand undisturbed on his, and despite the chaos erupting around us, I smiled at him reassuringly.

"It's going to be OK," I said, staring steadily into his eyes, and in them, I saw relief and gratitude.

July 12-05
Dear Amy,
   I can't begin to tell you how painful it was to see those women all of Them get up There and say There peace. Tiffany killed me. I wish I had the courage and heart of all of Them. I know each will get her wish. I am mentaly tormented as Tiffany wished, I am physicaly tormented and I'm sure There will be beatings and Attempts If Not successful plots to kill me. Unlike the women If Someone tries to rape me in prison I will die and They'll have to fuck a corpse. I never chose how my mind works. I was thinking Friday If people knew what goes through my head They would put me in a place where no one could ever find my ashes after having dismembered me after having publicly executed me. I was punched by a female guard in Denver County jail. I think she thought she would feel some resolution by that action but when she Looked into my eyes and saw the Look in them and figured out That I Like them to fight and struggle it realy freaked her out. That was a bad day! on a good day I would have been ashamed of my actions and would feel Like no punishment will ever be enough.
   Brent

SEVENTEEN

The Sentencing

As I left for work on the Tuesday after the Fourth of July, I grabbed a large manila envelope and stuffed it full with Brents' letters and his journal. A progress hearing was scheduled for Wednesday, but I knew it was going to be more than just that. He was going to be sentenced, and his victims were going to speak, and even though my editor had pooh-poohed the idea, I wanted to include some of Brents' writings to show his history and motivation. If nothing else, I hoped it would help someone, maybe just one person, understand him.

Once at work, I hid the envelope deep inside the middle drawer of my desk, just to keep it safe. Besides, Brents had asked me to keep the names of some of his friends confidential to protect them, and I had given him my word. I didn't trust anyone else not to be careless.

The next day brought a classically deep blue Colorado sky. Even though it was July, the winds sweeping off the Flatirons mountains in the mornings still delivered cool air, and I left for the courthouse an hour ahead of schedule, giving myself plenty of time to walk there and get settled for the 9 a.m. hearing.

As I headed west on 14th Avenue toward Bannock Street, I suddenly saw Brents' attorney, Carrie, walking briskly and wearing a stylish black suit jacket and skirt, red shirt, and black patent slingbacks. She was pulling a tall cart on wheels, packed with bulging files and boxes, and seemed to have no problem maneuvering it over curbs, despite its apparent heaviness and her three-inch-plus heels.

I hurried to catch up to her, but once I did, I couldn't think of anything worth saying, because "Hi, Carrie, any reaction to the sentencing that's going to happen today, even though I'm not supposed to know about it and you probably hate my guts after that first story?" sounded as ridiculous as I felt thinking it. Her face was intent, deep in thought, and she didn't even glance my way, although she must have known I was there.

I suddenly felt I was intruding. I dropped back, and she hurried on alone.

I was one of the first in the courtroom, and once there, I hesitated. Where would I sit? Would I keep my word and be where Brents could see me, or would I retreat back to the more comfortable—and certainly more popular—stance of being a cool, clinical scribe who was there only to record the day?

Yes, the letter of the law with journalism says you don't get personally involved in a story.

I could follow the letter of the law, or I could follow my heart.

I knew where I was going to sit.

Ever since I can remember, my dreams have shown me the way. The previous night's dream of staying resolute while an angry crowd tried to rip me away from Brents was a sign, I was sure, that I was supposed to continue what I'd started.

So I would.

I glanced around the room, eyeing the table where Brents would sit and the podium where I knew his victims would stand, and positioned myself four rows back from the rear of the podium, directly in the line of sight of anyone sitting at the defense table. I put my purse at my feet and reached into its depths to discreetly break off a piece of a chocolate protein bar. Food is not allowed inside courtrooms but I had not felt like eating breakfast. I chewed it as slowly and as inconspicuously as possible while the courtroom slowly began to fill, deciding against leaving my spot to get a drink of water at the fountain down the hall.

A side door opened and two Denver sheriff's deputies appeared, followed by Brents and then two more deputies behind him. Brents was wearing a red jail uniform and glasses and had a clean-shaven face except for a small goatee. He looked thinner than I remembered.

Keeping his head down, he scooted to the defense table, chains around his ankles and wrists, and took a seat next to an assistant public defender on the case, Karen McGovern, a young woman wearing a cream-colored suit. He didn't look up. I wondered if he knew I was there. I wondered if Carrie wore a red blouse to match his jail uniform.

With dozens of other options, a *Rocky Mountain News* reporter walked up and sat next to me. Normally standoffish while on a story, I didn't mind. I wrote a question on my large notepad and showed it to her: "Did you guys preview today?"

Was it "out there" that the sentencing was going to happen?

She shook her head no and looked confused. I sat back, feeling oddly satisfied. Taking a quick glance around the room, I counted only forty people there, excluding reporters, attorneys, and five deputies who stood in strategic locations—one in the back, two against the door, and two against the far wall—no doubt just in case. But it was no circus. The victims would have their day.

And then the bailiff appeared to announce the presence of Judge Robert S. Hyatt, an energetic-looking man with neatly trimmed gray hair, a gray beard and mustache, and long sideburns. Hyatt sat and immediately got down to business.

As the judge announced the plea agreement, a buzz began across the courtroom. I could tell from surprised faces that many people did not know. But several women sitting in the back clearly did. I recognized some of them as victims in the case and watched their faces, tense and tight-lipped.

Then I returned back to my notebook, writing quickly across the page to keep up with all the numbers the judge was announcing. I always used large notebooks for court cases, so I can scrawl quickly across their long pages with plenty of room to spare.

"... guilty to count 1, 4, 5 through 16, 20 through 46, 49 through 56, 65, 66, 69 through 79, and 80," Hyatt intoned in a gravely voice. "In exchange the prosecution will dismiss 2, 3, 17, 18, 19, 47, 48, 67, and 68."

In another case, he said, Brents was pleading guilty to counts 1, 2, 3, and 5, while the prosecution was dismissing count 4.

"Upon your guilty plea, as part of this agreement, you will be remanded to an out-of-state correctional facility that the state of Colorado will determine," the judge told Brents. "And this plea bargain is subject to the condition that there will be no misconduct on your part, and if there is, you will be returned to Colorado to serve out the rest of your time."

He didn't have to add, "which won't be long, because with your notoriety and your record, you will surely be killed quickly." He didn't have to. Everyone knew it.

And then Hyatt had some questions for Brents.

"How old are you?"

"Thirty-six."

"School?"

"Eleventh grade, a GED."

"Are you being treated for an emotional disability? I see where you were previously sentenced to a state hospital, but you've not been diagnosed with a major disorder, you're not on any medications, you have no diagnosable mental illness you're under treatment for . . . Do you suffer from mental illness?" the judge abruptly asked Brents.

A pause. I looked up from my notebook and at the defense table. From my seat, I could see Brents grimace.

Another pause. "No, sir," Brents finally replied.

"Are you under the effects of alcohol?"

"No."

"Drugs?"

"No."

Then Hyatt began reading the descriptions of the charges, using the clinical technical terms one hears in court that describe awful things:

use of a deadly weapon, menacing, kidnapping, aggravated robbery, serious bodily injury, and child abuse with serious bodily injury.

And of course more than any other charge, the words "sexual assault." Over and over.

After advising Brents of his rights, the judge went over the counts of the charges again, and this time, after each one, Brents leaned forward to the microphone on the defense table and softly spoke a single word: "guilty."

The audience seated in the courtroom began to buzz. Some of the women began to cry.

Shortly after 10:30, the judge announced a twenty-minute break, then stepped away from the bench and out a rear door to his chambers.

Hardly anyone else moved.

A few minutes after 11 a.m., the sentencing resumed, and now it was the victims' turn.

The first woman, wearing a navy suit, walked up to the podium that faced the defense table, her back to where I sat. Even so, I could see her clenched hands. When she spoke, her voice rang with anger.

"Brent Brents should never walk free again," she said. "He destroys life."

And then she was shouting. "I will never be the same again! His other victims will never be the same again! I'm suspicious everywhere I go. I'm a prisoner in my own city, and in my own life. And this could have all been prevented."

Brents should never have been released from prison, she said, and she also blamed Aurora police for not arresting him when they had the chance.

"It's not OK to rape women and children," she screamed at Brents. "Not OK!"

From where I sat directly behind her, I could see Brents staring at the woman, his face impassive. Was he really hearing her? I hoped so. I looked back down and continued to take notes.

"... to my Congress Park neighbors, thank you. To all the EMTS, and Denver Police, thank you. To God, thank you for my life, and thank you for my freedom."

She walked away, and immediately, another woman took her place at the podium, visibly shaking.

"I'm a forty-four-year-old woman, the owner of a pet store," she began. "I try to live honestly and be kind to those around me."

On February 11, she said, she picked her car up from the repair shop and met a friend for coffee.

"I am an ordinary woman. That all changed when Brent Brents walked into my store that day. My world was suddenly very different." Her voice trembled. "Now, I wear a panic button around my neck. I am no longer able to be alone at my shop. I am no longer an ordinary woman. Today I share my story so that there may be a better understanding of what happens to a woman who is raped."

She has been able to afford treatment, the pet shop owner said. "What happens to those who can't? They often turn to drugs or alcohol, or die like Aida Bergfeld," she said. "I hold Brent Brents accountable for her death."

The adrenaline from the attack, she said, stayed in her system. "It keeps you from eating, sleeping, mentally functioning. Fatigue is ever present, and my startle response sky-high . . . I could not breathe, I could not get out of bed, and the pain in my back was debilitating. The tears that finally began to fall were unending. It will be a long time before I feel whole again. The experience has been pure agony, and not just for me, but for all those in my life."

She now straightened and stared hard in Brents' direction.

"You are pure evil. What you did to me, the other women, and to the children, was clearly an act of pure evil. I hope in prison you get to know sheer terror and crumble from weakness. You have forever impacted our lives, and for that, may you live in torment."

As the woman stepped away from the podium, Brents continued to stare in that direction—my direction. I wasn't sure of the expression behind his glasses, but I could feel the weight of his stare, and so I stared back.

Then I realized Tiffany Engle was nearing the podium, and I inhaled deeply as if to breathe for both him and me.

"As you can see, I'm still here," Tiffany said in anger. "You may have hurt me but you didn't beat me. You are the most odious vermin that nature ever suffered to crawl upon the face of this earth. Your soul's going to rot for eternity."

And in the next moment, she began to cry, tears of rage and mourning. And as she did, Brents eyes filled up with tears. He stared at Tiffany, he stared at me, and he began to blink.

No, no, I silently begged him with my eyes. Stay with her, hear her out. She deserves that.

I was as focused on Brents as if I had tunnel vision, locking my eyes on his face. I could no longer hear what Tiffany was saying, even though she continued to speak.

And then she was finished. As she turned to step away, I caught Brents' eyes, now full of tears, and gave him a small, sad smile of encouragement. There, you did it, my smile said to him silently.

He then hung his head and cried.

It was now Carrie's turn. She didn't glance at Brents, who after a few minutes lifted his head but still sat motionless, looking down. She rose and walked to the podium to address the judge, although she actually talked to all of us.

"There are no words that are adequate to express the tragedy that occurred here," she began. "No words adequate, as his lawyer, as to how sorry we are."

She spoke in soft, somber tones we could easily hear because the room was so still.

"Mr. Brents has asked me to speak on his behalf. He recognizes that anything he says would further traumatize. He recognizes the horror of his acts—and that is why he chose not to put the victims or their families through any more."

She took a deep breath. "He is a damaged human being, but the damage is not from pure evil. I understand how people feel it is evil. Maybe, as a society, we can say wait a minute, what are we doing wrong?

"The history of Brents is quite a paper trail. He was first prosecuted as a twelve-year-old for rape. Horrific acts were committed upon him. From age four to eight, he was sexually assaulted by his father, including anal intercourse. He was only four years old. And at six, his mother began rubbing on him, and having sexual intercourse with him, until he was taken from the home at thirteen."

Carrie was in tears. She shook her head as if to shake them off and continued to speak, her voice thick with emotion, gaining volume with every word.

Someone could have leapt into the room and screamed "Fire!" and I don't think anyone would have moved.

"How can I stand here and defend Mr. Brents?" she asked. "I feel nothing but despair and sadness that he went through what he did, that he became a person who could no longer control his anger. And anger does not heal as well as understanding. This kind of torture affects these kids."

I looked up from my notebook. At some point during Carrie's speech, Brents had begun crying again, tears silently streaming down his cheeks.

"At age twelve," Carrie said, "Brents had his face bashed in and was in a hospital for three weeks. He was in prison at eighteen, and certainly prison does not make a person a kinder, gentler person. It makes you more violent and more angry. Psychologists documented his abuse, and how it created in Mr. Brents an uncontrollable violence and impulsivity. It is the result of a societal failure to protect our children.

"I hope, I pray, that we as a society spend less money on prison and more on early development and schools. Do more in the early stages. While nothing good can come out of this, he would like the people in this courtroom to know his acts were horrific, but maybe his story can bring information to the public that we are just not taking care of our children. He feels great remorse for his actions."

And with that, she walked back to her chair and sat down. Before she was all the way seated, DA Morrissey was on his feet.

"I don't know about his early life history," he said, "but Brent Brents does have a criminal record. To say he hasn't gotten a chance from the system—well, he was given the opportunity for sex offender treatment. He chose not to do it. He's not a man who doesn't understand. He's a sociopath, a predator. He's understood that for a long time.

"Tiffany Engle—she would be dead today but for the work done at Denver Health," he continued. "Doctors removed parts of her brain, swollen from the beating.

"And but for Aida screaming, I'm convinced that Mr. Brents would stand here and be arraigned today on a murder charge."

As for the twin girls he raped, Morrissey said, "The impact on those little girls and on that family is just immeasurable."

He grimaced and paused.

"And there are a number of victims we are not hearing from because they live a different lifestyle—the women on Colfax. Far more women than those who have come forward. I bet he was gambling on the fact he could continue to do this behavior without the victims coming forward. He was terrorizing, victimizing, choking those women as well."

And now Morrissey stopped and looked straight at the judge. "You're the only person who can ensure that he will never walk on the streets of our community, or any community, ever again," he said firmly, and then he walked to his seat and sat down.

The DA was wrong. This judge wasn't the only person who could ensure Brents be locked up. He still had to be sentenced in Aurora, a different jurisdiction, for molesting his former girlfriend's son and raping Margaret.

But I guess it sounded more dramatic this way.

Now it was the judge's turn, and he didn't need any time to ponder.

"These are inescapable truths," he said. "There are over sixty counts on charges involving a dozen victims. These are extraordinary crimes. The sentence will be unlike any sentence I have imparted in more than two decades on the bench."

Brents' crimes, Hyatt said, all bore his unique stamp of violence and threats.

"You stalked these victims, assaulted these victims, and you degraded these victims, at every stage," he said sternly to Brents, who sat as still as a statue, his tears gone. "You showed unspeakable cruelty ... Your relentless pursuit of these victims, daily, hourly, was nothing less than an ongoing horror."

Brents' only mitigating factor, the judge said, was pleading guilty, which was allowing him to serve his time out of state.

"Your victims will, in some fashion, bear the scars of your inhumanity forever, and it's beyond my power to eradicate their pain or make them whole. I doubt you have any idea of the pain you've caused. But I want to ensure justice for the victims and to ensure against future victims."

Brents had stared down for most of Morrissey's speech, but now his eyes were locked on the judge, who addressed him as if they were the only two people in the room.

"It is true that while incarcerated, you resisted treatment. I reviewed your psychiatric reports. I cannot fully explain what made you the man you are today. However, you are far beyond any potential rehabilitation. You must simply be contained, you must be housed, you must simply be kept apart from society. It's the task of this court today to ensure you will never be free again."

Regarding the victims, Hyatt said, "They all matter, and they're all part of this sentence."

He began delivering it, and after a while, I could barely keep up with the numbers.

"Count 1, sexual assault, sixty-four years to life," the judge intoned. "Count 4, menacing, three years, consecutive with 1. Count 5, burglary, thirty-two year sentence, consecutive. Count 7, aggravated robbery, thirty-two years, consecutive. Count 8, kidnapping, forty-eight-year sentence, consecutive. Count 9, sexual assault, sixty-four years to life . . ."

I lost track of the total number of years after it topped 1,000.

And then Hyatt rose and left the bench, and the crowds began streaming out of the courtroom while the deputies quickly ushered

Brents away. Still in the courtroom, I overheard Morrissey talking to a reporter about the upcoming cases in Aurora, "Arapahoe County will have the same deal—he'll plea there too. I'm sure he'd feel safer serving outside the state of Colorado."

Glancing around the room, I noticed everyone was gone—almost. Toward the back of the courtroom, two detectives lingered near a couple of women. One of the men I recognized to be Denver homicide detective Martin Vigil. The women were victims in the case.

"We're sorry," Vigil said awkwardly, nodding at his fellow detective, whom I recognized to be in the sex crimes unit. "And . . . congratulations."

The women stood, wooden and as if in shock, their eyes almost unseeing. Then they wordlessly walked away.

What could anyone possibly say? Vigil must have had the same thought because in that moment, he looked at me and shrugged helplessly. Ah, well, I tried, his look said.

Out in the hallway, Morrissey was surrounded by a throng of reporters. I edged up to the rear and listened in.

". . . all the victims were consulted, and family members," he was saying. "Our main concern was that the bottom end was high enough that he wouldn't be able to live long enough to serve the minimum."

How long was his total sentence? Someone asked.

"Over 1,200 years," Morrissey replied with a grin. "This is the longest sentence I've ever seen in Denver."

I looked past Morrissey and down the hall, where I saw a familiar shade of blond hair, and I ran to catch up with Carrie, who was for the first time talking to some reporters.

"As far as Arapahoe County," she was saying, "we'll plea to the charges and the judge will have full discretion."

Why did he want to go out of state? Someone asked.

"Anybody with that kind of record is at risk in prison," Carrie said patiently as if talking to a child.

How do you look at him? Another person asked.

"As a tragic figure," Carrie replied. "A very, very tragic figure. At four years old, he was a beautiful little boy, and today he received a sentence that sends him to prison for the rest of his life. It's a tragedy. It's a tragedy for the victims and it's a tragedy for him because he was a victim as well.

"And I don't want to minimize their pain and cause revictimization. I only want to say, hey, let's recognize the tragedy of the entire situation so we can learn from it. I think people see what's happening and they don't explore more because they don't want to know," she said.

As far as Brents' abuse as a child, Carrie said, "Teachers had to have seen it. Neighbors had to have seen it. We all have a tendency in society not to take responsibility."

Overall, someone asked her, how do you feel about today?

"This isn't working," she replied, and for a brief moment, I wondered if she meant the inane question.

"I can't wait to get home. I had to stand in the midst of all that tragedy. You can only feel despair when you're exposed to it."

I blinked at Carrie, my eyes open wide in recognition of that truth. I could relate to what she was saying, and in that moment, she nodded at me. Then she turned and walked away, and none of us reporters went after her.

There was nothing more to say, but a whole lot to write. And it was going on 2 p.m.

Walking back to the *Post* newsroom, I was busy constructing the lead to the story in my head. I would start with the judge, of course, because his sentence was the focus today, and I would definitely include some of Carrie's raw emotion and her earnest pleas for understanding...

I was so busy writing in my head that I didn't notice at first when I walked into the newsroom that something was off. First of all, it was quiet—far too quiet for the middle of the day, and we weren't even close to deadline. Second of all, everyone was typing, apparently transcribing pages that were fastened to the tall metal stands we kept at our desks for such a purpose—everyone, every reporter and editor, and even the assistant who normally answered the phones.

They were typing letters, I realized, and as I drew closer, I saw the familiar scrawl of the handwriting and felt a sick thud in my stomach.

They were all typing up Brents' letters, which were clearly no longer hidden in the middle drawer of my desk.

I felt like I'd been slapped.

"What? Who?" I sputtered to my editor, who only nodded his head toward another one's office. I strode quickly into the room and stood, silently enraged, over the editor's desk. I didn't trust myself to speak first.

He looked up and smiled apologetically at me. "I'm sorry," he said. "We were talking about the sentencing in the morning meeting, and the other editors thought it would be a good idea after all to use those letters you have, so I found them in your desk and gave them out for everyone to type into the system."

"*Found* them in my desk? I hid them in the middle of one of my drawers. You would have had to *rummage*."

"I'm sorry," he said again, sounding mechanical. Then he added, "I thought you'd be OK with it since it was me."

I looked at him and slowly shook my head. A little more than a year ago, I had respected him so much as an editor that I would have allowed him to push my limits—and did, with disastrous results.

A little more than a year ago, I had been teetering on an edge, and instead of taking my hand to pull me back in, he had thumped my back and sent me over.

A little more than a year ago, he was right—I was OK with him.

But not any longer.

"No, that doesn't help," I told him honestly. "Those are my letters, not the *Post*'s. I had my cell phone with me—even though I was in court, you could've texted me and asked. For one thing, there were names in some of those letters that needed to stay confidential."

For another thing, I thought, I don't trust where you're going with this. Some of that material was horrifying and graphic. I didn't want it to be used in a sensationalistic way.

"Well," he said, tilting his head sideways, "why don't you go check on who's doing what with them?"

And so I did. For the next hour, before I even sat down to start writing the sentencing story, I went from computer to computer, reading over my coworkers' shoulders to see what they were typing and asking them, "Can you please take out that part?" Or, "Can you please take out that name?" Or, "Are you going to write up a note to go with this to help explain it?"

In the midst of that chaos, Lynn Kimbrough from the DA's office returned my call. I had phoned her the day before and told her about Brents' graphic description of the kidnapping and assault of the fifteen-year-old prostitute. I wanted to know if investigators believed it could be true. Maybe he was making the whole thing up, I thought hopefully, although he hadn't lied to me yet that I knew about. Every once in a while, I could confirm something he'd told me—such as the jelly-filled sweet rolls. He said he and Aida had stopped on their way to Glenwood Springs to buy some because she liked the iced rolls with the cherry filling in the middle. And then months later, poring over police reports, I read Aida's statement to police, and in it she mentioned getting the jelly sweet rolls.

Lynn had promised to share the details I gave her with the investigators who worked on Brents' case and get back to me. Now, as always, she was keeping her word, although I wouldn't like what she had to say.

"In addition to the crimes we charged, there are at least thirty prostitutes out there he has raped," Lynn told me. "Those details fit with the attacks we do know happened.

"His admission of this particular attack fits his pattern and would have been possible within that time frame. The details he shared with you do fit with violent acts that we know he committed," she said, "but it was not reported and he did not share details of this particular act with investigators."

My throat full, I managed to croak out a thank-you to Lynn and hung up, feeling defeated and, like Carrie, full of despair.

I didn't want that awful story to ring like the truth. I didn't want that girl to be out there, somewhere, unknown and unaided. I didn't want to write about this entire tragic story anymore and I didn't want to have to be the one to babysit all those damn letters.

In that moment, my cell phone rang. It was Matt.

"Hey," I said weakly, unable to manage more.

"What's wrong, honey?" he asked, and I paused. How to explain? And would he really care? After all, this was not a safe topic between us.

I decided to try.

"I came back from court and the editors had rummaged through my desk and taken Brents' letters, which they gave to everyone to type up," I said miserably, not expecting any sympathy.

I was wrong.

"That's a shitty thing for them to do," Matt said indignantly. "Can't you just take them back?"

"I thought about it, but they'd already typed most of them up. Besides, I think I should just try to minimize the damage and manage it the best I can. I still think it's important that people hear about his history. But it's . . . it's just been a hard day."

My voice caught at the last part, and Matt heard it. "Aw, baby, I'm so sorry," he said, and in moments like that, I was reminded of how warm and tender he was, how generous to his core, and yet with the heart of a lion. When I told my sister I was marrying him, she had fretted that it was a rash decision, until I told her I'd had a dream about Matt and he'd been surrounded by white light.

"Well, why didn't you say so?" was all she had said. My sister also has faith in my dreams.

And now, that image from my foretelling dream of my husband so long ago popped into my head. Matt was my own personal white light, my white knight, and just hearing the love in his voice suddenly gave me the resolve I needed to get through the rest of the day.

"Thank you, sweetie," I told him, and in the silence that followed, I could picture him listening intently on the phone. It felt like he was standing next to me, although he was in Boulder and I was in Denver. I remembered the feel of his strong arms wrapped around me and was actually able to smile.

"I love you," Matt said. "Get finished there and come on home."

"I love you too. And I will."

July 12-05
Dear Amy,
   Carrie and Karen have both done this About Face as far as you are concerned. I don't know what you wrote in the paper Lady but you seemed to have Impressed the hell out of them. Here is a direct Quote from Carrie "Promise me you'll deal with no one but Amy." And that it was a very good story and you ran my statement word for word. I knew I could believe in you . . .
   I haven't seen Carie, Karen or Larry since court and Lots of bad shit is going down and I feel helpless when I don't have a right to. Every Instinct in me tells me to fight, hurt maim KILL and defend myself when things happen to me, but it's like a catch 22. The physical pain they can exact on me is no big deal. Hitting, choking, Tazzering me breaking my bones none of that realy bothers me. Its breaking my word to you. It is our goal that is important. I read your Letters every day, my most prized possetion is your Letters to me. My encouragement, my rock.
   Grateful Always,
   Brent

EIGHTEEN

Aurora

After hanging up with Matt, I tuned out the newsroom and focused on my story about Brent's sentencing so I could get the hell out of there. I was almost finished with the first draft when I looked up and saw the icing on the cake of my day: a television camera aimed in my direction. The female reporter with the male photojournalist squinted her eyes at me and said, "You're the one that corresponds with Brents, right?"

Ah, so word had gotten out that I was the Female Reporter Who Writes to the Rapist.

I gritted my teeth. I had never liked the idea of reporters talking about the stories they covered—you ran the risk of accidentally giving an opinion, leaving yourself vulnerable to unfair accusations.

Yet my editors had evidently already agreed to it. So I sighed and grabbed the small brush I keep in my purse, running it through my hair at my desk. I become disheveled when I'm on deadline, working a fourteen-hour day before realizing I never finished combing out my wet hair after my shower in the morning.

I then faced the camera, feeling like it was a firing squad. Would this day never end?

"How is it you were able to talk to Brents, to read his letters?" the heavily lipsticked female television reporter asked me breathlessly. "I understand they're quite . . . difficult."

She flicked her wrist to position the microphone at me—your

turn!—and I shrugged. I didn't feel like divulging to this perfectly coiffed and made-up woman any of the inner struggles I had fought.

So I answered her question with a question. "What reporter wouldn't want to know how he was made?" I asked, and she frowned.

"How do you feel about him?" she said quickly, lobbing a softball of a question my way.

Well, here we go, I thought.

"I have empathy for him," I said, and at that, her eyes widened with shock. "I think he's a product of his environment."

There. It was done. I was "out"—I didn't hate the monster.

What more was there to say? Clearly unsettled by my response, she withdrew the microphone and signaled to her photographer that they were done.

She gave me an inkling of the revulsion I would get from most of my coworkers regarding Brents.

Apparently typing up his letters was enough to make several of them literally ill, and now, one by one, they began to seek me out, searching my face for some kind of answer to the same question: How did you do it?

"I don't understand," one fellow female reporter told me, shuddering. "I couldn't have done it. I don't know how you were able to stomach reading those things, or hearing his voice."

How to answer that? I had no expectation that she, or hardly anyone in that newsroom, for that matter, would understand. They were all on the same fast-paced reactionary track.

"I thought it was an important project," I finally told her, "and I tried not to judge him. And I guess I'm just freakishly thick-skinned." I smiled. She simply shuddered again and walked away.

I couldn't get home fast enough.

Thursday morning I was back at work, sitting at my desk and trying to psyche myself up for the next day, when Brents was scheduled to be sentenced in Aurora. While there were only two cases, they promised to be just as wrenching as the others—one involved the charge of him molesting the eight-year-old son of the woman he dated when he first came to Denver, and the other one was Margaret.

Margaret. I paused as I recalled her, the woman Brents had stalked for three days before he attacked her, raping and beating and choking her. I could still see her expressive, haunted eyes and the bruises on her throat and face. I wondered how she was doing. Had she seen the court coverage? Was there anything she wanted to say before the next day's hearing? It was possible that once there, she wouldn't want to talk. So I called her, and to my surprise, she answered the phone.

"Yeah, the DA told me there would probably be a sentencing," Margaret said to me in a matter-of-fact fashion, and I wondered why the prosecutor would couch it so cautiously at this point.

"It's great that he's admitting what he's done," she said. "He leaves us here in prison, though. I feel like a damn rat in my own house. I don't go anywhere, and I'm scared."

She was glad Brents was going to prison, she said, and she had one question: Does the man feel any remorse at all? "I bet he's scared," she added. "But he asked for it, we didn't. My life—I don't think it will ever be the same again, ever."

And then as she had in February, Margaret opened up to me in a rush of words.

"I feel filthy," she said, almost spitting out the last word. "I feel like a filthy, dirty, ugly person. All my friends—I won't tell them. Or my family. I'm so embarrassed, and I know I shouldn't be—it was nothing I did—but I feel like a piece of trash. I feel ashamed, and I feel embarrassed. I just want to forget about it but that's not going to happen overnight."

She can no longer run errands alone and waits for her husband to come with her. On Fridays, the day of the week that Brents attacked her, "I'm so tense," she said. "I jump at every little thing. I think, Am I going crazy?"

She was depressed, and little in life interested her anymore.

"Why didn't this son of a bitch just kill me?" She spit out the words. "At least I wouldn't be going through all these things I'm feeling."

"How do you feel about seeing him in court tomorrow?" I asked.

"It's gonna be scary. Just looking at him gives me the creeps. But I do want to see what he gets. Maybe if I see him in shackles, it will make me less scared."

And then abruptly, her thoughts sped off in another direction.

"I saw a picture of him as a little boy. I thought, What happened that he turned out the way he did? What happened to that little boy?"

I sucked in my breath. Margaret was asking the same questions that had plagued me for months. And I knew the picture she was referring to—Brents' mother had given it to me in Arkansas for that first story. It showed a young boy about six or seven, smiling broadly, wearing a dress shirt and plaid pants that looked like his Easter best.

As Margaret went on in a rambling stream of consciousness monologue, I was increasingly amazed to hear someone, especially one of Brents' victims, articulate the same struggle I had undergone.

"I feel awful for him, too, but at the same time, it's hard to deal with what he did. Sometimes I hate him. I know there has to be something wrong with him. Something happened to that little boy that he turned out to be the way he is. He's a human being, just like us. Sometimes I hate him, and sometimes I feel awful for him too. I think something must have happened to him for him to be that way. I wish somebody would have helped him."

She read his apology letter in that day's paper, she said. "At least he had the decency to do that. I still feel bad about him."

And in the next moment, she stunned me.

"I forgive him," Margaret said, simply and emphatically. "Right after it happened, I hated him for what he had done. But after I saw that little boy's picture—I kept thinking, What happened? I guess ever since I saw the picture of that little boy, I forgave him. Who am I, really, to condemn anybody?"

Her last sentence struck a chord in me. I circled it on the page as she continued.

"I feel scared for him, too, going to prison. Where's his family? That's why people turn so hard and so cold, because they get no love from anybody. I just keep thinking that he messed up my life but it's not only his fault. There must be something wrong with him. I feel bad for him. My sister says, 'How can you feel bad for him?—I would be hating him.' And I do sometimes, when I'm really scared. But that doesn't last too long, because I then think about the man.

"And I guess I'm looking at my boys the same way—I have two sons. I say to myself, This is not a man. This is a little boy that somebody hurt. How can somebody turn out to be so bad just because? There's got to be a reason why they do the things they do.

"I just wish somebody would have helped him. Where's his mother? If you talk to him, tell him I forgive him. It's scary for me, but I forgive him."

And then, apparently emotionally spent, she stopped. I hung up and sat in my chair, shaking my head. Just when I thought it wasn't possible to be surprised anymore, Margaret had done it. I was amazed and humbled by our conversation. She had reached deep into her soul, faced evil, and *forgiven* the man who brought it upon her.

How was that possible?

She had also asked a very insightful question: What about Brents' mother?

So I called his mother's house in Arkansas, and again to my surprise, the person I was looking for answered the phone.

She had been following the coverage online, Brents' mother said, and when I asked her for a reaction, she paused.

"What do you do with him?" she finally said. "All we do is pray. Don't know what else to do for him."

In court, his attorney said he was sexually abused, I told her.

"He wasn't," she replied flatly. "I don't trust anything that kid says. He's so screwed up in the head it's not even funny. His dad—when he heard something like that—he'd just sit and cry. He'd try to work with people around here. I think that's where Brent got that idea. Most of them had bad lives—are mentally ill . . . His sister said, 'I know Daddy, and he wouldn't do things like that.' He didn't want them running the streets and doing drugs like he did when he was little. Then we became Christians."

At the word, I had a sudden memory of the detective in court in Denver describing how Brents referred to one of his victims as a "Christian bitch."

"I sit and cry myself to sleep a lot, worrying about him," his mother went on to say. "People can change if they want to. If they don't want to, they don't."

And then she hung up.

I looked at my notes of my conversation with her until I found the phrase I was looking for when Brents' mother had talked about her husband, Brents' father: "He didn't want them running the streets and doing drugs like he did when he was little."

Another pattern.

I thumbed back through my notes again and wrote a quick preview story about the impending sentencing for the next day's paper and included the detail of Margaret's forgiveness. I then stood up, feeling the need to stretch and get out of the building.

Outside, the July heat bounced off the pavement and hit me square in the face. I walked forward a few feet to Broadway and the tracks of the 16th Street Mall shuttle, deep in thought.

Talking to Brents' mother made my brain hurt. I didn't believe her denials. Was this a small measure of what Brents had felt his entire childhood, maddening frustration at the duplicitous life they led?

I needed to move to process this through, so I took a step forward. Just then, a sudden unexpected breeze broke my thoughts and made me look up—it was the bus, the red, white, and blue mall shuttle, zooming toward me, only inches away. I had nearly stepped right in front of it, and the driver blared his horn. It seemed to shriek, "Hey, idiot! Wake up!"

My heart pounding with released adrenaline, I jumped out of the way, nearly stumbling as I hurled myself backward. And then I simply stood there, both hands over my pounding heart.

I needed to get a grip, I told myself. I could have, and probably would have, been killed. Geez, what a cliché: "She got hit by a bus."

Earth to Amy. Get your head out of your ass and let this thing go.

I had nearly been killed because I had been musing over Brents. What the hell? I asked the universe. Is there a point to all this? Really?

Pulling my cell phone out of my pocket—I gave up trying to wear a watch a long time ago because nearly as soon as I put one on, the battery would die—I noticed it was nearly 3 p.m. My daily story was finished, and I had racked up enough hours lately. I'd grab my things from my desk and head home early.

Back in the newsroom, I sat down at my desk for a final check of my messages. There, with a time stamp of 2:46 p.m., was a new email with the subject line "Brent . . ."

I opened it, and as I began to read, I had to smile. Once again, the universe was answering my questions, and wow, it hadn't wasted any time. Yes, some higher power seemed to be telling me, there is indeed a point to all this.

> Hi Amy,
>
> I have been closely following your stories on Brent Brents and I first of all just wanted to say thank you. Thank you for showing his humanity, thank you for looking for the cause of what happened and not just focusing on the effects, thank you for exposing the disgusting place we put people when society casts them out and thank you for caring enough to keep in contact with this man who so obviously is desperately reaching out for any friend in the world he can find. I was very touched by the letters he sent you and while I am horrified by his crimes I still tend to have the naive belief that humans are basically good and that he is actually one of the victims as well as the criminal.
>
> I was shocked and horrified to read your article when Brents was first arrested where in the third or fourth

paragraph it just so bluntly stated that he expected to die in prison. I have had my share of the seamier underside of society and have known many people that are in prisons and jails for various reasons so I know the culture that exists in our country's prisons, but what was shocking to me was that our society so glibly accepts that this is the way things are that they don't even question when something like that is printed in the newspaper as fact. It's just assumed, not questioned . . . where's the moral outrage that we, as a society, or the government we put all our trust in, will refuse to protect people we assign to be trapped between four walls in a place like this for half a lifetime or more? If we put them there, isn't it our obligation, as a government or as a society or just as compassionate human beings concerned with the plight of our brothers and sisters, to protect them, to make sure there is minimal violence and certainly not murder? It's not like they can run away if they want to, it's not like they can really protect themselves.

So I just wanted to say thank you and I hope something good comes of this whole thing. This has been on my mind for a long time now and after reading those letters today I feel you were the appropriate person to share this with.

Sincerely,
Angela

The Arapahoe County Justice Center in Centennial is a sprawling, modern-looking building with a large expanse of windows from nearly end to end. Yet the courtroom holding Brents' sentencing for his Aurora cases seemed small and felt claustrophobic. Or perhaps, I told myself, that is just because I don't want to be here anymore.

The only places to sit were benches directly behind the prosecution and defense tables, so I slid down one and waited for others to appear.

A few minutes later, Margaret stepped into the courtroom. Happily, I bounced out of my seat and walked over to her with a smile, and to my surprise, she frowned at me and made a small but emphatic "shoo" motion with her hands.

Chagrined, I ducked my head and returned to my bench. A few minutes later, I heard a voice in my ear and turned my head just enough to see her sitting behind me, nervously perched on the edge of the bench.

"Sorry," she explained quickly. "I just don't want anybody to know who I am."

I nodded. And with that, she quickly moved several benches away, as if I had nasty germs and was extremely contagious. But I understood. Talking to a reporter is one sure way to attract unwanted attention, especially for a victim who wants to protect her privacy.

I was busy surveying the courtroom and almost missed it when Brents was led in. I had been somewhat nervously bracing myself for his appearance, thinking he would surely have seen the coverage in the *Post* by now of his Denver sentencing, the printing of many of his letters that contained such deeply personal and painful details. It was one thing to agree to lay open your life for a reporter, I knew, and quite another to see the reality of it in print. Often, I got hit with a backlash of accusatory phone calls and emails. How would Brents react? Would he feel angry and exposed? Would he scream at me? Glare? Flip me off? Did he think I, too, had betrayed him?

I was hoping he had seen my story in Friday's paper that included the amazing detail of Margaret's forgiveness of him. Even if he hadn't read it, I figured Carrie would have told him, and perhaps it lessened the sting of scrutiny.

Escorted as usual by sheriff's deputies, he was walking to the table from a side door when he stopped in mid stride to turn in my direction, as if reading my thoughts.

"I'm OK with it," he said in a low voice to me, and suddenly benches creaked and clothes and papers rustled as nearly everyone in the courtroom turned to stare at me, the person Brents was talking to. I inwardly shrugged. I gave up caring what people thought of me a long time ago.

Then flanked by Carrie in a rust-colored suit and Karen in a cream one, Brents approached the podium, and the sentencing quickly began.

He pleaded guilty to first-degree burglary, sexual assault, menacing, and robbery in Margaret's case from February 4. I wanted to see the reaction on her face but I dared not turn around and risk giving her away again.

In the next case, Brents pleaded guilty to sexual assault on a child under fifteen with a pattern of abuse, from two incidents dating September 2004 to November 2004, as well as sexual assault on a child by a person in a position of trust and the enhanced charge of being a habitual offender against children.

And then it was time for the prosecutor in this case, John Tower, a tall, thin man with a thick mop of white hair who moved slowly and deliberately, to talk. He started with Margaret's case.

"It has basically destroyed the life that she knew," Tower said to the judge. "It is a very difficult period, with basically no end in sight."

I frowned at that last part. He seemed to be telling Margaret, "It's not going to get any better."

Sounding and looking like a dignified southern gentleman, Tower then thanked Carrie for her work and for helping the case be resolved.

He was hardly seated before Carrie was on her feet and talking. Clearly, she wanted Brents to be acknowledged too.

"He knows—and knew—that he was never going to leave prison," she said. "He did not want to cause any more harm than he had already caused."

But Brents had been chronically abused as a child, she said, including anal penetration from the time he was four.

"I'd like to ask the court to think about the last four-year-old child you talked to—a small, small child," she said, and I thought, Wow, she will never give up. She was clearly going to take advantage of what was probably her last opportunity to get her message across.

"When you expose a child so vulnerable to that kind of victimization, then that person has a high chance of sitting where Mr. Brents does. State services are not enough, and unfortunately, it was too late by the time he was twelve to undo the unspeakable horror that had been done to him. He does not want to hurt anyone else. And he doesn't want to make a statement because he realizes it's very difficult for the victims and their families. He has great remorse."

Carrie sat down, and then the mother of the eight-year-old boy, the woman Brents had dated, slowly walked to the podium. She read from a white piece of paper, her trembling voice so low that I leaned forward and strained to hear.

"I want you to know how you have affected our lives," she said, and as I looked to see his reaction, I noticed that Brents was not looking at her.

"We showed you love and kindness and took you into our family and all we received in return from you were lies, deception, and pain. My son's life has been forever changed by your actions. He has become guarded and distrustful of men because of you. He has paid a high price for loving and trusting you as a father and that price was his innocence.

"He showed you nothing but love and in return you showed him the evil in your soul. I no longer feel ashamed for believing your lies and thinking you deserved a second chance in life. It is you who should feel shame for manipulating your way into our lives in order to hurt my son. My only wish for you is to live a long life in prison, tormented by how badly you have hurt everyone who has ever come into your life."

She returned to her seat, and some women who appeared to be her family leaned in toward her, rubbing her arms and patting her back.

Now the prosecutor was back on his feet, his face twisted in disgust.

"Mr. Brents was responsible for a reign of terror," he said. "The defendant's own childhood of abuse may have contributed to his actions. He has now abused other children. Due to what he's done, he may have set other victims on the same path."

My stomach lurched. Had he really just said that in front of that boy's family? Didn't they have enough to cope with without the insinuation of a criminal future for their child?

I felt horrified and outraged for that boy's family. I wanted to throw something at Tower—my cell phone, my notebook, anything—before he opened his mouth again and said anything else so stupid. To my relief, he sat down.

Then the judge was reading Brents' sentence: burglary—twenty years; sexual assault—sixty years to life; robbery—ten years; sexual assault on a child—fifty years to life; sexual assault on a child by a person of trust—fifty years to life.

He dismissed the other two counts.

I did quick math—the sentence was nearly 200 more years, making a grand total of a little more than 1,500.

As everyone stood to leave the courtroom, Brents smiled at Carrie, a grin of relief, and she smiled back.

At that, an angry murmur broke out in the courtroom.

I hurried to catch the boy's mother before she left—I'd had trouble hearing her, and I needed to double-check what she'd said in her statement. After I identified myself and told her what I wanted, she surprised me by pulling the paper out of her purse and handing it to me.

"Keep it," she said.

And then some of the other family members—what appeared to be a mixture of parents, grandparents, and adult children—turned toward me, looking worried. I realized they had a question for me, so I stood still and waited expectantly. Finally, an older woman spoke.

"Do you think our boy's going to grow up and be like Brents?"

Oh, God. Why ask me? was my first thought, followed swiftly by the understanding that it was because they considered me the resident expert on Brents. And the question tugged at my heart. I silently cursed Tower as I looked at their concerned faces and also saw their arms around one another and their hands clasped together, all huddled closely as if taking comfort by standing together as one.

Normally I would shy away from giving any opinion to anyone on a story. Normally I would say "I'm sorry, it's not for me to speculate" before scurrying safely away.

Not now.

I chose my words carefully. "In cases like Brents, where an abused child has grown up to be a predator, it's usually after years of horrific and violent abuse, where no one intervened to help, no one cared. In your boy's case, his abuse, while awful, was short-lived, and you caught it right away and got him help. His case is not like Brents'. And besides, your boy has something that Brents did not have—he has all of you. And you clearly love him very much, and you clearly love each other."

My throat started to tighten.

"He's going to be fine," I said to all their hopeful faces. Turning away, I coughed as if to clear a frog out of my throat.

A man who I found out was the boy's father then walked up to me and tapped me on the shoulder, and I turned to him.

"I don't think he's going to be majorly damaged from it," he said, and we nodded at each other in agreement.

July 20, 2005

Dear Amy, A.K.A. Glenda (the good witch of the east),

    Words cannot express my gratitude or my sincere relief to you. You are a champion . . . Amy don't be deppressed. Some things in our Lives hurt even when we do everything we can to protect ourselves from them. You tried to protect yourself from me. Just as I tried to protect myself from you. Your human Amy, your sincere, caring, honest and you posses personal qualities that alot of people don't posses . . . You felt guilty for having empathy for me. I do promise you This Amy Having Empathy is one of your better qualities. It will not affect your writing, I believe if anything it will make you better and lead you to bigger and better stories. When I would talk with you I could feel and hear you battle with yourself, I felt for you. Amy I have been Like a Tornado in most peoples lives. I don't want to do that with you. I want to see us achieve our goals and I want you to know you are real to me. I get scared sometimes, I catch myself Just being me, and I feel like I don't deserve to be me . . . I am sorry that you feel hurt and sorrow, I am sorry you feel empathy because I know its painful. Amy you can't help All of my victims nor can you help all The prostitutes or junkies. God knows you'll try. But don't destroy yourself in the process . . . Thank you Amy

    Take care Always
    Brents

NINETEEN

Aftermath

One of my favorite books to read the boys when they were little was *Oh, the Places You'll Go!* by Dr. Seuss.

At bedtime we would pile a small stack of books on my bed and I would build a backrest of pillows before we'd cuddle up, their short legs in their footie pajamas mingling with my longer ones in my sweats. I usually saved *Oh, the Places You'll Go!* for last. I loved it for its hopefulness: "Wherever you fly, you'll be the best of the best." I think I also liked it because it reminded me not just of the ups and downs of life in general, but specifically of being a player in the seesaw world of news: "I'm sorry to say so, but, sadly, it's true that Bang-ups and Hang-ups *can* happen to you."

Yup, Dr. Seuss had it right. High and low. I sometimes wondered why I didn't get whiplash.

The high: a flood of emails and phone calls from an assortment of readers, thanking me for my Brents coverage:

"I was truly touched by your article on Brent Brents as well as other pieces about him and the quote from him when he said he was not afraid of dying per se but afraid of dying without having done anything good. I was heartbroken when I read that . . ."

"I think he is a victim of our society as much as his victims are also a victim of society, he being the channel for the sickness to move through."

"Brent Brents is not pure evil. He is simply a man who cannot control his actions without the assistance of others. He is genuine in his remorse and he is saddened by his lack of control. He knows that he cannot control his actions and he is pleading for help."

"If we simply cast him off as 'pure evil' or a 'bad seed' then we neglect the fact that this could have been prevented."

The low: an editor appearing at my desk to tell me that Michael Roberts, the media columnist from *Westword*, wanted to talk to me about Brents.

It was Monday, July 11, following Friday's sentencing in Aurora, and I was in pretty good spirits. Until I was told Roberts was on the phone.

"I have some questions for you, and I'll just go down the list," he said nearly as soon as I picked up the line.

"First question: Did you send Brents a photo of yourself, as is rumored?"

And just like that, my temper lit. My reply was as swift as his question.

"Off the record, Mike?" I asked, and waited.

"OK," he confirmed.

But still I repeated it. "Off the record?"

"Yes."

"Fuck you. Fuck you for asking that question. I'm not gonna talk to you."

And I hung up.

Less than five minutes later, one of the editors was standing next to me, clearing his throat uncomfortably while I ignored him and stared at my computer screen, trying to appear as if I were riveted by fascinating email.

"You really should give Michael Roberts an interview," he said.

"Nope."

"And he says you sent Brents a picture of yourself. Did you?"

I shook my head as my eyes narrowed, and despite my attempts to contain my irritation, I found myself glaring at him. Et tu, Brutus? I thought. "No, I never sent him a picture. And p.s., he never asked for one, either."

"Well, I still need to get a statement from you."

"OK," I said, spinning around in my wheeled chair to face him. "My statement is short: 'Fuck you.'"

He blinked and then eyed me curiously, as if trying to figure out whether I was joking, or whether I was going to start speaking in tongues or perhaps leap out of the chair and scream.

In return, I tried to grin cheerfully at him, although I was still angry, so the result ended up with me pulling my lips back from my teeth. In the animal kingdom, I thought, that's what we call a snarl. Not a good way to reassure him that while he might think me crazy, he didn't need to fear I was going to flip out. Not then, anyway.

Faced with clear insubordination, he took the only route he knew: dictatorship.

"Harrumph," he began, and I realized with some amusement that it was the first time I had actually ever heard someone make that sound. "It's best that you talk to him. So I expect you to call him back. Soon."

He then turned and left. Cursing, I looked up Robert's number and dialed it, punching each digit with irritation.

Maybe I had to talk to Roberts, I thought, but it didn't have to be officially.

"OK, I'll talk to you," I told him when he answered his phone, "but only on background, all of it off the record. Agreed?"

"Agreed," Roberts said, sounding cheerful. I decided to let that go.

I took a deep breath and thought, What the hell, take a chance.

So for the next several minutes, I explained it all to him: Other female reporters had flirted to try to lure Brents into an interview—and some had indeed sent him photos—but not me, and Roberts could look in his case file for proof. I had convinced Brents in that first letter to call me by telling him I had visited his mom and sister. No, I didn't have copies of my letters to him because I wrote them all by hand. I only typed one and it felt so contrived and impersonal that way that I hadn't done it again (Brents had told me he'd return my letters at some point, but the county jail threw the first batch away in one of their many shakedowns of his cell. I would later get the others back). I had returned from court to find that an editor had rummaged through my desk and given the letters to everyone to write, and I had tried my best to keep the coverage from being sensationalistic.

And I realized in a way I was Mary, mother of God to Brents, which was why he ingratiated himself to me, but that didn't mean I had said or done anything unethical or inappropriate, because I hadn't.

Most of all, though, every letter from him with a graphic description of violence had felt like small, sharp daggers piercing my heart, leaving it permanently wounded, but I had embarked on this project because I felt it was important to look at sexual assault from the perspective of the perpetrator in order to learn the "why."

And then I was out of breath and out of resolve. I went silent, thinking, *I need to go live in a cave.*

It's a joke I often make to Matt or to my friends, but it always turns tail on me. I no sooner throw up my hands and contemplate abandoning my fellow hopelessly flawed humans for a solitary life in a mountain cave, forevermore blithely existing on dried beans and chocolate, when somebody invariably, unintentionally, gives me reason to again believe in our species.

As Roberts did in the next moment.

"Wow," he said in a low voice after a long pause. "That certainly changes things. Thank you very much for telling me all that, and I promise I won't quote you on any of it. But it's good to know . . . And this whole thing must have been really hard."

"Yes, it was," I admitted.

That would be the last time he would call me with an offensive question. After that, our relationship changed. And ten days later, when the piece ran in *Westword*, it did contain a garish caricature cartoon of Brents, blowing a kiss above manacled hands, and the headline "Yours Truly?"

But the story's tone was not lurid, and it even defended me.

On July 8, confessed serial rapist Brent J. Brents, who'd received an epic 1,319-year sentence in Denver two days earlier, appeared in Arapahoe County Court to learn how many more theoretical decades he would be ordered to serve for his heinous behavior in that jurisdiction. While there, according to observers, Brents didn't look at or acknowledge any of his victims or their relatives, on hand to watch his prison term lengthen by another 190 years. Instead, he focused on *Denver Post* reporter Amy Herdy, to whom he'd granted exclusive access following his February arrest. Brents mouthed a greeting and the words "I'm okay with it" to her, in apparent reference to Herdy's writings about him.

Eyebrows that shot skyward over this incident had been in the same position on July 6, when the *Post* put extracts from Brent's journal and numerous letters he'd written to Herdy in recent months on its website. His tone in assorted spelling-challenged passages was often very personal. On June 8, he asked Herdy to sit at a hearing in a place "where I can see you without too much trouble" and declared, "[It] realy was good to hear your voice today . . . I know you trust me and won't give up on me." In a note dated the next day, he concluded a description of his return to stir in Denver County with the line "I'm tired and thought I'd let the only person who might care know I am back in Denver." And his June 13 missive ended on an even more flirtatious note that, considering the person who penned it, came across as undeniably creepy: "Amy I will always be fiercely loyal to you . . . I look forward to a visit from a long cool woman in a black dress."

This material provides a greater understanding of Brents, whose attempts to come across like a regular guy only underscore how dangerous and disturbed he is. Yet it also makes implications about Herdy's conduct that may very well be inaccurate. She's the most unlikely person imaginable to treat a rapist coyly due to her coauthorship (with colleague Miles Moffeit) of powerful, compassionate articles about sexual assaults on military bases, which made up what was arguably the strongest series the *Post* has published during the past few years. Just because Brents affected a beyond-friendly tone in his correspondence to her and was overtly solicitous toward her in public doesn't mean she led him on in any way.

Unfortunately, the *Post* figuratively hung Herdy out to dry because of the way it presented the letters. Had the paper included Herdy's own dispatches, Brents' hints of a personal relationship would probably have been revealed to be mere delusions. An introduction describing the aspects of Brents' character that led him to assume a false intimacy might have worked as an alternative or the portions of the letters addressed directly to Herdy could have been excised. Instead, the *Post* included a brief "discretion advised" warning and ran Brents' cozy comments sans additional context, thereby inviting speculation that Herdy crossed the line in search of a scoop.

Later, one of the editors stopped by my desk in one of the few expressions of regret I would see from management over how the Brents letters had been presented.

"Roberts was right," he said simply. "We could have handled that better. We did hang you out to dry."

It was the closest thing to an apology I would get.

I had not heard from Brents. I would later find out that after being sentenced in Aurora, Denver detectives whisked him away to question him for several hours about the homicide of a woman in a neighborhood he frequented. What's more, Brents actually knew the victim. Yet nearly three years later, another man would confess to her murder, and that man's DNA would be matched to the crime scene.

The official word was that Brents had been taken to the Denver diagnostic center to await transfer to an out-of-state prison. No visitors were allowed at the center, so all I could do was wait for him to contact me again, because in my gut, I didn't feel like it was over. I found myself wondering what the aftermath was like for him—whether he was being retaliated against, or whether he had gone on the offensive and was lashing out at everyone in pure reactive rage.

More importantly, I was convinced that I was not done writing about him. There was more to be learned from Brents, of that I was certain; I just didn't know what yet. The older I get, the more I know that not everything is revealed on the timetable you'd like it to be.

I know that the only certainty about life is that it will surprise you.

On July 13, five days after Brents was sentenced in Aurora, I found myself again sitting in a courtroom for a story, only this time it was back in Denver, and the familiar judge, Marcucci, was tasked with the unenviable job of trying to mete out justice to prostitutes who appeared before him on solicitation charges.

But this was not a generic story on prostitution. There was only one woman whose story I really wanted to hear: Kim, the mother of Aida Bergfeld, the young woman who had been kidnapped and raped by Brents, who had no doubt saved Tiffany Engle's life by stopping him from continuing to choke her, and who had been with him when he was captured only to later die from a drug overdose.

After Aida died, Kim embarked on a drug binge that culminated in her arrest and court-ordered rehabilitation. As part of that rehabilitation program, she was appearing in court, and I had wasted no time in asking her for an interview. She agreed, so bailiffs escorted us to a small, windowless room off the courtroom. We sat in metal chairs and I stared at her in fascination.

At forty-nine, Kim had jet black hair and dressed like a high school Goth kid, wearing a black tank top, a black armband imprinted with her daughter's date of death on her left bicep, and baggy black jeans, rolled up to reveal the only splash of color on her person, hot pink flip-flops. Despite the youthful clothing and her legal entanglement (one of apparently many), she had a mystical worldliness to her that said I know the secrets of the minds of men who move within the regal skyscrapers as well as the filthy underbelly of the city, and I'm weary of it all.

She said she didn't go to Brents' sentencing because "I just couldn't deal with it."

Brents did not beat her daughter, she said, although she had marks on her wrists where he had bound her.

Aida had felt sorry for Brents, Kim told me, and shared with her mother that they had talked a lot. "Whatever he said to her burdened her." Kim added that her daughter had told her, "I feel incredible pain that will never, ever go away."

After that, Aida started spiraling, using cocaine and heroin. "I think she kept self-medicating," Kim said.

Shortly after being questioned by police, Aida again overdosed, but this time she did not recover. She ran out of her mother's house and gasped, "Oh, Momma, I think I've done too much," before collapsing on the lawn, her head cradled by a pillow of snow.

She slipped into a coma and died days later, on her twenty-eighth birthday, April 10, 2005, with a beautiful expression on her face, her mother said.

Kim's grief was fierce and laced with guilt. "I chased the dragon and it chased me back, but it didn't bite me—it bit my child," she told me, vowing to stay clean and find a new purpose.

"My whole life centered around her," she said. "I still can't believe she's gone."

Yet she chose to forgive Brent. "To hang on to that anger is only going to slow me down. Pain is a heavy force of its own. To live is to suffer. I tried to avoid pain to begin with and ended up colliding with it . . . It takes a knife to make a flute."

That afternoon I sat at my desk and stared at a blank computer screen, still mulling over the experience of meeting Kim. As the interview had ended and I stood to leave, she had reached out and taken my hands firmly in hers, like an old-world gypsy fortune-teller. Fixing her black-lined eyes on me, she said, "You have the gift of being a seer, and sometimes you try to run away from it. Don't. Remember, people are put in our lives for a reason."

I had smiled at her in amusement, thanked her, and left. But now, sitting at my desk, I had to admit I'd been slightly unsettled by her frank observation. I wasn't used to being on the receiving end of anyone's scrutiny, except for Brents, and I always chalked it up to the fact he had very few other people to focus on.

Recalling her words brought Brents to mind. I had sent him envelopes and stamps after his sentencing along with a note but still hadn't heard from him. I wondered if anyone else was still writing to him.

Every once in a while during the coverage of his case, readers would call me and ask how they could go about sending him a letter. Most of the time I simply would refer them to the jail—if I started becoming a resource guide for the public, I'd get very little else done. But one scripture-quoting woman named Irene had sounded particularly elderly and frail, her voice thin and reedy on the phone, so I took pity on her. Patiently, I explained to her that she needed to use Brent's Colorado Department of Corrections number—"They have numbers? Oh, my," she said—along with his name on every letter. She blessed me and hung up. Brents later mentioned to me that he had started receiving letters from her and so had written her back, and I had lumped her into the harmless but well-meaning category of Those Interested in Saving Brents' Soul.

Little did I know that soon, Irene would make it clear she wanted much more from him. Much, much more.

But for now, still pondering Kim's words, I realized that even while I wondered about Brents every day, I consciously avoided giving him much thought because the whole situation depressed me. And my own avoidance bothered me, as if I had used him, draining him dry of information, and now that I was done, I was going to just walk away.

I could at least tell him about the unexpected reactions from readers.

So I pulled out a piece of paper and once again began to write, even though it was painful.

July 14, 2005
Hi, Brent,

So much has happened so quickly—it was a bad week, trying to write about your sentencing . . . And it has already accomplished what you hoped: Raised awareness from readers. The emails blew me away. I had braced myself for a barrage of hate mail, and only received 2 negative ones—1 from a nut & the other from some woman who claimed to be a Harvard psychologist who scolded me for writing you, saying I should leave the job of trying to figure you out to "experts."

Anyway—the emails: People said thank you—for helping them see the whole situation in another light, for showing that you are human, and that you have your own hell to contend with . . .

And understanding is everything. It changes perception and attitudes and ultimately, can change actions or behavior. One woman who wrote me is studying to be a counselor—she said she wanted to just hate you and dismiss you as "evil" but now she can't, and she feels sorrow and empathy instead. So if she goes on to work with clients such as yourself—she'll try harder to help. And so it spreads—like ripples on a pond.

Meanwhile, Westword called me and asked about you. The columnist said, "My sources say that Brents whispered to you in court . . . don't you think that's crossing the line for you as a journalist? Did you indeed send him a picture of yourself, as is rumored?"—and other such questions along those lines. They all implied the same thing: That I stepped over the line with you, used "feminine wiles" to entice you and lure you to talk to me. How else, or why else, would he have opened up to you?—I was so angry. I told him no comment.

My editor also asked, Did you really send him a picture?

I gave him a dirty look & said No, I didn't & he never asked for one, either. He said, What do you want me to say to him (the columnist)?—and I said, Tell him, Fuck you.

Who knows what he'll write, but I have a feeling it won't be kind. I guess other reporters in this city are miffed and that's the best way they can strike at me. My editor asked me, Why did you agree not to publish anything until after he's sentenced? And I replied, Why not? My word to him is the same as it is for anyone else, regardless of what he's been accused of or what he's done . . .

Well, now, frankly, I'm sorrowful. Everything about this is depressing . . .

Take care of yourself.

Stay alive, please.

Amy

A few days later, I realized Brent deserved to know that like Margaret, Kim had found a way to forgive him. It was a topic we rarely discussed because he maintained he didn't deserve anyone's grace. Yet they still offered.

7-18-05

Hi Brent,

I'll send you a copy of the story. We also put excerpts of your writing on the website—the journals, or letters, I mean—that explain more than any story ever could. It's all there—your childhood, your despair . . . Yes, I kept my word. We published the apology, word for word.

Now here's the amazing part: I talked to Aida's mom. She said to tell you that she doesn't hate you, that she can't hate you. Somehow, she said, you touched her daughter—in that things you told her broke her heart for you. I'm writing a story about Aida's mom—she was also a prostitute & heroin addict, and now, because of Aida's death she's trying to go straight.

    Anyway, Aida's mom, Kim, is very Goth looking—a former fortune-teller who believes strongly in other lives. She told me that everyone who impacts our life in this lifetime is someone we knew before, and the souls agreed to meet again in order to accomplish something or learn something from each other or have closure. Even if it's traumatic, such as being raped or abused or even murdered. And that actually, for someone to murder you is agreed only between souls who were intimate (I'm not sure how that works for mass homicides or terrorists in another life?). But I do believe, as strange as this may sound, that we choose our lives and our fate. If someone gets cancer, I believe it's because they decided that before that life began, to learn from it or gain something from its struggle or suffering.

    I still believe that with you. And in a letter that was returned to me that I sent you to co. jail—I used to have guilt for feeling empathy for you. You were right. I did, and I don't anymore. Don't get me wrong—I don't pity you. I recognize the horror of what you've done. But I mourn the person you started as, and the person you longed to be, and the glimpses of the man you allow me to see. It's all so very sad. I'll never be the same for knowing you, and I'm not embarrassed to say so. I didn't think you would impact my life this way, but not a day goes by that I don't think about it all, and wonder how you are, and how your victims are. I wonder if you're still alive or if at that moment, some guard is trying to extract some measure of what his/her warped head thinks is justice . . .

    And as far as any other victims—how can I find them? Mostly the kids—the teenagers—where were they? I want to try to find them. They deserve to be helped, if that's possible . . .

Lie low, stay alive. Focus.

I'll send this off & then send you another that is more upbeat. Right now I feel pretty depressed, to be honest. And I can't imagine how you feel.

Amy

9-1-05

    Ok so I guess its time to Ask you about my Ashes. Ive asked The only other person I know to do it. Its against her religion and she's to damn old to go to the Mtns. Fuck I wish I could talk to you in person about this shit. Amy I aint gonna do harry carry ok. I'm stressing hard because of uncertainty. I don't want to be in a prison cemetery with a concrete stick that says 61549. Maybe I don't have a choice, maybe this is part of that Just Reward. I know it's a tough thing to think about Amy. I do, I ask only that you don't let them keep me alive if I'm in a coma and To spread my Ashes in the Roosevelt somewhere you choose or bury me in my urn somewhere where civilization can't swallow me up. How you do it will be up to you. Theres a cemetery between Kiowa and Elizabeth that is new and might take Indegent burials. But I doubt they would take me. Plus there are no trees there. I'd rather be spread free. Talk to me Amy. I know as you Always Tell me This is a tough one. But you're a tough lady.

    Peace,
    Brent

TWENTY

Letters

The dog days of summer in Denver stretched on and on like endless miles of heat-shimmered blacktop highway. As the Little People returned to school, I slipped back into a routine of working long hours and swallowing the stress that came with it.

Maybe I did it to cover up the heartache I'd carried ever since I started covering Brents' case, a sadness that persisted with every letter. I had no idea what role I was going to continue to play in his life, or he in mine.

We just kept writing.

> 9-6-05
> Amy,
> The sarrow, The guilt, The hurt Let it all go with me if I die. Think about the change in both of us. Think about the laughs so far few but still good. Think about this You were my first real friend and Not once did I ever Lie to you or deceive you. But think about This you have someone to watch over you. Amy don't try to harden your heart. Guard it if you must but enjoy what I give to you. That's what I do with you. Miss Cynical hard Nosed Journalist.
> Peace,
> Brent

10-7-05
Amy,

Hello. Well This is probably gonna be a touchy one. So I'll get right to it. First of all I am Not bitching or Even writing with an attitude. This Letter is Actualy about my Respect and care for you. So I need to Let you know some things and then ask you a question and I need the True Amy answer Ok.

First let me say this. I can never begin to tell you how much I appreciate you. You could have been a whole different person. You are The first person I have ever been able to be completely and brutaly honest with. You have never betrayed me nor I believe even thought about it. You haven't Felt sorry for me or tried to humiliate me. You've been fair and honorable from the beginning.

I know you've grown to Like me and even care for me. A gift I'll never be able to forget. I'll always cherish your friendship. And Laugh at how you say I can't be your friend. Your good people Amy Herdy.

Now the question actually questions.

1. Do you realy want to take care of my Ashes for me?
2. Will you be able to make sure my medical declaration of treatment will be carried out?
3. Will you execute my will as I ask?
4. If I could make other arrangements would you prefer that?
5. If so will you attend my services?

Don't fret I won't take it as a betrayal If you realy don't want to do this Amy. I'm asking you to look into your heart and tell me the truth ok.

Thank you.
Peace
Brent

10-17-05
Amy,

There is good in me a deep need to Love and be Loved, but a very real inability to function properly without the control and restraint of an institution. No matter how badly I desire to be "normal" I Never can or will be. I fully realize that. As each has passed over the last 2 ½ years I've known I was getting steadily worse. Somehow I managed to get by, I know now that whatever is wrong is progressing at an alarming rate. Things are happening mentally which I have no control over. Loss of memory (short term), Bouts of extreme paranoia, more frequent blackouts. The Dr. told me my brain may be acting in self defense who knows. All I know is a part of my brain is going back to a childlike state, Fantacies, tantrums, Need, fear. I have to work extremely hard to stay grounded here in first person Reality.

So at times when I get as I am now where my mind cartwheels thru a gammit of emotions from Rage to dispair I sit down and write stuff to you. It's Not that I expect you to understand what its Like, or even feel empathy or sympathy. Its because I know you actualy care and your realy interested in the hows and whys. I know in some ways I am your experiment or study model I guess. I hate it but yet I see genuine enterest from you to serve a greater purpose. I guess I realy want to say thank you for hangin tough. I know I got some realy deep shit goin on. I know some of it is painful for you too. Yes I suppose you could say I have a severe thing about abandonment. Wanting to be loved etc. Funny thing is though I can't bring myself to worry as much about that. Instead I somehow gained a conscience . . . Even that will eventually give in to the rot in my mind. My victims will have the ultimate revenge in the Long run. Someday I know It will destroy my brain completely. I have come to understand the truth about who and what I am. And how my future will constantly be shaped by the steady and unrelenting compulsion in my brain. It couldn't be any clearer if I were staked in a Hot Desert with the Vultures circling high above. Death will come soon and they know it. My brain is a vulture circling on itself.

Ok sweetheart what gives, Job Shit realy stressin you out that Bad? Have you been getting assigned shitty stories? Are you getting punished because of me? I know yours can be a stressful one, but whats going on? Its Not Like you to say you want to quit your job. Well shit Amy try not to go postal huh. Kiddin. I know you have to work hard. Just be good to yourself when you get home, Love the animals Love yourself (run) read the funnies. Take care of yourself.

I'm outa here.

Peace

Brent

p.s. Tell Pike Hi and seriously be Good to yourself. Play Another One Bites the Dust at max volume and picture some asshole editors face and practice scissor kicks or snap kicks.

Thur 10-20-05

Hi Brent,

Rotten penpal—me. This week has truly sucked, pardon the language. Thanks for your letters, tho . . .

Work: I do hate my job rt now. I would quit but I'm too responsible—I have a house (so, mortgage) and bills to pay. And I don't always hate it, just rt now. I've worked really hard this past week on that Asian massage parlor story, & I wrote it today, & it will be edited tomorrow, & that's o.k. So I'm literally lying on the couch, reading your letters that I only now have had time to get to, & Callie is lying on my feet. I'm in a great mood bc the hard part is done. The phone rings—my cell phone—it's work. I think, breaking news? & answer, it's an editor, who proceeds to tell me that when I come in tomorrow, I need to rewrite my story—she doesn't like it. And am I covering the news conference on Sun? she asks, & I said, NO, & she said why not?—and I said, b/c I don't work on weekends. I hung up, good mood gone, instant headache.

    A newsroom is a voracious beast that will gobble you up if you let it. I've seen it destroy people—they end up with bad health or busted relationships or breakdowns or just living there—& I'm trying to have a life. That means saying, No, I won't work more than 8 hours a day for free, or come in on weekends, or stay late.

    The editor I wanted to drop kick said to me, We can hire 2 eager reporters for what we pay you, and they won't fight us about what we tell them to do! I just shrugged. I know I'm good at what I do, & it makes them crazy . . .

    I would smile when I quit. And once I was done, I swear, I'd get a job working the counter at Starbucks before I'd go back. Enough about me now.

    I'm concerned for you. The headaches and blackouts sound awful. Can they give you any medication? And if writing to me helps, then write. Or talk out loud. Or pace, or do my pushups for me.

    You know, you started out as simply a case study. But it's changed.

    I wish I could offer you words that would help. I'd wish you peace. But hmm, perhaps I need to find peace in my own life before I offer it to you, huh?

    I mostly think that life is unfair. I honestly believe that anyone born to your circumstances would have either died or become violent like you did. The child Brent never stood a chance . . .

    I don't know how to tell you to find the strength to fight

the demons in your head, but you have to. If the vultures win, where will you be? So hang tough, please.

But know that no matter what, I'll still be here.

And stop worrying about me. No, I'm not getting shitty stories b/c of you. I do good stories—I find my own—but editors don't like me b/c I have attitude. Oh well . . .

So I'm off to take some Advil & get some sleep. I'm tired & tomorrow is another battle.

YOU take care of YOURSELF.

Deal?

Fight the good fight, Brent.

Amy

Mon. 11-7-05
Hi Brent,

Well, it's a true Monday—I'm tired, & struggling today. Sorry I'm not more cheery!—but I wanted to write and say Hey, and let you know I'm still here . . .

On to a story—a semi flipped off I-25 & crushed some guy. My story: To figure out who he was. Then, they want me to do a story on the child homicide rate in Colorado—it's one of the highest in the nation. I'm supposed to find out why. I talked to a woman this morning at the Denver Center for Crime and she said she thinks it's because no one intervenes in time. And I thought of you.

Ok, you. Take care. Stay alive. Walk away from fights. I'll be more cheerful soon.

Amy

11-12-05
Amy,

I got your letter today. Oh but I am disapointed girl, you forgot to add your sending nude photos to me, using your Feminine wiles, sending me Love Letters and of course the unforgettable moment of my making eye contact and whispering to you in the courtroom to your list of Amy Herdy's 10 ways to get a story from a Lonely desparate psychopath. I hope I make you Laugh the way you do me. This world is Just to fuckin serious sometimes . . . No seriously who gives a shit if theres something as innocent as ooh a friendship between us. As long as you didn't compromise the so called integrity of the paper what fuckin beeswax is it of theres . . . Can you tell I'm not Liking some of the people on your planet . . .

Be cool Rockstar Give the animal pack my love. Take care of yourself Amy and no spin kicks to editor's Heads. Peace girl.

I'm outta Here
Brent

11-18-05
By Brent Brents

As A Child I set out on a journey, never sure what it was I was searching for. I came across an oger and his mate. They ate my childs inner self. Consumed his ennocense. I was Lost, but as Alone and tortured as I was I could go nowhere else for I was but only a child. Soon I became like the oger. Primal and feral. Seeking flesh day and night. Hunting souls to replace my own Lost soul. Thinking my Journey had come to an end, but not realizing It had only Just begun. I began to hear a voice, A whisper. It is out there closer than you know.

I rode with dragons, fought with devils. I raped pillaged and plundered the lives of the ennocent. I Robbed from the Rich and took from the poor. And still my soul was Lost. I ate the hearts of virgin maidens, bedded down easy women and Ladies of the night. I derived pleasure from enflicting pain and torture upon women and children. And still I Was only a child.

I was capture by the king's men. Thrown into the darkest regions of the dungeon. I Lived with beasts of men, heard tales of woe. I Learned to survive by the sword and shank, poison and pen. I was used by guards and my keepers. I ate the souls of my fellow prisoners. And still I was Lost.

One day the King released me, and I heard the voice; It is closer than ever, you only have to seek it out. And so once again I set off on my Journey. I came across the ogers mate, Still she stirred her poison brew of denial and seduction. But I was stronger now I did not fear her any Longer. So I moved on. The Sun was bright and hurt my eyes. I again found myself eating souls by the shadows of night. And still I was Lost.

Do Some thing good with your Life. How asks the child for I am still as one with him. What he thinks I think, what he sees I see. What he does I do. How Can I Live as an oger and do good. I need to die.

Before she could stop herself she grabbed the child No child you must never wish to die. Yes the oger is part of you but you child are stronger There is a greater good in you. Promise me child you'll never kill yourself. You can still do good. Promise. She hugged the child fearcely. What are you doing maiden? the people and the Kings screamed in unison. As the maiden Looked at the people and the kings, They had the Faces of ogers and children. In a bucket of water at her feet the maiden SAW her own Reflection. Staring back at her was an oger and a child.

And I was found.

11-22-05
Hi Brent,
    Ok, as penpals go, I know I tanked these past 2 weeks. I remember jotting you a quick note about the phone—but I was on wicked deadline for the past 10 days. That story

of the guy who quit breathing while DPD was taking him into custody (I'll send you some of the stories). Man, I hate that story. I worked with another reporter—and we were at it for 12, 14 hr days, every day. The family of the guy in the hospital is pretty out there, & they were hard to deal with, to say the least. There were new developments at deadline almost every day, so had to rewrite until 9, 10, 11, midnight. I know this seems stupid to bitch about, but it's hard to describe what working a story like that does. The other reporter, Felisa, & I worked that neighborhood around the clock, trying to find someone who saw what happened. It happened at 11th & Xenia, in E Denver, near a 7-11 on Yosemite. Lovely area. Crackheads galore. We were out there at 10 pm one night and I was not happy about it.

So, I feel like I lost a week of my life. I don't remember eating much except junk on the run. I didn't run or work out, because by the time I got home I was too wiped out.

I didn't go to the grocery, I didn't cook, I didn't write you, I didn't pay bills, I didn't do anything else. I had one friend who left messages for me, saying, Are you Ok? I'm worried about you! Where are you?—I called her back & said, Just working.

So, Saturday I tried to get caught up—I cleaned all day, did laundry, ran w/ Pike, walked puppy (more on him in a minute).

By Sat nite I was feeling a little sick. By Sun I was full out sick (are you seeing a pattern here?) and just lay around all day feeling like crap. Yesterday I felt better, & did errands like grocery, took my car in for an oil change & to change the tires to snow tires (ah, yes, it's that time of year!) and actually worked Pike on a trail, ran, did weights, FINALLY read your letters, & so here I am . . .

I hope you haven't freaked, thinking I'm ignoring you. It's hard to explain what that kind of work pace does. Oh,

Felisa got sick, too, and she was more exhausted than me, & she's younger (no age jokes here, please) . . .

So, the puppy is a little terror. He has the SWEETEST face, & the worst temper. I kept Pike away from him for the first 10 days—only let him sniff while I held him, or watch while he scampered around so Pike would get used to something that small that runs fast, & not trigger his prey drive (which is high) to pounce on it and kill it. But now, they play, & it's pretty cute . . . Pike is pretty patient with him, and lets the puppy chew on him. They even have shared a bone, which is comical, b/c the puppy is roughly the size of Pike's nose.

I'll be a better writer (pen pal) this week. It was all more a reminder why I need to get out of this business. Can't you see me, typing away at a desk in front of a big window with a view of the ocean? I can. It's what I hold on to . . .

So how is it when you are with GP—General Population? Is it cool, or is anyone targeting you? . . . Just make smart decisions and be careful. Don't get caught up in the politics—stay clean.

Ok, here's my plan today: Post office (I also missed my mom's birthday). Take my car for an emissions test. Run. Walk puppy. WRITE. And maybe nap.

You stay alive & I'll slow down.

Deal?

Amy

11-26-05

My Rockstar,

I was Just sitting here Thinking about you and writing down songs for you to burn on a CD that you can Listen to while you run or on your way to work or home, one that will wake you up, motivate you, put a sparkle back in those awesome eyes of yours, Bring your beautiful spirit to the surface. As I am doing this, the cop opens my trap in the door and Lays 1 Letter on my trap. Then I notice it's a card. Hmm Who would be sending me a card. So I get up and see your Me Herdy and the tears filled my eyes. I love Maya Angelou Amy. The way you have managed all this time to reach deep inside of me and comfort me, steady me and even be tough when I needed it, realy is a testament to your true heart. I Needed you Amy and you have been there through it all. You weren't ever realy a bitch to me but your cynicism was often evident. I know it hasn't been easy for you. Just as I know Inside you have realy changed. You know Roberts was right about one thing I do have a very deep affection for you. But what he fails to see is that Life isn't always black and white. The grey area is full of mystery and Greater things than ourselves. My affections isn't about possesing you, sexualizing you or tearing your soul from you. Its about giving, honesty, compasion. When I think of you Its not about what I can get from you. Its about how to give to you. Happiness, enjoyment, Reassurance, confidence. How to Love you and care for you without causing your destruction.

    I realize no matter how much you Love your work it is grinding your spirit away. It has poisoned you callust your heart. So be free Amy, go find your dreams and Live them.

    I'm always here for you. Not that I could go anywhere. ☺

Be true to yourself. Give the pack my love.

Later Gator

Brent

Sat. 11-26-05

Hi Brent,

    Ok, life is slowing. I'm getting caught up on all the basics, like food & sleep, & the extras—like re-reading your last 10 letters. I love how you slip staggering phrases in the middle of your letters—like saying casually, Had a few emotional days—and then you say (broke down and died inside). WHAT? What is that supposed to mean? Where is that from—getting transferred again? You need to expound, please. Why were you feeling that way?

Thank you for the card. Once again, we have the same thought and it crisscrosses in the mail. I started laughing as soon as I saw the envelope.

As for meth or vodka—well, sorry, they're just not in the training regime. Temporary solutions that don't really help. Endorphins are much better (well, I'm not speaking from experience, I've never done meth) (& I'm not a vodka drinker, either, although I have tried it, more of a merlot person).

Thanks for the fairy tale—well, I'm undergoing my own transformation, aren't I? You know, I don't keep a journal. I don't meditate—I always say if I sit in a quiet, darkened room I'll just fall asleep (recreational sleeper, I can sleep anywhere, anytime) so perhaps writing to you is the most I examine my life. And reading your astute observations. Yes, I need to leave that job—it's killing me. More than that— the whole empathy issue.

Yes, I've struggled with it, and will some more, I know— all the conflicting feelings of empathy & compassion & guilt for having them & for not being able to hate you. Because I mull over some of the crimes—all the details—& sometimes it hits me, the full magnitude of it all, and even then I can't hate you.

So yes, as you said, we need to get people thinking about a solution other than the systems answer.

So, you made other arrangements for your medical wishes? Does that mean you no longer want me to sprinkle your ashes?

And oh, Pike & I had a come to Jesus meeting, and not the kind that I suspect Irene talks to you about.

Ok, more later.

Stay alive.

Don't glare at the guards—they don't take kindly to that, and can always get the last word.

And STOP JUMPING ROPE WITHOUT SHOES.

Take care.

Amy

11-22-05

What's up Dudet!

Peace and hair grease. I called all the #s you wrote down finaly some dude answered Boy I was stuck. So I Lamed it—Big Time duh moment. I don't know what you have told them so I just asked them to Let you know I called. Is There anyone Else you'd Like to talk to brent? Ah No sir. Bye. Click. Fuckin Moron I asked for Amy Herdy if I wanted to talk to someone else I would have said Let me talk to a reporter dipshit. ☺ So you'll probly be accused of some realy cool tabloid shit. God what I wouldn't give to be a fly on the wall in the ensuing conversation. You could feel the buzz thru the phone Amy.

Did you try your pushups with your arm closer to your body Like suggested? You'll probably be able to do BOY pushups that way plus Less risk of screwing up your rotator cuffs. You have very Long arms wideout pushups are not good for you in your case close in nose to the Ground and all the way up to 90% not quit full Locked out (Damage to elbows) Trust me you fuck up your shoulder it will seriously hurt your running.

So I forget that prison is full of uneducated ignorant people All day long pussy this pussy that. Guys who think

They know all about AIDS and don't know shit. Or Man when I get out I'm gonna get me a stable of Ho's and serve pussy and crack and carry a strap Ya da fuckin YA. Its fuckin ceasless one guy was talking about how he was trying to catch this dudes bitch in the visiting room. I thought please don't Let some fuckstick try that when Amy comes. I don't see you as my lover or anything, it's just a respect thing and I'd be hardpressed not to fuck someone up for disrespecting you and me Like that.

    I can feel your tiredness Amy you work hard at all you do. Its one of your better qualities. Just promise me one thing. Please Amy be careful out there at night. I don't have to tell you why. But on a deeper Level you not writing because of work is one thing but you being hurt would realy fuck me up Bad. The Neighborhood your speaking of is where I used to buy my heroin. Shit hole heaven. A lot of crazy bad shit happens there. And No, No one Likes the cops, Reporters or Themselves for that matter.

    Take care and be good to yourself Amy. Remember picture window and the smell of sea salt and warm sun on your pretty face.

    I'm out
    Brent

12-01-05
Rockstar,

    Ok Amy As for my ashes yes you'll still have them. But I think since you'll be in California that if you didn't think it to weird maybe you could put me on a shelf where I could Look out the big window at the ocean and watch you and the pack run the beach and watch you while you work and you can talk to me and play music for me. At least until you know its getting close to your own time then you can do what you Like with me. I know you'll take care of me.

    Amy you've taught me to believe in people again, about the simple love of friendship, about compassion and empathy.

Take care of yourself, be good to yourself. Show the pack some Love for me and know I'm Here for you. Rock on!
I'm Gone
Brent
p.s. Keep the sunny beach In mind. It's gonna Happen.

Sat 12-3-05
Hi Brent,
   Ok, let's get this out of the way. I DO NOT DO GIRLIE PUSHUPS. EVER. I've always done the "boy" pushups, just not that many (sets of 12 or 15, usually 3 or 4). (I know, I know—but man, I friggin' hate 'em).
   I will try with my hands closer. So far no shoulder damage. I do weights that include shoulder presses so maybe that's why.
   I think you're right—my body is used to my workouts. Yesterday on my run w/ Pike I did what I call 30/30s—which is I run really hard for a slow count to 30, then run slowly for 30, then hard, etc.—and keep it up for most of the run. Pike was looking at me, like, what the hell?—but he still didn't have to break stride.
   When we started out it was 6:30 am, cold as hell, just starting to get light. An orange sky, bleeding onto the black.
   Toward the end of the run, we're bopping down this trail that is bordered on both sides by tall grass, when the most beautiful coyote I've ever seen pops out & runs right in front of us. He was huge—so big at first I thought he was a wolf, with a long plumed tail. He ran over to the other side, paused to look over his shoulder & check us out then poof! was gone. It made my day. I took it as a good sign. I have a necklace that I wear that is a wolf howling, and I think we are shown such things for a reason.
   So, it snowed here last nite. Yeeha. I'm writing this first thing in the am, waiting for it to warm up before I run. Pike

tried to wake me up this morning & I made a wall of covers where he couldn't reach me with that cold nose.

Ok, pictures: I'm running into a logistical problem. The only way I can take a picture of the whole pack is this: Callie sits on top of this tall cabinet in the living room, so I was going to put Vincent next to her, Pike in front of me, hold Teddy/Chiko (I call him both, I hope he's not schizo as a result). So that means someone has to take the picture. One of my friends just looks at me when I ask (I told her why) and the other just says no. She doesn't think it's wise, blah blah blah.

Oh, work told me you called—they don't seem to think anything of it. And another time you called, the person who answered said he put you on hold (duh) without accepting the call. Sorry. I've told them again to accept the call. No one asked why we're still talking—the editors have not "officially" told me no on the last story idea & I haven't pressed.

I'm now on this lovely story about a missing 6 yr old out of Aurora who isn't really missing but dead. They just can't find the body. No one has seen her in 18 m. Her mother lives in Detroit in a homeless shelter. She lived with her dad & about 7 other kids & her dad's girlfriend.

My editors tried to send me to Detroit last nite to re-interview the mother (another reporter already did). The story has been going on for 2 wks & they only asked me to help yesterday so I have managed to stay out of that mess so far. I suggested that the other reporter who first went should go back. I worked the story for 3 hours and brought them some pretty significant details so they were happy.

Ok, off to run and then . . . gym. Sigh (girlie pushups my ass. Grumble Grumble. I'll show <u>you</u> girlie roundhouse kicks. Pow!)

Ha, made you smile.

Amy

12-06-05
Coyote Girl,
   Ok let me tell you this Fancy pants ☺ I can teach you a thing or two about Girlie pushups that I'll bet you enjoy. Get in the Girlie pushup position cross your legs at the ankles. Start in the up position count to ten on the down movement and then on the up movement "slowly" I'll bet you'll feel those 10 girlie pushups. Try it see if I'm B.Sing you. When you can do 50 of these you'll be able to do at least 100 regular boy pushups.
   Ok dig this. I think I Like your friend. Her worry sounds Like she's a genuine friend. Amy you know i'll never hurt you. What we have is real. Honesty and reality are things I've realy come to value. Besides Amy I realy Genuinly care for you.
   So let me ask you a question. Have you realy sat and thought about how all of this has and could change your Life. You know what i told on the phone today about taking my Ashes with you. I mean that. Regardless of the past 30 years, what happens in my head, the violence, confusion, hopelessness, Lonliness, Rage, sexual urges all of it. I have changed. With your help, your trust, your confidence in me— yes a lot of the old shit is still there Amy. But i found that little boy and between you and him I'm becoming a better person. I've learned That Its Not about me. Its about others. So I swore to myself that i would do everything humanly possible to Never take from anyones Life again. So there are three people in my Life. You Ellen her husband and Irene. Ok four. But only one who has truly been there with me. Ya know Rockstar your the bomb baby. My Life is a better life with you as the most important part of it. So smile you make difference.
   Ok so listen if I don't send you a Christmas card heres why. They only sell sweetheart Girlfriends or wife cards or

Mother sister Brother etc. One of the sweetheart cards is realy kick ass but I don't want to hurt you with it. I'm always afraid to tell you I Love you because im not sure if you understand its not a sexual thing. I Love you for Who you are who your becoming and in plain speak you're a real friend.

So Be good to yourself, Do the Girlie pushups I told you in the beginning they realy are good. Keep smiling Rockstar its a beautiful thing. Give the pack my Love and Councel Ted wisely (No Leg humping stay off the cats and the furniture do your business outside etc). Take care Amy. Thanks for being a true friend.

Captively yours HA! Prison Humor
Brent

Wed. 12-7-05
Hi Brent,

I got your letter and was really struck by it. Introspection and the examination of one's life is the hardest thing of all to do. Most people don't do it. That's why people live the same way, over and over, and patterns repeat.

But listen—it takes guts to realize all this, and to determine to live another way. You are being brave when you do it. You've been brave by baring your soul and your past. So there. ☺

I worked till 11:30 pm Mon, til late yesterday, & today I'm sick. Same old, same old. I've been taking Vit C & zinc like candy but the fucking cold germ got me anyway.

So anyway I'm at home, but still not sleeping. I typed up notes for a story, sent them in. Little psycho is in his crate, Pike's asleep on the dog bed, above him on her cabinet is Callie & Vincent is snoring on the couch. I worry about

Vincent—he seems to be a lot slower lately. He's about 13, I guess.

Well it's sub zero here. DAMMIT. Can you guys get hats & scarves & big coats there? They don't expect you to head outside without that, do they?

Did I tell you my journalism joke?

It's like the guy who works at the circus, shoveling up behind the elephants. One day he grumbles about how he has to shovel shit all day long. A friend says, "Well, why don't you quit?" And he replies, "What, and give up show business?" Ha.

Ok, take care. Don't start shit with the rednecks. Watch your back. I'll keep Pike at mine.

Be well, Buddha Man.

Amy

With every letter I wrote came the growing realization of how much I hated my job. I was, indeed, the guy endlessly shoveling up behind the elephants at the circus, disillusioned and bitter, yet unwilling to give up the security and small occasional thrills that my career offered.

Then one day my sister recommended an author of crime fiction to me, and after checking out one of his books at the library, I noticed a dedication to his agent. Just like that, I had the thought, I could write a book. I certainly had a story worth telling.

I Googled the agent and sent her an email. What if I wrote a book about Brents and, more importantly, about what I had learned from covering his case?

The agent wrote back, intrigued.

It sounds like a fascinating topic for a book, she said, if you're willing to do the work and open up for it. For example, she asked, what is the connection between the two of you?

What was our connection? How could I tell her, when I wasn't even sure myself?

Wed 12-14-05
Hi Brent,
    It's Wed! That means I have 2 more days, then I'm off for a week. Woo-hoo!
    Oh look at the bumper sticker I just saw: Namaste—The divine in me blesses and honors the divine in you.
    I just got to my desk and Googled it. It's Sandskrit Hindu.
    So, anyway, I have lots of pondering to do. I don't know how I describe our relationship when I have not defined it. As you know, I don't even say the word "friend" to you. Yet I admit I care about you, what happens to you, how you are, what you've been thru that led you where you are. I can honestly say I've never hated you—not even a split-second's worth. Hated what you've done, yes. But I will refuse to believe that's all there is to you.
    I know I feel protective of you—how odd is that? Like you need protecting. But that first court appearance, when you walked down the hall, that's why I walked near you—an unspoken gesture of support, a buffer to the rest of the media horde hovering nearby & yelling questions.
    You said in your last letter that you have found that little boy inside you, and that through him & me you are becoming a better person. I sometimes think that's who I'm talking to—the hurt & abandoned 12 yr old, reassuring him I'm not going to hurt him. The kid in me talking to the kid in you? Perhaps. As you've said, it's not sexual or romantic or religious—(I'm leaving your soul up to you, I don't think that's even Irene's turf), it's not ego or power trip or manipulation. I write to the Brent who struggles with his dark side—with the rage, who is honest about all of it, who also has a sense of humor, compassion and intelligence.
    What do you call that?
    And here's a disclosure, not trying to hurt your feelings,

but I'm uncomfortable when you tell me you love me. I KNOW I KNOW it's not romantic or sexual—I do believe that it is sincere—probably also fueled by your loneliness and fear there. But I can't respond to it, and then I feel guilty. I can't even call you "friend" without struggling—I wrote "friend" on the visitation form because I was afraid that to visit you as a reporter would create problems. But I felt funny writing "friend"—old habits die hard, I guess.

Do I fear the world knowing that I have empathy for you? No. Do I fear being hated or threatened or ridiculed? Hell no. Do I fear admitting I have a heart? Oh, yes. I guess I fear that struggle with myself most of all. Does that make sense?

Take care. STAY ALIVE.

Amy

12-15-05

Rockstar,

What is the thread that connects us. Past hurts and pains. Loss, feeling abandoned. Something deeper.

I recognize you, Amy, I see Loss, I see a tough Girl act protecting an unsure woman. I see the desire to Accomplish good things being smothered by self doubt and a fucked up Political machine of a Job. I see a woman wanting to Love and be loved without weight or strings. We are a lot alike.

You have always been good at avoiding questions. You defended me, Go mad at me, Laughed at me, with me, encouraged me, made me promise not to kill myself which im still mad at you for. Gained my trust and respect. Acknowledged my Love & care for you. You haven't given up, Even now.

Think about the song "Under Pressure." The music the Lyrics, the feelings the song brings up in you. How it leaves you feeling. You told me once it was your favorite song. We are Like the song Amy slashed and torn, wanting something more from Life. Redemption, Love, That feeling of achievement, To be ok. Your going to be Ok Amy, me well we shall see.

Ly.

—B.

12-21-05

Rockstar,

I got the books today thank you. You rock! I also got your Letter. You're a funny Girl. Brent i feel uncomfortable when you say you Love me. Ok she who battles self. I'll Just shout it in my mind at you once a day. ☺ Bite me! As for whether it is out of Lonliness. Maybe at first, actually yes at first it was a Little bit of a desperate grasp to fill my Lonliness. Now however it is a real deal thing. Not A day goes by that i don't feel good about you, About our Goals. That i know without you i would have just given up. I know you battle inside. The fact that you do realy says a lot about you. Amy Look in the mirror past the physical except for your eyes. Look into your heart and mind and your soul. You'll see what i Love and respect and truly value.

Well any way I hope you have a good X-mas and New year. Check out this ending.

Mooshy! Mooshy!

Brent

P.S. Love to the pack and thanks for being you.

12-24-05

Dearest Amy,

It's been a real hard day. A guy just a few cells away hung himself this morning. He's alive but in a coma. I can't say i didn't think about the same thing. Yeah i know your probably saying oh boy here he goes feeling sorry for himself,

> but no Amy i'm not. I'm Just being a realist. We have a Goal, see it through. Be the champion i know you can be, for the children who need someone to stand up for them. Continue to spread the message.
>
> Do i love you? yes. Yes your uncomfortable with it. I told you you scared me. Even in your Absense Amy you give me hope and inspiration. Not that you do or ever will Love me as i do you. No its a different hope and inspiration. I've never done anything realy meaningful or unselfishly. Amy a part of me is alive with passion and desire Like none i've ever Known. I can Live outside of myself without hate or rage, shame or dishonesty. I can feel Lonliness or pain without using it as a fuel for destruction. Its ok Just to be me. I've made up my mind Amy. No more Living in a desparate struggle to fill the emptiness or holes in my heart or my Life. No more trying to make up for what i didn't have as a child. There is always going to be a void in my Life. It doesn't make me special or unique. I don't know how much time i have left. What i do know is i am going to do all that i can to give of myself to our Goal and to you.
>
> Amy you've done more for me than you'll ever know. I am and Always will be grateful to you. Dream big Amy and chase those dreams. Take what i can give and enjoy it. It may not seem Like Alot but its real and i give happily. Rock on Rockstar.
>
> Your friend
> Brent

Brents was right: The song "Under Pressure" by Queen, one of my favorite songs, did strike a chord in me. Listening to its lyrics gave me hope that I wasn't alone in thinking that hating him was not the answer. Everyone, even those living in darkness, deserved love and compassion.

But how many other people would feel the same way? Brents and

I both knew that for me to write a book about him would put him at risk for retaliation. The consequences were uneven and unfair: I was only risking some painful introspection and perhaps hate mail, he was literally willing to risk his life.

"I want to accomplish something good before I die," he would often say to me.

As the book formed more and more into a solid reality in my mind, I realized that like Brents, I couldn't do it halfway. And that if I was going to commit to it, I had to be fully honest. With myself.

And with Brents. Because I had been keeping a whopper of a secret from him, one he would find out eventually, if any book did come to fruition.

So I took a breath and decided to tell him now.

12-29-05
Hi Brent,

I hope you haven't worried. No, my plane didn't crash, & the earth didn't suddenly swallow me whole.

I'm sorry for the gap between letters. Suffice to say, I've been busy & stressed. But more importantly, I had to figure out what I wanted to say.

The book is fine. You and I are fine. I'm coming to peace with baring my soul to the world—slowly. I haven't finished that intro yet. I figure I'm good if I get it done in Jan.

Here's what I've been struggling with: This affects not just me. I have a family of my own.

And you need to realize how vulnerable that makes me. And them.

It's a part of my life I have always sheltered from the world.

If it's not clear, I will try to be: I have kids. And I have never told you about them because 1) I have never included them in my work life, always tried to shield them from it, and 2) They are too young (I have 3 boys, 2 of them are young) to make any kind of decision about how they would feel about this project, and its effects on them, and if they are Ok with the entire idea.

A little background: I was a single mom for several years, and have learned to be fiercely protective. I've had threats in the past, bc of my work. I'm always pissing someone off. And don't feel bad I didn't tell you before: When I left the St Pete Times, most of my coworkers did not know I had kids. I'm that private (and I worked there for 7 years).

In January (last Jan) I got married (you've commented on the ring. I never acknowledged it bc it would have been intruding on his life). He's a really good guy, & great with the boys. He has struggled with this, this whatever-you-want-to-call-it relationship you and I have. Not in a jealous way, but in a I-don't-understand-it way. So I left him out of it.

But I can't write about this project, and our letters, without writing about its full effects on me at home. It hasn't been easy. In the very beginning, after that first phone call from you in early March, my husband asked me not to do this. Not to keep in contact with you, or do the project. He was afraid for me on a few levels—that it would be a wrenching process, and take a toll on me (and who are we kidding, it has)—and I had just finished the military project, and recovered from it.

That perhaps at some point I'd anger you, and you would try to have me hurt, or worse, hurt me by having someone get to the boys.

That the project would piss off other people so much that they'd come after me, or the boys.

And I have thought about it all.

The bottom line, God help us all if I am wrong: I trust you.

I don't think, even if you and I got in some full-flown,

all-out nasty fight, that you would ever try to hurt me. Or anyone I love.

As far as the emotional toll—well, I'm a big girl, and I learned a lot from that military project. Like how to take care of myself before I'm completely burned out.

And as far as others being pissed—well, they will be. And I'll do what I've always done—protected the boys.

So, in a sense, you and I are both risking a lot, huh?

I hope you're not hurt I didn't tell you before. It did not seem fair. But it did enable me to look at my life as who I am at the core—and that's the me you have come to know.

Everything about my life I have told you is true, I just left them out. And my friends and my husband have all said, Don't ever tell him anything personal. I have been told I shouldn't use their names. Hell, I can't get anyone to take a picture of me and the pack.

After seeing how much it meant to me, my husband has tried to support my decision. You have no idea how hard this has been for him—I read your letters in private, write to you and exclude him from it all.

So, in a way, this has been a very isolating thing. Perhaps that's another reason you & I have bonded.

I was waiting to tell you the next time you called. But you haven't been able to, I guess.

So, no halfway for any of it, I decided. If I'm going to write about the whole thing, it will be the whole thing, including my struggles with these decisions.

Everybody thinks I'm nuts.

I'm essentially putting us all on the line. You, as well.

But the truth deserves to be heard.

So, do your part. STAY ALIVE. Keep your nose clean (you know what I mean).

Take care,
Amy

1-4-06
Amy

    My friend what can i say. Truth yes of course. Mad, angry or upset No. Surprised yes. Sad a little. Proud of you very. I've always known there was more to the story and figured you would tell me when and if you wanted to. So Rockstar Just know Two Things. I would Not ever hurt you, him or your boys in any way, and your having the courage to do this only serves to prove i was right about you being a good hearted woman. So now i have four new reasons to do all i can to help you. Amy you know i trust you fully and without reservation. As for how i write i'll not change anything except mooshy mooshy. You and i both know its not a sexual thing but since i respect you i'll honor him too.

    As for brent he's been doing ok. He got hurt recently by someone who he thought he could count on. Partialy me fault (Desparation) mostly hers. imagine this i got manipulated by a woman. Me of all people. And No i'm not talking about you. As you know i dig older women. But this one has Loose screws and Luckily i opened my eyes in time to see a truck coming. Am i a fool, it's a Long story. I'll tell you when you come up or on the phone. I Just feel real foolish about the whole thing.

    Ok heres some food for thought. What i am going to say is the whole truth and nothing but.

    Am i desperate to be Loved and cared for? Yes Somewhat. Amy i able to know the difference between compassionate Love and man woman love? Yes i know the difference Amy. Do i find you attractive yes of course. Any man who didn't would be Gay or Blind. Do i see you as a sexual object? Absolutely Not. Do i Think about sex with you? No, Not only do i not i Never have. <u>The only woman i've never sexualized in my entire life.</u> Even That day in the elevator. I couldn't figure it out, but there was something definitely different about you. I Think and feel thats why trust you and feel safe with you. I don't feel insecure or threatened by you Amy another rare thing in my Life. Do i put you on a Pedestal No. I can safely say Amy no matter how good she is can be a bitch. But i do know your heart is good.

    Amy i can't even imagine the pain and vulnerability where it concerns your Husband and children. I try to understand, but its one of those things only a parent or wife could. I'm sorry for that but i do empathise with you. So bottom Line your brave and courageous. Your example is the best teaching for me. If you can have the courage to do this and so much so can i.

    —B.

January 24, 2006
Amy,

    Without you I could never have accomplished this degree of peace in my life, I could not have found the will or courage to be honest with myself or others. I could not have faced the child or the reactionary man. I talk to you a lot, people probably think I'm nuts when they see me having conversations with No one around but oh well, it helps . . .

    So February coming up . . . It's hard because I hate myself for all of it. The 'if onlys' and I should haves don't help i know. The i wishes are only tormenting. Not a day goes by That i don't see Tiffany or wake up in a cold sweat remembering what i did. Feel sorrow at Aida's passing. Or how badly those two girls tried to please the bad man.

    I'm sorry Aida suffered in her Last day . . . Yes Amy Some days i want to take the same Road, but as i've said repeatedly i made you a promise And in truth sometimes its enough Just to know you are there and others the promise is the only thing that Keeps me alive. For the Most part i do Like the man im becoming. Still its hard to rid myself of what i was and still Am in some ways.

    Peace out Rockstar
    —B.

TWENTY-ONE

Changes

The start of 2006 was slow and sweet, like a lazy Sunday morning. Matt and I celebrated our anniversary—and the New Year—by slow dancing in our living room.

Overwhelmed with joy and gratitude, we both got teary.

My New Year's resolution was to keep focusing on giving the best of myself to my family and friends, and the rest to my job, instead of the reverse order. And increasingly, that was easier and easier to do. I began turning down overtime assignments, and even on regularly scheduled days, I no longer bounced into work but trudged into the newsroom with leaden feet. I felt stubborn and defiant, like an old mule who doesn't want to carry her load anymore and digs in her hooves. I started questioning every story, every assignment, every order.

After driving into work in the mornings, I would sit in my car, a dull headache starting to throb at my temple, and begin the process of coaxing myself into walking to the newsroom. I constantly had the thought that I was not doing what I was meant to do, and a nagging, sharp pain in my side to accompany it.

It didn't help that I turned forty-two in January.

Having finally wheedled the date of my birth from me, Brents sent me two cards. The first was a pink and glossy piece of art with a picture of a white cake adorned with roses. He wrote a short note on the inside cover:

Amy,

Not a minute of any Day Goes by that i don't think of you and what you have not only accomplished in your own Life recently, but in mine as well. I just want to thank you for following your heart. I hope someday all your dreams come true. Thanks once again for being my friend and Teacher and for simply Just Caring when no one Else did.
L.y.
B.

The second card was a festive design of balloons and streamers and party hats and presents. On the inside he wrote,

You know at your age you can get discounts on alot of stuff. Your so lucky. Dream Big Rockstar.
Ly
B.

On the same day, I got a letter from him where he mused if his brain wasn't just burned out from drugs and hate and that forgiveness of his past was impossible.

I wasn't going to let any of that slip by unchallenged.

1-4-06
Hi Brent,
    At my age? Ha!—funny card. OK yes, you made me laugh. But hey, when I come visit, if you want to run laps around the visiting room with this old lady we'll see who drops first. (how's that ankle?) ☺
    (Oh! Oh! She jabs to the left! The right! It's a direct hit!)
Ok I'm done.
    I got your letter the same day as the card.
    So, are we alike in some ways? Yes. Both loners. Both

driven. Both introspective. Both quick to put up our fists if we feel threatened. Both hate feeling vulnerable.

Have you really burned out your brain with drugs or hate?

NO, you haven't.

Think about the lungs of a smoker. Dark & gray/black. Smoker quits, and slowly, the lungs start to rebuild, start to turn pink & healthy. Within 5 years, they look like healthy lungs again.

I saw this movie called What the Bleep Do We Know Anyway. It's a documentary about quantum physics—how we affect our own lives by our thoughts and intentions. The brain has neural pathways that become set and used to the same thoughts—so it fires up the same way. When you have different thoughts, it literally forges new paths in your brain. Soon, the old neural pathways break down.

And I've always believed that the universe hears our intentions. That's one of the reasons why I always knew, and I think you did, too, that we would do this book together. Even when people around us have said Don't do it. Oh well. We're both stubborn, too.

I'm glad you trust me. I hope that when your mind starts to spin, it's enough for you to hold on to. I know you know this but I'll repeat it anyway: I will never hurt you. Or betray you. Or abandon you.

I don't want you to feel hopeless. Try to find that new part of yourself, that healthy pink part of your brain and your heart, and nurture it. Let it grow. Protect it the best you can there, do what you have to do.

And I don't believe there is no forgiveness for you. I refuse to believe that. It's the thinking that people cannot change, when we both know they can. Anything is possible.

Hey, this will cheer you up: That vice cop found me an

address and 3 possible phone #s for Tracy. I also have her picture. So I feel confident I'll find her soon.

Speaking of finding—I'm going to send you a picture of a 15-yr-old prostitute, & I want you to tell me if that's the one from Jan. If so, I will know how to find her, too. This friend of mine who runs the non-profit agency for prostitutes is really a cool person.

I know she would help them if I asked. She gives them emergency shelter, helps them detox, get treatment, get counseling, healthcare, new clothes, a job—all of it. She only helps a few women at a time b/c it's so intensive. And she offers them mentors, too.

It will work out like it's supposed to, Brent. I have faith in that. This woman, Leanne, who runs the agency that helps prostitutes—Street's Hope—well, I met her when I first moved to Denver, & started hanging out with the search dog team. She was a member. Then she quit, b/c she said she felt called to start this agency. 3 years later, it's up and running, & she calls me to see if I want to write about it. Absolutely, I said. So I did.

Keep the faith (eegads, now I sound like Irene).

Take care of yourself.

Stay alive, please.

Later, Buddha.

Amy

Writing about an agency like Street's Hope and people like Leanne Downing was one of the best parts of my job. The topic was worthwhile, and listening to Leanne was inspirational. I learned a lot from her about why women become entrenched in prostitution. For the story I wrote that appeared in the *Denver Post* in December 2004, she told me, "What I've found is that most of these women suffered some major tragedy when they were young, and they quit living and started surviving. One thing affects another, and they live hand-to-mouth. I believe that everybody has potential and everybody's beautiful if someone just reflects that back to them."

That's the kind of story that makes everyone feel good.

Stories about a serial rapist, on the other hand, horrify everyone but garner an enormous amount of interest.

As the anniversary of his final crime spree and February arrest drew near, Brents once again became the object of media attention, and reporters sent their letters to the Colorado Department of Corrections and asked they be forwarded to him, wherever he was.

FOX31 NEWS

Brent J. Brents
DOC# 61549

February 1, 2006

Dear Mr. Brents,

My name is Sari Padorr and I am a reporter for FOX31 News in Denver. I am very familiar with your case as I had covered the crimes and the court proceedings follow [sic] them.

I was wondering if you would grant me an on-camera?

I'm interested in finding out more about you and what might've pushed you to commit those crimes. It could also afford you an opportunity to apologize to your victims.

I realize you are now housed out-of-state but my photographer and I would fly to see you if you grant this interview. I think the people of the Denver metro area would be interested in hearing from you as the one year anniversary approaches.

I know you have been in touch with Amy Herdy at the Post. Her article was insightful. But I think an on-camera interview will show people that there is a man behind, what some call, a "monster."

Please consider this.

Thank you for your time and consideration. I look forward to hearing back from you.

Regards,
Sari Padorr
Reporter FOX31 News
100 E. Speer Blvd.
Denver, CO 80203

There was certainly lots to write about: Many of Brents' victims were suing the Aurora Police and the Arapahoe County District Attorney's office for all the mistakes that had allowed him to remain free for so long. Also, the Aurora Police Department had been overhauled as a result.

But even though reporters once again began searching him out, Brents was no longer in Colorado, and I wasn't going to reveal his whereabouts to anyone. Only a handful of people knew his out-of-state prison location, and they were of his choosing.

One was Irene, the older woman who had told me she was interested in saving Brent's soul. The other was Ellen, a woman who apparently had been writing to Brents for some time but who only called me in February 2006 at his request to make sure I had been getting his mail.

At first I lumped Ellen into the same category as Irene, someone whose interest appeared to be a zealous pursuit of Brents' soul. As the days and weeks passed and I got to know her, I began to realize that while Ellen was indeed religious—a deeply devout Catholic—she was also one of the most spiritual and sincere people I had ever met. The two don't always coincide, but with her, they were one and the same. And her story, which she only revealed once we'd known each other for quite some time, was both heartbreaking and inspiring.

Ellen's oldest daughter, Mary, died after another driver plowed into her car as she was driving home from school. The other driver wasn't drunk—just exhausted from work. He had fallen asleep.

It happened on Ellen's birthday.

Nothing can prepare a parent for the overwhelming, heartrending pain of losing a child. Ellen fell into a deep well of grief, not knowing if she would ever be able to clamber her way out.

On the afternoon the driver who killed their daughter pleaded guilty to careless driving resulting in death, Ellen and her husband stood in their living room, talking about the upcoming sentence, when her husband stunned her.

"He said he knew the driver was a simple man who didn't make much money, so he didn't want to ask for restitution, even as the principle of the thing. He also said that he had changed his mind, that he did not want the man who killed their daughter to go to jail," Ellen told me later. At that point, she left the room, feeling lost.

"I just walked into the kitchen to be somewhat alone for a minute," she said. "I had been going to the hearings for my daughter. But I didn't even know what she wanted. So I closed my eyes and almost shouted to myself, 'What do you want, Mary? What do you want?!'

"Of course I didn't expect a reply but I did get one. I heard Mary say, 'I don't want him sad . . . I really don't want him sad.' She was very emphatic about it. I did hear her voice and it did not come from my head and no one else heard it. I did feel the Holy Spirit very strong and then she gave me to the Lord. I felt Him and I felt His words. It is hard to explain. It was like His thoughts were my thoughts, but in my heart. The Lord said, 'Why are you worried about her? She's all right. You should be worried about him.'

"He didn't say it as a reprimand. He knew why I was worried and was simply telling me I needn't be. I should be focusing instead on the driver, Jose. His voice was very gentle, very kind—and not like anyone else's. The Lord allowed me to feel all of the love He had for Jose. The closest I can describe it is a mother's unconditional love for her child. I had asked God to show me how to love Him two years previously and had been asking ever since. He showed me how I should love that day. He answered my prayer.

"But that was not the end. And this part may sound strange. But the Lord let me know that He would love him the same way if he had drunk three quarts of vodka—I was thoroughly confused about that! And that He would love him the same way if he were a person who did terrible things. I had the image of a person who strangled and I thought of the Boston Strangler. I don't have a clue how long this 'experience' happened. I had no concept of time. It could have been instantaneous or lasted a few seconds or minutes. I really can't say.

"I know it was God. I felt that Christ was speaking to me, and I felt the Holy Spirit. I had felt the Holy Spirit on other occasions and there was no doubt. As strange as it sounds maybe, I still have no doubt.

"I was a little unnerved afterward. Every time I thought of it, I cried. I still do. Not because it was a bad experience—it was a good experience. I think I'm just so much in awe. Of course we sincerely forgave Jose during the sentencing. And we did not ask for jail or restitution. But that is not the point of this message. The point is that I did understand that I was going to meet someone, someone who choked others. And even though the Lord did not give me the feeling that this person would be a sexual offender, I somehow knew that too. Somehow I knew it would be OK, though, and I put that thought out of my head, thinking it could be years or decades down the road. Or maybe I was wishing that. I had this revelation in May of 2004. Brent was still in jail but was released that summer.

"The revelation was about him. I did not realize it at the time. I had put it out of my mind as I said before. I was just looking for someone to pray for and had asked God for guidance in the matter. I realized it was Brent that the Lord was speaking of when He told me that he could drink a gallon of vodka a day. Later I became aware that he did choke the people he victimized.

"So what can I say. God loves Brent. God loves Brent unconditionally. God loves Brent like He loves Jose. And I did not want to think of Jose, much less pray for him (although I knew I should) before the revelation. Afterward, Jose was like family in my heart. I love him as my own family and I do pray for him every day. It's an unconditional love. God can give his love to everyone unconditionally."

To this day, I feel inspired by her.

Regarding another pen pal of Brents', however, I felt quite different—Irene, the woman he referred to in his January 4 letter as having "loose screws."

At first, Irene wrote to Brents about redemption and fulfillment. Evidently an older widow with a comfortable nest egg, she began sending money to him every week for prison luxuries, including a television, radio, clothes, and the special food orders that can help make life in a cell bearable.

Soon he began calling her collect every week and, at her request, writing her every day. She sent him inspirational books engraved with his name in gold—such as *Your Best Life Now* and *The Purpose Driven Life*—and writing on the inside cover: "May this book help you find purpose for your life . . . Merry Christmas, Brent! Love, Ireney."

And then it became clear what purpose Irene had for Brents' life: to be her sexual boy toy.

As he would later tell me, it seemed to happen overnight. One day she was writing to Brents about passages from the Bible, and the next she was asking him about his penis size.

The similarities to his accounts of his relationship with his mother, an older woman who claimed to be religious yet turned to Brents for a deviant sexual relationship, became unmistakable. The situation both appalled and saddened me, especially when I realized it brought out the worst in Brents.

Meanwhile, Irene began to talk to him about marriage, dangling the lure of conjugal visits, as well as what her money could buy. She visited him in prison and paid the guard to look the other way, then asked Brents to fondle her beneath her skirt. I later saw a photo of the two of them taken that day, and Brents' face was a thunderstorm, a dark scowl of anger I didn't recognize. I wondered if that was the look his victims had seen.

Yet I kept my concerns to myself. Whenever Brents would bring up the situation with Irene, which clearly troubled him, I would demur from comment, telling him, "This is your business only."

As the one-year anniversary of his final spate of crimes and his capture neared, I offered an in-depth piece on Brents' psyche to my editors, proposing that we interview criminal psychologists and a former FBI profiler to see if anything was to be learned from him. The editors turned it down, saying we had already run a bunch of his letters, what else was there to know? I felt strongly relieved. Someday, I thought, I'll tell the whole story, and it will be on my terms, not theirs.

And then came a surprise that wasn't really a surprise, after all: While doing background for the anniversary piece, Barbara, the *Post* researcher, found records of Brandy, Brent's brother. He had just been released from prison, a convicted felon with a history of sexual assault and kidnapping. And so the pattern repeated.

I decided to tell Brents about his brother during his next phone call, thinking it would be too difficult to learn about in a letter.

He was sad but not surprised. "I had hoped things would be different for him."

And as the anniversary drew near and the frenzy in the newsroom began to rise, I started getting this nagging feeling that trouble was brewing. So I tried to warn Brents.

Wednesday, February 1, 2006
Hi Brent,
    Stop calling for a while. This is for your own safety—
it's getting close to the anniversary, and they (editors) are
gearing up for stories.

So for now, don't remind them you're there. I know you're really, really stressed, but I weigh that against the risk of overblown, sensationalized coverage that could get you killed & the latter seems worse.

That's about it. I'm tired & stressed, so this is short.

Please keep your head down, and be careful.

Meanwhile, I hope the universe protects you.

Take care and STAY ALIVE.

Amy

My warning arrived too late.

When he called a general number looking for me at the *Post* the next day, February 2, another reporter, young and ambitious, took Brents' call and talked to him briefly before transferring him to my phone.

I had always viewed that reporter with a bit of suspicion. Shortly after she joined the *Post*, a small group of us were sharing "war" stories in the newsroom one slow afternoon when she told us of a scoop she'd gotten at her old paper by getting an exclusive interview with a father accused of killing his child.

"The day after my interview," she said to all of us, seated in a chair as we stood clustered around, "the father *killed* himself."

And with that, she raised her fists above her head and shook them in an apparent victory gesture.

I stared at her, filled with horror. I wasn't sure why she had felt victorious—because she got the exclusive interview? Or because the father killed himself? I was afraid to ask.

So, evidently, was everyone else. One senior reporter muttered, "Well, I guess you're suited to your job," and the rest of us stood awkwardly silent before finally sidling away.

Now, after her brief conversation with Brents, the young woman apparently had a scoop. The next day, she quoted him in a story in the newspaper, which I learned about by seeing it in the paper like everyone else.

Four days later, I got a letter from Brents with the words "ATTENTION/EMERGENCY/HELP READ ME NOW HURRY! HELP!" written on the envelope. Inside was a brief note along with an official Department of Corrections document dated February 3, the date of the story, that read, "NOTICE OF OFFENDER PLACED IN TEMPORARY LOCKUP."

In other words, Brents had been thrown in solitary confinement, or "the hole" as it's known in prison—a small, windowless room where the prisoner is kept twenty-four hours a day with no contact with others. It's a stressful, inhumane situation for anyone, but especially for someone already battling to maintain his sanity.

> 2-7-06
> Amy,
> Hey Guess what/ I'm in The segregation unit. Pending investigation for a 303.30 Rule violation unauthorized forms of communication.
> This sucks and it could not have happened at a worse time. I kept your cards you sent. Its something to hold onto. Hopefuly They will clear this up soon. I'm realy at a loss.
> Peace, my love to the pack. Don't give up. Eat well Take care of yourself.
> Sincerely,
> Brent

Another letter on the heels of that one showed that he was already starting to spiral.

> 2-7-06
> Rockstar,
> Tell me if you can relate to this. I feel hollow, Kinda Like i have the befuddled feeling after a concusion . . . I feel sad. I feel a scary sense of calm, yet restlessness seems to be creeping

in around the edges. So many emotions, one result. Quitting it all . . . I got so upset last night I beat the walls, my hands are swollen and hurt real bad, but anything helps to Avoid what I'm feeling inside.

Well I realy think these fuckin people are trying to set me up and get me killed. I realy feel Like Going on the defensive and protecting myself. But i know it will be futile well I know I'm gonna start Losing my cool and say real stoopid shit so I'll go for now. Peace out. Some time maybe in the future will be good to us.

Peace out
Brent

Whatever the prison said about the situation being "temporary" was evidently bogus.

One week later, still in the hole, Brents sent me his will:

I wish to be cremated and my Ashes given to Amy Herdy, as we have already agreed to this. Not one Else, Not Immediate family or close friends should posses them. Remember the picture window Amy.

Enclosed with the will was a one-page letter.

2-10-06

My friend, My teacher, My Inspiration, My Everything special. As They say The Shit has started to hit the fan. It's just a matter of time now before they get me . . . Well I don't know If I'll be able to watch over you when I die, but if I can I'll do you right always. Keep you out from in front of mall buses, open manholes. Steer you to better opportunities and kick ass on anyone who tries to hurt you or your family. Oh yeah wedgy shouvanist ass holes who can't see you for a strong good hearted woman and equal. I have never been a good person until now Amy and I realy does feel good to be good. It's a lot harder than being a bad person but its honest.

Be strong, Be good to yourself, The Boys, The husband and The rest of the pack. Live your dreams Amy Live them Large.

Your Loving friend
Brent

Then he found out the young reporter's story was the reason for his segregation, and his rage was clear.

2-10-06
Amy,

Well i know a little of why i'm in the hole. Well my so called enterviews are the reason I'll be coming back to Colorado. I did not know there was a rule here about giving enterviews. You can thank that reporter for tricking me and oh yeah tell her thanks for not telling me she would get a brownie point for saying she enterviewed me Fuckin cunt asked two questions. Oh well fuck it. I'm gonna die anyway might as well get it the fuck over with. I know you didn't mean to cause me harm and hell you probably didn't know either. I'm sorry for yelling at you, I know you've been real. I'm Just so fuckin tired of Losing no matter how hard i try to do good. Finish the book Amy, Finish it with the heart you started it with and you'll do fine.

Goodbye
Brent

As soon as I got the first desperate word from Brents, I sprang into action and got on the phone, explaining to prison officials that when he had called for me, the other reporter had interviewed him without his knowledge or permission.

I also called that reporter, who said she was shocked about the consequence of her story, and admitted that while she didn't tell Brents she was talking to him for publication, she thought she had been "clear."

"If you don't use words like 'interview,' or 'quote,' then how are you clear?" I said to her sharply, feeling frustrated and angry.

I also wrote to Brents and told him to hang on, that I was doing everything I could, and that even though the situation seemed dire, I somehow knew he would be safe.

> 2-10-06
> Brent,
>
> I've been on the phone. What I've been told so far is that this is more for your protection than anything—that the order came from Denver. Don't despair. I also explained what happened with that reporter taking my call & quoting you without your permission. I called her and she was dumbfounded.
>
> I'm disgusted and upset over all of it—that reporter is young, & under the same pressure of that newsroom that we all are. I wish I had listened to my voice's warning sooner. I wish I had come to see you sooner.
>
> I really think this will be cleared up. I'm going to call the security director today and explain what happened.
>
> So please, try not to freak, although I know that seg. does bad things to your head. As soon as you are out of there, I'll come visit. And here's a question—& I'll ask the security director as well—would it help, or can I, attend your disciplinary hearing? It's probably closed since it's internal, but I would be willing to come there and talk to whoever I need to talk to in person. If I can't attend, find out—& I'll ask too—if I can send a sworn statement. Or if you need that reporter to send one.
>
> I know with an unwavering certainty that no matter what, it will all be O.K. I have finally started to have faith

that sometimes, the universe does amazing things. And I have always struggled with that belief. But I have it now, so don't you give up.

    Don't make me come out there and kick your ass! ☺

    Take care. Breeeeaathe. STAY ALIVE.

    See you soon.

    Amy

Meanwhile, his letters that crossed mine ran the gamut of emotions.

2-10-06

Amy,

    So whats it Like Amy to Live on the other side, you know to fear the Law, the consequences, to go with the flow, to be in the norm? Whats it like to lie next to someone you love for the whole and not just in a sexual thing. Whats it Like to come home to your boys, knowing you made them, you raised, whats that pride feel Like. These are Just some of the things I wished to have known.

    I know it may seem strange to you or anyone normal, but somewhere early on I Lost the fear of pain or consequence. You Asked me if I am a psychopath I think in this way, yes. Since I've never been raised with a normal standard of Good vs bad or right vs wrong I have no fear of most of what the norm does. I'm proud of my survival skills but the thinking borders on animalistic and that I'm not proud of.

    I can't get warm, I cant eat and when i do I can't keep it down. Oh what the fuck am i whining about I just need to man the fuck up and get real. I fucked up, it aint Never gonna be easy so stop crying like a bitch. Thats what i realy need to do. That reporter was just doing her Job. Fuck it. I was pretty pissed, Fit to be tied. She should be kissing your ass right about now because if you hadn't taught me about honesty and courage her Life would not be a pleasant one.

That was the first thing I thought when I put two and two together. But fuckit she'll learn on her own, I can't Terrorize someone every time i think they wronged me. I hope she got good reviews on her story. So there you have a Look into the Angry mind of Brent. Actualy thats the G version of it Just tell her All if forgiven. If i don't forgive her now I will stew and bad things will happen. So I forgive her and promise peace to her.

 I haven't punched any walls and busted my knuckles open, I haven't cried myself to sleep or Laughed into unstable fits of hysteria or become so paranoid that I feel like Everyone is talking about me. So hey todays been a good day. But reality check ok. I Am scared and Feeling very very vulnerable and alone. I realy want to shut everyone out, Yes even you. I know that would be the worst thing I could do. That's why I'm writing every day I know it's important not to close down. Well anyway I hope things are well with you. Stay strong Rockstar. Eat Good take care of yourself and the family. Ly. Peace and all that good stuff.

 I'm outty.
 Brent

Enclosed was a note to the young female *Post* reporter. He asked me to read it to her (yet not give it to her), so I brought it to work with me the next day and that afternoon, I walked over to her desk.

She looked up in curiosity. Feeling strangely formal, I told her, "I'm supposed to read this to you from Brents." Still standing, I then unfolded the letter, cleared my throat, and began.

> *I must be honest and say for a minute i was very very upset with you. But sincerely I wish you Nothing but peace and Good Life. You were kind and considerate enough to put my calls through to Amy, when you didn't have to. Amy tells me you feel Awful, Don't! Most people see me as an*

Animal without rights, encluding people you work with. I can understand this. So they do and say things without regard to consequences. I am Not going to make a fuss. I don't know when I go to my hearing but i will Just plead guilty. At first I thought well I'll just use her (you) as a witness. Ya know, did you tell me you were conducting an enterview, did you tell me you were going to quote me, etc. But then I thought they'll find me Guilty anyway and I'm Not gonna drag you into a losing battle. Anyway I should have known better than to say Anything to you. So It aint all your fault. Shit happens. I hope your bosses were pleased w/ your story.
    Brent

Since the letter hadn't been addressed to me, that was the first time I had read it. I realized I'd barely taken a breath the whole time, feeling the weight of what Brents had written. Through that letter, he was struggling to regain a measure of his human dignity. More importantly, he was trying to forgive someone, a concept as alien to him as if it had come from Mars—yet one that had been introduced by Margaret and reinforced by Aida's mother, Kim.

Somehow, he was now offering his own forgiveness to someone. I found it amazing.

I sighed and looked away from the letter and down at the reporter, still sitting at her desk. She was frowning, her lips pursed in a pout. Apparently, she didn't find it so amazing.

Then she opened her mouth and removed all doubt. "Whatever," she said, rolling her eyes and giving a dismissive shrug. "Fuckin' psycho!"

I started to speak but stopped myself. What was the point? Refolding the letter, I walked back to my desk, deep in thought.

To me, the betrayal, and then the disregard, by that reporter smacked of something larger: She was simply the sore throat of the desperate pneumonia that pervaded that newsroom.

For many journalists—and at one time for me—the story is first and people are second. Somewhere along the way in the evolution of journalism, we began to confuse being objective with being callous.

But we're certainly not original—that's a mentality reflected by the rest of the world. So are we reflecting how everyone else thinks or setting the tone?

It's easier for us as a culture to dismiss Brents as evil, because exploring his humanity only serves as an uncomfortable reminder of our own kinship to him and our roles in his existence.

Where does the blame belong? It belongs to Brents, certainly, for his choices. But what about his parents, and their parents before them, for perpetuating the cycle of incest and abuse? What about the rest of the world, for our lack of compassion and refusal to recognize all the Brents walking among us, until they exact their anger in a public way?

I realized that Brents was right—the empathy I felt for him, even the tremendous sorrow over the tragedy of his life and the pain he caused others, gave me insight as a journalist and rekindled compassion I badly needed for others as well as for myself.

I reached into my purse, where I keep a tiny picture drawn by my youngest when he was in first grade. It shows a girlish version of me with a birthday hat on her head and a huge smile on her face, and under it, in childish scrawl, it reads, "Mom as a cid." That's how he saw me—full of life and laughter. It wasn't how I viewed myself, I realized. And I wanted to be her.

My mind was made up. I then walked into the office of the editor of the paper.

"This doesn't work for me anymore," I told him as he raised his eyebrows. "I need to quit."

"Where are you going?" he asked. "What are you going to do?"

"I'm going home—to write a book about Brent Brents."

Thur 2-16-06
Hi Brent,

    I QUIT. Yup, I quit. I gave them 2 weeks notice. Everyone is shocked and fellow reporters are envious (& a few editors, too).

    I'm not sure where I'll end up but I'm not worried. Plus, it was time to go. How did you put it?—"a fucked up political machine of a job." Well, that hit it on the head. And writing to you, and having you reflect it all back to me, helped cement that decision. So thank you. I may end up dead broke but there's no doubt in my mind I'll be happier!

    I'm worried about you. Really worried. Please try to remember 2 things: 1) To breathe, slowly, with your feet on the floor, and 2) that I'm here.

    Keep the faith, Brent. If I can, you can, bc I've never had any, and now I do.

    Write when you can. Please be careful. Keep your head down, don't do anything stupid or risky, and stay alive. Please.

    Amy

P.S. It friggin' snowed 6 inches last night. It's ten degrees right now. Snarl. So if I can endure snow, you can endure the hole! ☺

    Please don't give up.

Epilogue

My last day at the *Denver Post* was March 1, 2006.

The next day I finally went to the doctor for the persistent sharp pain in my side, and within a week, I was in surgery for a myriad of health problems I had ignored for years (take some ibuprofin and move on!) that were internal time bombs, ticking away and only getting worse from the stress of living a life so untrue to myself.

Two months after that, I sat across from Brents for the first time in an institutionally brown visitation booth at the Colorado State Penitentiary in Canon City, where he was housed briefly before being transferred to another prison out of state.

During that visit, separated by thick glass, Brents told me in person what he often said in his letters—that he would be forever grateful to me, and that because of me, he had realized the one thing he'd always wanted and never had: to honestly care for someone.

"You saved me," he said, his eyes full of tears.

I looked at the man I now hardly recognized, puffy from gaining weight, prison-pale, his long hair and growing beard lending anonymity to his face, and told him that I was grateful as well. By allowing me to see past the construct of evil that he hid behind, through to the persistence of his human spirit, Brents awoke empathy in me that I once feared was dead.

His observations, and I include some below, helped awaken me.

If I had stayed at the *Post*, justifying it for the money and recognition, I would have continued to abandon not only myself but everyone around me by surrendering to the callousness that cloaks the media. I would have been killing my soul, not to mention my physical self.

I don't believe I would have walked away from the *Post* if it hadn't been for knowing Brents. Up until the day I gave notice, I was filled with fear over whether it was the right decision. And now that I am gone from there, I often wonder why I stayed so long. I am softening and settling more into the open and caring person I always wanted to be.

It took four years after Brents' case ended before I was ready to write about it.

I don't have the view of the ocean—not yet, because I pinkie-promised the boys we would stay in Colorado until they were done with high school. I do, however, write for a living, and my next project is about a horse I named Sophie, a wild Appaloosa filly I adopted sight unseen in 2007 that has proven to be a challenge and a blessing.

Being a writer gives me great satisfaction and allows me to be available as a mom and a chauffeur to school and sporting events. I work at home next to a large window in my living room, which usually stays open so the cats can hop in and out all day.

My beloved cat Vincent died of old age at sixteen, and I was stunned by the amount of grief I felt at his passing. For months afterward, I would halfheartedly peruse ads for kittens, but I couldn't bring myself to commit to one, because none of them seemed to have his personality. Finally I stopped searching, telling myself that the universe would bring me another Vincent.

Several weeks after that, I was at my computer one afternoon when my inner voice nudged me to check out a local Humane Society website. As I scrolled down the cat adoption page, I was struck by the picture of a short-haired black male with a few white hairs on his chest, just like Vincent—and missing his left eye, just like Vincent. I rushed to the pound, and when the staff member put the two-year-old cat next to me on the floor, he promptly walked up and head-butted me, just like Vincent used to do. I burst into tears and adopted him on the spot, naming him Vincent II. He is every bit as grand as his predecessor.

His very existence is proof to me that sometimes amazing things can happen. The universe will answer our prayers, whether we're searching for love or an answer or peace.

Or understanding and support.

I maintain a website where I post many of Brents' letters and tell parts of this story. I often receive heartening letters from readers, but one day, I received a letter from an unexpected source: my husband.

Dear Amy Herdy,

I likely owe you an apology, or at least a statement of recognition for what you have been doing with the website and Brent's story.

I looked at the website this afternoon out of curiosity as to what comments you were getting. The comments speak for themselves. And they speak to your commitment of trying to do what many consider improbable, if not impossible. The likelihood of someone setting aside judgment for compassion, hatred for empathy, fear for faith, or ignorance for understanding is little to none with such a topic. I feel for you, the victims, and even Brents.

I've avoided this for most of this journey other than offering a few words of support and occasionally proofing what you have written. I've chalked that up to your journalistic writing skills and continual desire to be a source of credible and attributable information. I looked past the why you are doing this, the who you are dealing with, the whens you've worked long and hard on this, the what of the content you've had to wade through. I did not look at the ripples at my feet. I did not look at you and the growth that has occurred before my eyes.

Until now. You don't know where this journey will lead you or when it will end. I applaud your diligence and your foresight. Your willingness to be "out there" and face whatever may come is awesome. You've touched the hope, the despair, and everything between. That takes faith, courage, and honesty in a person who truly cares to make a difference. As you said, if even just one "got it," it's worth doing. Well, judging from the website, I believe you have struck a chord with certain souls that have been looking in the same direction as you. More than just one gets it.

Move forward with this. Don't stop or lose faith. Edge out those who are scared, unwilling, or unsure. Align with those who aren't.

So with that, I think this is amazing work and has tilted the world's perspective.

Congratulations.

Love,

Matt

How can hate exist in the same world with such love?

It did take years, but I no longer feel bitterness or anger toward my brother. Whenever I think of him today, I just feel sorrow and compassion. I can say with certainty that I would not be able to do this if it were not for the Brents case and its stark examples of how rage and fear can shape any of us into monsters.

My cold dismissal of my brother was not the answer. I know now that forgiveness is the only path that leads to healing.

So I stay in touch with Brents. We still write, and I visit him on occasion. I made up my mind long ago not to walk away from him like I did my brother.

I never found the fifteen-year-old prostitute. I think about her and pray for her.

I did find Tracy—she's in prison on drug charges. I pray for her too.

As for Irene, well, she and Brents didn't get married. Her demand that he sever ties with me proved to be a catalyst for him.

He broke off contact with her instead, telling me, "I got Irene out of my life because I was becoming the old me with her."

He went on to write,

> You know i dreamed of you when i was little. I didn't know what you looked like. But i knew some day you would SAVE ME. It's one of those lonely weekends. But I've learned to close my eyes and picture you. Thank you my friend.

The truth is, I didn't just save Brents.
He saved me too.

February 17, 2006

> I think you have seen yourself in that secret mirror we all have and because of whats happened between us you have been honest with Amy. It's a sucky scary feeling I know but for you it holds more meaning and promise . . . But answer me this, if this thing hadn't happened between us, do you think you would have seen the real depth of the home vs work battle? I don't think so. Acknowledge yes but realy deal with it no. I think I have made you realy think about how precious your boys Are. And how there lives are not worth Losing to your job. I know your Good Amy (REAL DAMN GOOD) but your driven. Dangerously driven. People like us we don't learn easy. We usually crash and burn and Lose things or people we love in the process. Youre afraid to let the world see because its scary and vulnerable . . . SO IF YOU CAN HEAR ME AMY, I'M HERE, I CARE . . .

February 27, 2006

> So are you scared yet? Ya know to be a free woman unbound from the chains of political chouvanism and destruction . . . Well onto more beautiful things for you missy.

Yeah I know you'll miss it. That's one of the things that sucks about being driven. Adrenaline . . . Now that you can lighten up and not be so serious I bet the other soccer moms won't call you an evil bitch! ☺ *. . . Ya know it's almost been a year since our paths crossed. One Anniversary that I can be ok with . . . You were there when there was no one else and i was ready to call it quits. You been pissed at me, Laughed at me, pushed me, pleaded with me, consoled me and loved me in your own kind way. You have helped me see Life for what it is. You have set an example of courage that i tried to follow, You have been The best friend i have ever hoped to have.*

March 9, 2006

So i get your card last night and i cried Amy for a long long time. I cried for you because i was proud of you and worried for you. I cried because a very simple thing like the card can mean so very very much And I cried because i am tired of being A bitter man.

May 16, 2006

Keep believing in yourself . . . you have to stay confident and sincerely believe in the woman you are and the skills you possess, believe Amy that all things Are possible. Your still doubting and feeling guilty. Bullshit Amy. Yeah the Post was Good Pay. Fat Lotta good That would have done you or the boys when you fell over from a heart failure Leading cause of death among corporate females between 45 and 60 in the us. Your Life is in a place now Amy you can realy be there for the boys for your husband and for yourself. But you realy have to be confident in yourself and your abilities. Amy i know about having the confidence to succeed in some things How do you think i survived All Those years in Prison. Good Liar yes but confident in my ability to Listen and memorize and Listen to everything around me.

Epilogue

But hey weve both changed our Lives this Last year. Born of Change. Just believe in yourself and don't get discouraged and when your tummy heals get gunner Petersons Ab ball workout . . . Take care of yourself
    Always, B.

And last but not least, my favorite letter from Brents, dated shortly before the end of 2005 and the dawn of what would truly become a New Year.

12-27-05
    Amy, Somewhere once I read that the greatest bond between two people was there accomplishments together. I laugh at us. You and I are night and day in many ways and yet reflections in a mirror in another. I think my life was chosen for me by me in an subconcious and blind way, for example I remember as a kid when i was being raped by my father or beaten by him There was this feeling like I was going to die and it fueled this adrenalin escpecialy when he was realy trying to hurt me bad. Something about that feeling became addictive and i think i transferred that surge of adrenaline and fear into other parts of my life. Sex, fights, drugs, trying to get away with stuff.
    As for how we are alike. We are both driven people. You've been more consistant of course and your choices career wise have we hope led you to your ultimate dream. Mine on the other hand (choices) have all been half measures and triumphs in self destruction. Your dream to write and do good. Mine to simply do good. The book and the message our accomplishment together. But its deeper Amy. Think about it honestly. Your reasonably successful but unsatisfied and somewhat encomplete. And here you are suddenly in this relationship/inner conflict/growing and learning experience with me. How odd is it that someone who is as fucked up as i

am, can encourage and inspire you to change your thinking, outlook on life and feelings.

On the opposite side of the coin. Take me and my general purpose in life for the last twenty or so years has been to conqur and posses and decieve and use everyone and everything in my life at all costs. Here i am suddenly wanting to give and care and challenge others to do likewise. Me seeing a Woman as an equal (not a sperm bank or an object to posses or control). Trusting you, believing in you. So have I realy burned out my brain with drugs and hate. This thing that has become our destiny has realy upset the balance within me, for the better. You know i always tell you i'm scared of you and i think maybe this is the best way to explain that fear . . . I don't see my mom in you as I do 90 percent of the women i know, I don't fear you'll hurt me, and i don't desire to destroy you and i am truly trusting and comfortable with you. This is all new to me and unfamiliar . . . when i am out of control paranoid or in a fit or rage somehow I have managed to see you as a friend and not foe.

Cons have an ideal of the way women in their lives should be. Bitches. My bitch this or My bitch that. Once in a while a woman comes along we call a soldier. You're a soldier Amy tough enough to hold me to task and yet gentle of soul. You realy do challenge me mentaly, emotionaly and even physicaly. You make me think and feel. I feel alive regardless of all that has transpired. I realy do see the world with new eyes because of you. I have also come to realize the neccesity of honesty because of you.

Has anyone ever heard a victimizer say i was also a victim. Sure countless of times. Has anyone ever heard a victimizer say I did these things not because they happened to me. I did them because I chose to vent my hurts, my rage, my humiliation, embarrassment in the same sick twisted ways that happened to me. Key word being "chose." There are *numerous reasons why i chose these ends. But regardless of the emotional traumas i suffered i'd always had choices. So now I'm given another choice possibly lose my life to speak out on the damage of encest, child rape and physical abuse, neglect and emotional and verbal assault of children. Or continue to be a coward, a liar and victimizer. The latter is most certainly the easier path.*

But it comes down to a choice of right and wrong. So if losing my Life to save a boy or girl from being beaten raped or murdered or a woman from being ambushed raped and murdered, then i say if my one life can change many then its truly the right choice to make . . . Acts of violence against children are life altering. No matter how Large or small these acts may be, they damage and destroy childrens thinking, feelings and abilities to cope and enteract with any kind of normalcy as growing children and adults. A marter tries to change the world thru self sacrifice. I can't change the world.

But hopefully I can change a few lives and save others by doing this . . . Nothing can ever absolve me. I do not wish to be forgiven. As for you Amy, whatever happens between us Afterward is realy up to you. I only hope that you'll continue to do the right thing.

Ok I'm gonna shut my trap now.
Brent

Acknowledgments

I would like to commend the CU Independent student staff whose passion for journalism rekindled my own. I'm especially grateful to Stephanie, Cameron, Ashleigh, Lauren, and Jimmy, who cheered me on through this process.

I am indebted to Barbara Cohen for gently nudging me to dig deeper.

This book would not exist if it were not for the stellar researching skills of Barbara Hudson, who time and time again pointed me in the right direction. You rock.

I'd like to thank my parents for instilling in me a joy for books, and my brother and sister for their steadfast love and support.

I owe a world of gratitude to Pat Brockenborough, a wise and wonderful woman who gave me terrific advice when I was a young college student at a crossroads by telling me that journalism would be a useful and practical career choice. Pat, you were right, and I'll never forget you.

I could not ask for a better web guru than Danielle Alberti, who became a trusted friend and teacher.

An enormous thanks goes to G. Brown for reading all those early awful drafts and still offering encouragement and advice, as well as to my agent, Patty Moosbrugger, whose belief in this book never waivered.

I continually shake my head over my great fortune in meeting editor Sandra Jonas, who provided incredible insight and made this a better book with her skill and precision.

I want to recognize B., my soul sister, for always being there for me and being the best friend anyone could have.

And none of this would have been possible without the support of my husband and my sons, who have backed me every step of the way and who provide me daily inspiration to be the best human being I can be. I love you.

About the Author

Amy Herdy began her career in television news in Kentucky and then moved to Florida, where she was also a crime reporter at the *St. Petersburg Times*. In 2002, she joined the *Denver Post* as a criminal justice reporter.

An investigative series she coauthored in 2003 at the *Post*, "Betrayal in the Ranks," exposed the military's mishandling of sexual assault and domestic violence cases. The series spurred congressional reforms and earned a nomination for the Pulitzer Prize.

After leaving the *Post*, Ms. Herdy became an investigative producer at KUSA-TV. Soon after, her interview with Ted Haggard created a firestorm when he unexpectedly confessed to buying meth from a gay male escort.

Ms. Herdy has won numerous honors for her work in journalism, including an Emmy for an investigative television series she produced on the misconduct of public officials, two Society of Professional Journalists awards, an Associated Press award, a Radio-Television News Directors Association award, a Military Reporters and Editors award, and two American Society of Newspaper Editors awards.

Her professional engagements include "Investigative Journalism" in Dhaka, Bangladesh, September 2011, for the U.S. State Department; "The Art of the Interview" for Investigative Reporters and Editors in Denver, July 2010; "The Art of the Interview" and "Journalism and

Trauma" in Lahore, Karachi, and Islamabad, Pakistan, May 2009, for the U.S. State Department; and a 2005 plenary for the National Center for Victims of Crime conference in Washington, D.C.

Currently, Ms. Herdy is a media consultant, writer, and editor. She lives outside Boulder, Colorado, with her family and a large passel of animals.

CPSIA information can be obtained
at www.ICGtesting.com
Printed in the USA
BVHW092031050522
636137BV00007B/1096